THE CHALLENGE TO WESTERN MANAGEMENT DEVELOPMENT

Given the increasing amount of economic competition at a global level, the quality and provision of management education is coming under very close scrutiny in a large number of countries, both in developing countries, where management is relatively new, and in developed countries, where it is more well established.

This book aims to enable debates within any one country to be placed within a wider context. It is based on eighteen contributions from experts in countries around the world who review the state of management education and the problems and priorities that are currently faced. It is edited by a group from the Centre for the Study of Management Learning, University of Lancaster, who specialize in research into both domestic and international aspects of management education.

The Challenge to Western Management Development is unique in the diversity of perspectives presented (both in terms of content and mode of expression), and in terms of its central message. This message is that each country can learn a lot from experiences in other countries and that the developed countries have little room for complacency. Though essentially taking a pluralistic perspective, it recognizes that although some general principles may be worthwhile in management education, there are many reasons (both cultural and economic) why individual countries should depart significantly from these principles.

Anyone concerned about the future of management education in any one country – whether they be policy makers or workers within the system – will find this book of particular value. It will also be extremely useful for the discerning clients of management development – whether organizational representatives or individuals – not because it gives a guide to individual institutions or courses, but because it crystallizes (and contextualizes) many of the key issues and choices involved in the provision and use of management education.

The Challenge to Western Management Development

International Alternatives

Edited by Julia Davies, Mark Easterby-Smith,
Sarah Mann, and Morgan Tanton

London and New York

First published 1989
by Routledge
11 New Fetter Lane, London EC4P 4EE

Simultaneously published in the USA and Canada
by Routledge
a division of Routledge, Chapman and Hall, Inc.
29 West 35th Street, New York, NY 10001

Reprinted 1990

© 1989 Julia Davies, Mark Easterby-Smith, Sarah Mann, and
Morgan Tanton

Filmsetting by Mayhew Typesetting, Bristol
Printed in Great Britain by
Antony Rowe Ltd, Chippenham, Wiltshire

British Library Cataloguing in Publication Data
The Challenge to Western management
    development.
    1. Management skills. Development
    I. Davies, Julia
    658.4'07124
    ISBN 0-415-00100-5

Library of Congress Cataloging in Publication Data
The Challenge to western management
    development / edited by Julia Davies . . . [et al.].
        p.   cm.
    Includes index.

    ISBN 0-415-00100-5
    1. Management – Study and teaching – Congresses.
    2. Comparative management – Study and teaching
    – Congresses. I. Davies, Julia.
    HD30.4.C48   1988
    658'.007 – dc19

Contents

Acknowledgements   vii

Introduction   1

PART I   The historical context

1 Is the Western view inevitable? A model of the
  development of management education   11
  Morgan Tanton and Mark Easterby-Smith

PART II   The challenges generated by cross-cultural transfer

2 Strategic choices in management education: the Bahrain
  experience   29
  Ibrahim S.J. Al Hashemi and George K. Najjar

3 Grounding management education in local research: a
  Latin American experience   40
  Carlos Dávila

4 Cultural dynamics and management development   57
  N.S. Gupta

5 The impact of local culture and attitudes on
  organizational effectiveness in Algeria   66
  Boufeldja Ghiat and Phillip C.T. Willey

6 Lessons from evaluation in Africa for external funding
  bodies   75
  Robert Youker

7 The cultural context of leadership actions: a cross-
  cultural analysis   85
  Peter B. Smith, Monir Tayeb, and Mark F. Peterson

PART III   The challenges generated by social and
political change

8 Incentives for management in China: the economic
  responsibility system   97
  Chen Wen Ya

9 An evolutionary account of management and the role
  of management development in China   112
  Qiu Xu-Yao, Yu Ke-Chun, and Xu Chan-Min

10 Reconciling the East and the West: management and
   management education in Turkey   125
   Esin Ergin (formerly Ahmet)

11 Management education for developing entrepreneurship
in Hungary 137
Magdolna Csath

12 Corporate social awareness and responsibility:
implications for management education in Hong Kong 152
Joseph N.K. Tam

PART IV The challenges generated by questioning
current practice

13 The promotion of effective management development 167
John Wallace

14 Some limitations in the Western model of executive
training: a case study 185
Dag Bjorkegren

15 Management development in a British multi-national
company 199
David Ashton

16 Mixed-national training programmes: some unintended
consequences 211
Rae Andre

17 Re-defining resources: turning the minimum into the
optimum 224
Ronald F. Clarke

18 Management and organizational development in
Bulgaria 238
*John Wallace, Evka Razvigorova, Jack Kalev, and
George Boulden*

Basic statistics 247

Index 249

Acknowledgements

This book is the product of a conference held at Lancaster in September 1986 on the topic of international management development. The conference was organized by a team comprising the four editors of this book and Christine Dytham. We are very grateful to Christine for handling the administration of the conference, and for overseeing the production and revisions of material for this book. In keeping with the principles of team spirit we have listed our names in alphabetical order on the credits.

We should also like to thank the British Council for providing financial assistance to a number of participants and for contributing to the overall expenses of the conference.

Introduction

Julia Davies, Mark Easterby-Smith, Sarah Mann,
and Morgan Tanton

During the last few years many assumptions about the world's economic order have been challenged. The arrival of Japan as one of the world's greatest economic forces took many people by surprise. Writers and management theorists in the USA reacted with characteristic vigour to probe the secrets of this success, and a spate of best-sellers followed, of which Ouchi (1981) and Peters and Waterman (1982) are probably the widest known. Other features of this economic order continue to change. The UK, which has been slipping for many years, has recently been overtaken by Italy as the fifth largest (capitalist) economy in the world. Brazil, now lying eighth in that league, could easily be one of the top economies by the end of the century.

Hong Kong, Singapore, Korea, and Taiwan, the four Little Dragons as they are referred to in China, continue to increase their dominance in high-technology manufacturing. And then there is China itself, with a growth rate which has fluctuated somewhere between 10 and 20 per cent per annum for the last ten years, and a population that is expected to peak at about 1.2 billion by the end of the century. China still has a long way to go, but it is definitely on the move. This is not a time for complacency among the developed nations. The success of organizations, and countries, in dealing with this global competition depends, to a large extent, on the competence of their managers. This gives some urgency to questions about the nature of managerial competence and how it can best be developed.

There are many different views about what constitutes good management, and consequently there are many different philosophies about how to educate and develop managers. Until recently the dominant views about management have originated from the United States. These have included a view of management as being based on a general set of principles and analytical techniques which can be applied to organizational problems irrespective of context, or culture. Views about the best ways of developing managers follow from views about the best forms of management, and hence US business schools have had an enormous influence on the patterns and philosophies of management education around the world. The belief that there are general principles and practices that can be applied to advantage in any context we refer to as a 'universalistic' perspective on management education.

This view has been challenged by many commentators in Europe and elsewhere who find that US models of management education are inappropriate both culturally and economically for their countries. They also neglect the methods and models that have evolved locally. In some cases this view may be taken to its logical conclusion: that the dominant view is of no relevance whatever in other countries or circumstances. The resulting home-grown models we may call 'particularist' models. But the danger here is that adoption of such models will produce managers in these countries who are unable to relate to the increasingly international texture of business – and are thus even less able to compete in global markets.

What we believe is needed in contrast is an approach that is able to blend the best of the dominant models with the particular circumstances of different countries. We think this is best achieved through dialogue, where the sharing of knowledge is the preliminary step to enable people from each country to decide for themselves what there is in other models that is appropriate to their own particular needs. Not only does this information need to be freely available, but it also needs to be available without strings attached. This is not easy when one part of the world is dependent on the other for the funding of its economy, and power is distributed unevenly between countries.

It is in the spirit of exchange and dialogue that this book has been produced. It is based on papers presented at a conference on International Management Development held at the Centre for the Study of Management Learning, University of Lancaster in September 1986. The conference was attended by about eighty people from some twenty-five different countries who had significant responsibilities for management development. The conference itself was a product of CSML's growing interest and involvement in international aspects of management development. From our international work we have come to recognize not only the diversity of approaches but the value of exchanging and learning from this variety. The conference was a practical opportunity for people to exchange ideas and learn from each other, and the main aim of this book is to extend and continue this process by

2

disseminating some of the models, approaches, and problems presented.

The chapters in the book cover undergraduate and postgraduate courses for aspiring managers, and executives, or continuing, education for managers in mid-career. These are largely the preserve of business schools and management training colleges, although a number of companies also have management education centres of their own. The chapters are not concerned with the 'systems' side of management development (such as selection, the management of careers, performance appraisal) except where it has an impact on appropriate educational arrangements.

SOME THEMES

It may be that the book raises more questions than answers. Some of the questions raised are fundamental to our profession. To start with, what is management, and what is it for? In comparing, say China and the UK, it is clear that there are a number of parallels: there is a need to 'motivate' people, to plan and control, etc. But there are also many differences. In China, according to Qiu *et al.* (Chapter 9), management is currently seen in an historical perspective, with the goal being to bring managers throughout the country up to the level of 'scientific management'. The more distant aim of 'modern management' can only be reached after passing through the state of scientific management. By contrast, in the UK and USA much of the interest has shifted away from management as a science, towards understanding the values and belief systems in an organization that can lead to excellent performance.

Many people considered that US management education was the model to follow, until it was noted that Japan's economic success has been achieved largely without the aid of business schools. This poses fairly obvious problems for those concerned with management education and has led to much questioning in the USA and Europe about the efficacy of their methods. For example, in this book Bjorkegren (Chapter 14) presents the results of research into the process and effects of an executive programme run by a top training institute in Sweden, which shows that although the course is very highly rated, its relevance to the professional lives of managers is limited. A similar line is taken by Ashton (Chapter 15) who criticizes the basic assumption

3

of so many company management development schemes, that as managers move up the hierarchy they need primarily to broaden their knowledge of the business and its strategies. Although some broadening may be appropriate, he argues that managers at all levels need to develop personal skills at the same time.

These are some basic concerns about management education from a 'Western' perspective. But this book is also about the experiences and problems of management education in a range of countries, and it is interesting to look at the different circumstances that lead to different concerns. In particular, differences due to political, cultural, and economic factors are noteworthy.

From the political perspective the flavour is different when comparing socialist economies with capitalist ones. In Bulgaria and Hungary much of the management problems are to do with trying to be entrepreneurial within the constraints of strong central control. And management development problems centre on how to get managers who were trained under a formerly much more restrictive system to change their ingrained habits. Csath (Chapter 11) argues that there is a generation of managers who may never be able to adapt to modern management practices.

There are also evident differences between national cultures. This book shows how these differences can be expressed through style, between, say, a paper from the West and a paper from the East: contrast Andre (Chapter 16) with Gupta (Chapter 4), for example. These differences are also expressed most forcibly by Ergin (Chapter 10) in relation to the problems that Turkey is having in finding an approach to management that can fit with the two (Western and Eastern) cultures. Management educators in Turkey, geographically between West and East, must understand the Eastern (and largely Muslim) culture which stresses tradition and social relations. But they derive much of their theories and teaching materials from the Western (and predominantly capitalist) culture which stresses competition and individualism. Where is the appropriate model of management in this situation?

The appropriateness of different teaching methods is much affected by cultural factors. In the UK there is a preference for active methods such as action learning and the use of projects; in the USA the interactive case method still holds sway; while in some African and Islamic countries it is the authority of the teacher as expert that is crucial to the learning process. Given that Bulgaria is located at the southern edge of the Socialist bloc and near the eastern edge of Europe, it is interesting to note the evident success there of an action-learning programme (a UK invention) which is described in the chapter by Wallace *et al.* (Chapter 18). Does this mean that some methods are less culture-sensitive than others, or that in this case the cultural differences are not all that significant?

Sometimes it is the economic differences that are of more significance. In countries such as Colombia, China, and Sierra Leone, the resources and infrastructure that are taken for granted in many Western countries simply do not exist. This, according to Dávila (Chapter 3) means that management research has to be conceived on a smaller and more pragmatic scale than research in the USA, and this is even more pressing because of the limited applicability of imported models of management. Because communications and energy are much less reliable, as Clarke (Chapter 17) points out in the case of Sierra Leone, teaching must be approached in a way that optimizes the resources that are currently available, rather than assuming that nothing can be done until the promised batch of microcomputers arrives.

It seems that in many cases both models of management and teaching methods are transmitted from those in richer countries to those in poorer countries, and naturally this is also the direction in which the funding flows. If both the expertise and the funds are coming from largely Western countries, then it is hard for those who are recipients of this assistance to reject it in favour of locally grown methods and ideas. Furthermore, it is very easy for these countries to feel that their own methods are somehow not as genuine as the real imported thing. It takes a lot of confidence to reject expert foreigners and their money.

And there may be a darker side to all of this. Just as 'management' can be viewed as an ideology which supports the exploitation of one class by another (Armstrong, 1987), so can the export of managerial expertise to developing countries be seen as a way of increasing their dependence on the technology and products of developed countries. How are we to be sure that 'foreign' aid is really being given to countries for their own benefit, or, as Morgan (1986) suggests, for the benefit of the donors? Who is it that defines what a country's problems are: the aid-giving bodies, the power élites in given countries, or the intended recipients? Some may feel that any kind of intervention in the management field inevitably supports the interests of those who are already in power, whether they be the élites within a country, or the élite nations of the world. It is evident that even if these sentiments are not expressed by all of the authors in this book, it is a feeling that is not far from the consciousness of many of them.

STRUCTURE OF THE BOOK

It should be clear from the foregoing that management education and development are complex topics when viewed from an international perspective. They are also undergoing considerable change. Every chapter in this book describes some kind of change or questioning of the status quo. Irrespective of the substantive foci, there are clear differences in the geneses of change described. In some cases this comes from concern about the appropriateness of imported models, and how best to cope with them. In other cases changes have been generated within countries as a whole (through political and social shifts) and the chapters look at the consequences for management education. Finally there are several chapters where the genesis for change comes from the authors' questioning of their own assumptions and experiences. This is the classification that we have used for grouping the chapters of the book into three main sections. In the introduction to each of these sections we explain further the nature of the general theme and how it varies.

However, we also think it is important for these changes to be seen not as isolated incidents, but within an historical context. For this reason we begin the book with a chapter that offers a model of the development of management education in any one country over time. This is a 'stage' model where it is assumed that each stage is qualitatively different from the preceding one, and that to some extent the solutions that are applied in one stage lead to the problems encountered in the next phase. We stress that this model is descriptive of how a number of systems have developed in the past; in no way is it intended to show inevitable patterns of development in the future. Indeed, we hope that by making explicit the consequences of past decisions and strategies, it will help people to envisage the likely consequences of their current strategies. We have placed it at the beginning of the book because it provides a general framework which may explain some of the concerns expressed in the other chapters.

As a broad survey of approaches and concerns in management education around the world this book is quite comprehensive. At a quick count there are at least twenty-six countries that are mentioned either in detail or in passing. These include Algeria, Bahrain, Bulgaria, Central Africa, China, Colombia, Ethiopia, Hong Kong, Hungary, India, Japan, Kenya, Malawi, Philippines, Sierra Leone, Swaziland, Sweden, Tanzania, Turkey, UK, USA, West Africa, and Zambia. We have included a table of statistical information for each of the countries discussed – see below, p. 247–8. It should also be quite evident by now that the book is not intended to tell people how they should go about 'doing' management development either on their own territory, or on other peoples'. Its prime purpose is to demonstrate the complexity of the problems faced in this area, and to ask people to question, and possibly rethink, their own beliefs and practices.

REFERENCES

Armstrong, P. (1987) 'The abandonment of productive intervention into management teaching syllabi: an historical analysis', working paper, University of Warwick.
Morgan, G. (1986) *Images of Organisation*, Beverly Hills: Sage.
Ouchi, W. (1981) *Theory Z: How American Business Can Meet the Japanese Challenge*, Reading, Massachusetts: Addison-Wesley.
Peters, T. and Waterman, R. (1982) *In Search of Excellence: Lessons from America's Best Run Companies*, New York: Harper & Row.

Part I

The historical context

1

Is the Western view inevitable? A model of the development of management education

Morgan Tanton and Mark Easterby-Smith,
*Centre for the Study of Management Learning,
University of Lancaster*

INTRODUCTION

Two years ago we were commissioned to carry out a short investigation into the training needs of management teachers around the world.[1] The study was based on data received from fifty-five management teachers in twenty-one countries[2] who had been asked to describe what they thought were the main problems for management education in their own countries.

Our analysis quickly showed some common patterns. In over half of the countries surveyed the following were identified as the major problems:

(1) lack of academic recognition of management education;
(2) lack of funds and facilities;
(3) lack of suitably qualified teachers;
(4) lack of relevant national literature; and
(5) lack of industry–university collaboration.

Given the prevalence of these problems it is likely that they are not easily solvable. Our data gave us little guidance about what could, or should, be done, so we decided to delve further. After a while we found patterns emerging. There were similarities in the problems encountered in several groups of countries. These could be linked to the structures and methods of management education in each case, and to some extent to the wider economic circumstances of the country.

We grouped countries with similar management education systems into five main developmental stages. In doing this we were influenced by the economic development model of Rostow (1960) which claims that national economies can be classified according to distinct stages, and there is a kind of inevitability with which a country will, over time, 'develop' from one stage to the next. This assumption of inevitability has been strongly criticized in various quarters (Chase-Dunn, 1975) and we too do not suggest that movement of management education from one stage to the next is necessarily inevitable. We shall return to discuss our misgivings and the limitations of the model nearer the end of this paper, but first we would like to present the model and explain some of its immediate implications. In doing this we hope to demonstrate that there are very different patterns of management education around the world and that the problems in any one country may be a function of the stage of development of each national system. Thus the kind of solution that works in one country may be quite wrong in another country. In addition we hope to provide a general framework against which some of the contributions in this book may be located.

DEVELOPMENTAL STAGES OF MANAGEMENT EDUCATION

We have given the following labels to the five main phases: starting up, growing, establishing, consolidating, and integrating. In this section we will illustrate each of these phases with examples drawn from different countries. We emphasize that it may be unhelpful to try to classify national systems as a whole within one phase or another. The model is intended as a 'generalized ideal type' rather than as an accurate description of any particular systems. Thus we only intend that the different features of a national system should cluster around a given stage. In the third part of the paper we will discuss some ways that the model may be used, before reviewing its main limitations.

Phase 1 – starting up

The characteristics of this phase are that small family businesses dominate within the national economy. These family businesses rely upon a set of values and ethics based on emotion and family. The need for management education programmes is not recognized by these families. The practical application of rational methods is difficult because the successful business-owners are unable to see the necessity of academic training. In this phase

12

there are very few business schools and those there are, are constrained to teach subjects with easily visible skills, such as accounting and finance. At this stage of development the institutions rely on the lecture method and the student's role is passive, studying techniques which apply to organizational structure and systems rather than considering personal development.

An example of a country at the beginning of this phase is Botswana. The majority of its people are subsistence farmers. In 1980 the sole university in the country, the University of Botswana, introduced a Bachelor of Commerce degree programme for the first time, enabling those interested in management to major in this area, although to a limited extent. Most of the students of business studies now choose to major in accounting or finance since these two areas offer good job opportunities.

Phase 2 – growing

As businesses develop, products become more complex and organizational competition increases and therefore more sophistication is required to cope with the growing demands. At this phase, for the first time, an international perspective is introduced as products are bought and sold in new markets; the administrative systems are recognized as unsatisfactory and the previously productive short-term goals are seen as inadequate. Similarly, managers who coped with the businesses' needs until this time of expansion begin to reflect the stress of their situation.

At this phase a demand for management education grows and new institutions open. Many of the institutions are private, non-academic schools which teach skills and subjects necessary for young, inexperienced managers. The courses taught are seen to have immediate application and again the emphasis is on organizational methods and structures. In order to cope with demands for courses, where possible, programmes are imported from more developed countries and the help of experts is brought in from abroad. Managers who have been successful in business are transferred to business schools although they have no experience of teaching methods.

Pakistan provides an example of a country located in this phase. Management courses are offered by institutions other than universities, such as the Ministry of Production. Public and business management are still being run by non-professionals. Even in the public sector and in a few private large enterprises there are limited numbers of people who have received adequate management education, whereas in small business organizations there is hardly anyone having received even basic education. Pakistan still uses many foreign experts.

Phase 3 – establishing

In the third phase government policy recognizes the need for formal training if businesses are to compete with overseas trade, and industries begin to question the relevance of management training for their employees. In this phase, high priority begins to be given to funding and resources become available as grants are given by both governments and large corporations in an effort to improve output.

As government support is given, universities establish management education programmes and the subjects and courses offered increase to new levels. Young academics, having obtained training overseas, return with new methods and knowledge and difficulties may arise in the institutions as the young, newly qualified teachers struggle to express their new thoughts and adapt the new techniques within the environment of the older generation of teachers who may feel threatened by the influx of new 'foreign' information.

As the young, newly trained academics return to their own countries, they produce relevant academic material and research develops in their own culture. In this phase insufficient courses are offered in some subjects although large numbers of courses are offered in general business skills courses by numerous institutions. Teachers become mobile within their own linguistic and cultural regions.

An example of a country largely in this phase is Singapore. The situation there was encapsulated by one respondent in the following terms: 'Manpower is the only resource therefore the government is investing in programmes such as management development. This has caused the number of courses to mushroom and there are too many courses competing for students.'

Phase 4 – consolidation

In Phase 4, the number of courses offered continues to exceed demand and the competition between course providers leads to greater sophistication and a higher quality of programmes. As the less competent teachers retire and some schools close, others are able to consolidate and focus their resources more efficiently to achieve a higher level of management teaching and academic recognition. In this phase new methods of teaching are sought and traditional methods are rejected. A split becomes apparent between trainers who focus on skills and behaviour, and educationalists who aim to provide a broader understanding of the techniques and processes of management. The latter may become dominant. Thus the demands of abstract analysis and the generation of ideas and concepts may take priority over technical skills transference. The development of the individual becomes an acceptable goal.

Handy (1975) described contrasting philosophies of management education from the 'instrumental' view of learning to the 'existential'. It is largely in this phase that the transition takes place with the deductive, subject-based lecture method changing towards the individual-centred programmes where teachers lead individuals to develop their own ideas and concepts with the goal of drawing out individual talents.

In this phase the Government may start to withdraw funding (in the UK this has been fairly continual since the late 1970s) and cost-effectiveness may be questioned by industry. Small companies begin to accept the need for management education, but evaluation becomes a major concern and business schools attempt to justify their courses in terms of financial return.

In this developmental phase, most new staff will have obtained their qualifications in their own country, and will, therefore, show a marked preference for using locally developed materials. Experience-based teaching methods, with role play, training games, workshops, projects and group work will become established, and training programmes become more complex as their design and planning progress to an organic participative model.

Phase 5 – integrating

In this, the most diverse phase, industries recognize management

15

Table 1.1 Five-phase development model of management education (ME)

	National context	State of management education	Institutional teaching methods and approaches to training of teachers
Phase 1 **Starting-up**	Family businesses dominate. Management based on family values and networks. Lack of recognition of ME.	Few institutions exist, but pioneers founded at undergraduate level.	Lecture method dominates. Subjects restricted (e.g. a/c and finance). Staff transferred from industry. No formal training. Visiting experts advise on how to get started.
Phase 2 **Growing**	Development from small to larger industries. Poor administrative systems. Short-term goals. Complexity and growth leads to awareness of need for competition and improved methods.	Increasing demand for ME. New institutions open, many private, non-academic. Reliance on training skills and differentiated subjects, particularly those seen as having immediate application. Foreign materials imported from more developed countries.	Emphasis on quantitative rational methods. Experts from abroad introduced as teachers. Practitioners transferred to ME (ex-managers, no formal teacher training). Young teachers sent abroad to study.
Phase 3 **Establishing**	Public/Govt funding becomes available. Industries question relevance of ME. High priority given to facilities, funding and resources.	Universities establish ME. Increased dominance of subject divisions. Local academic material developed. Recognition for existing institutions. Mushrooming of number of courses overall although some courses still omitted or insufficient.	Overseas methods, especially case methods, brought back by externally qualified young academics. Development of research. Recognition of complexity and non-rationality in teaching methods. Difficulties between original and newly trained staff.

Phase 4 Consolidating	Governments pull out of funding. Cost effectiveness questioned. Small companies recognize ME.	Demand for evaluation. Search for new methods. Split between management education and management training. Courses offered exceed demand, leading to sophistication and improved courses.	Experience-based methods. Demand for local materials. Demand for abstract analysis. Executive courses increase. Local staff developed.
Phase 5	Industries support ME, particularly senior executive management courses. Global competition. Technology and speed of change input on economy.	Collaboration between industries and academics. Networking internationally. Tailor-made programmes. High-quality students attracted. Employment of ME in alternative areas, i.e. trade unions, co-ops. Pluralistic approach. Generalized view of organizational problems rather than subject framework.	Consultancy skills. Local materials, programmes, teachers and research. Indigenous staff development policies. Development of 'whole person' approach to teaching. Integration across disciplines.

education, not as an unrealistic cure-all, but as a collaborator. Conferences and workshops are held with the two forces meeting to exchange and develop ideas. A global approach is accepted and teachers and trainers recognize that learning can cross national barriers, in both directions. Consultants pass from nation to nation as methods and techniques are sifted and disseminated.

International networking is dominant in this phase and recognition is given to tailor-made programmes, particularly for senior executives, and post-experience courses become a norm for all competitive companies. The topic of change is tackled as a vital subject of study, as new problems and technological dilemmas are regularly introduced. In this phase the development of the individual is recognized as a necessary element for successful business and human skills are given priority using the culture of the nation as a basis for appropriate exercises.

A high quality of student is attracted to management education, and innovation increases as these students research and create new concepts, thoughts and ideas. It is possible that in this phase, diversification is also greater, and management education is seen as vital for the efficiency of new, alternative areas, i.e. trade union management and co-operatives, as well as within the public sector.

It is possible to regard some facets of management education in the US as being within this phase. This is indicated by the increasing emphasis placed on human skills and the attempts to re-design management education to cope with the rapid changes which are taking place. But much of management education in the US is still firmly rooted in earlier phases. Similarly, there are pockets of industries in the UK with management development practices that would fit well into this fifth phase. But recent research by Mangham and Silver (1986) shows that these companies of excellence in the UK are regrettably still in the minority.

The main features of these five phases are summarized in Table 1.1. We hope that this will enable people to see their own situations in a broader perspective, and that it will also provide a framework from which experiences may be exchanged and compared.

IMPLICATIONS AND APPLICATIONS

Perhaps the strongest use of the model is to help those responsible for management education to clarify the choices involved and to anticipate the problems that may result from future policies. For example, we can take the case of China which might be plotted in between Phases 2 and 3 at the present time. Strong Government approval and support has been given to management education in recent years. All managers are now obliged to take courses, but Chinese management education is nearer to Phase 1 in terms of teaching methods. Almost all teaching, even to senior managers, is based on the lecture method. Lectures are long and are rarely combined with discussions or practical work. However, experts from overseas are being brought in, in substantial numbers, to develop the country's management education system quickly, and they are also introducing large numbers of language teachers to enable their communication to be improved quickly in line with the need for an international perspective.

According to this model, as China moves into Phase 3, teaching methods are likely to include greater emphasis on case method, and approaches which acknowledge the complexity and non-rationality of management.

Growth is likely to continue quickly, the discipline of management will become more fully recognized and research activity will become increasingly important. But various problems may arise also. The following are quite likely: clashes in style and philosophy between senior staff and younger overseas-trained staff; subject divisions becoming sharper, thus reducing collaborative effort within institutions; paradoxically, an over-supply of generalist management courses; and possibly industry may start to question the relevance of management education.

At the present time in China, problems such as these are not particularly evident, but they have occurred in several other countries that have moved into Phase 3, as we have described it. Hence, if the Chinese people are committed to developing management education along these lines, they may be able to reduce some of these problems if sufficient action is taken in advance.

A more specific application of the model is in determining policies for staff development. Recent work we have been doing in this area[3] indicates projections of quite significant growth in almost all of the fifty international institutions we surveyed. For

19

example, in five years' time it is expected that there will be overall a 33% increase in the number of full-time teachers; 41% increase in the number of part-time teachers and 50% more researchers. So institutions will not only have to establish more programmes of staff development to take into consideration such increases but the model suggests that they will also need to consider the future demands on such staff and therefore their needs if they are to move to the next phase. For example, a country wishing to move towards Phase 4 will need to establish programmes to train and develop future faculty in their own country. But such programmes should not just be replicas of programmes already attended by young academics overseas. They need to take account of future structures and methods that may be required in Phase 4: assisting in the development of local materials; developing competence with experience-based methods; and preparing faculty to deal with challenges on the grounds of cost-effectiveness.

SOME LIMITATIONS

At this stage we also feel it is important to sound some cautionary notes about placing too great a reliance on the model.

First, with regard to its accuracy, although it reflects quite truly the views of our respondents, their number was limited, and the number of informants from any one country varied quite a lot. Although the countries that can be classified into Phases 1, 2, and 3 covered a wide spread of cultural, political, and ideological systems, the countries that made up the later phases were predominantly Western, non-communist, non-Islamic, etc. Thus the model in the latter stages may be skewed more towards Western values.

Second, in constructing the model it was also necessary to simplify much of the complexity, and to gloss over some cases that did not fit neatly into the general categories. This is intended to make the model useable and we hope that we have not over-simplified. We are aware that many countries have highly élite sectors in their management education systems, and these portions may not fit too readily into the model.

Third, there may be a problem in using the model to predict the future too precisely. This is because it is constructed from data taken from different countries at the same point in time. It is not constructed from analysis of these countries' development over time but from 'snapshots' and views about current directions. But if we look at the history of the development of national systems, the details do fit reasonably well. Thus the US went through a major period of growth and development in the period 1955–66. According to Schlossman *et al.* (1987) this involved a change in teaching materials from descriptive, industry-based examples to quantitative methods, use of behavioural sciences and the adoption of case methods. Many leading institutions also placed a greater emphasis on research. This was accompanied by considerable growth in size of institutions and in student numbers. These changes would be broadly consistent with a move from Phase 2 to Phase 3, although there are some inner inconsistencies with the model, such as the increased emphasis on quantitative methods in some institutions.

This brings us to the final and more fundamental point about this model, which we would like to introduce by reference to a debate among economists about the inevitability of economic progress.

This debate is summarized by Paul and Barbato (1985) in the following way: One position is taken by those who claim that 'the process of industrialisation has a kind of historical inevitability, with various nations of the world moving through similar stages . . .' (p. 8). The other position is represented by the 'North–South' debate which suggests that 'those countries that are in the process of economic development may never make it to a level of development comparable to that achieved by the United States . . .' (p. 9).

Central to this debate is the role of multi-national companies: do they contribute to development by introducing new technology and capital investment, or do they retard development by fostering dependence and distorting national economies in their own favour? But the answer is by no means simple. As Balusubramanyam (1980) has shown, the statistics on capital investment, repatriation of profits, technology transfer, etc. do not give overwhelming support to either argument.

The parallel question in the context of management education is about whether a country's progress from phase to phase is inevitable and whether the application of Western methods (principally drawn from Phases 4 and 5) will accelerate this.

We do not think that movement from one phase to the next is inevitable. It is most likely to arise from conscious decisions

21

taken by leaders in management education. The main problem lies in taking for granted the superiority of later phases. No doubt there are some benefits to be gained, but there are also major dangers in simply adopting the models and experiences of the older, industrialized nations.

There needs to be some adaptation which takes into account the current phase in which the management education system is located. This also needs to take account, as do many of the chapters that follow in this book, of the unique social, cultural, and economic circumstances of that country.

NOTES

1. The investigation was commissioned by the INTERMAN Project of the ILO, Geneva. Funding assistance is gratefully acknowledged.
2. The countries included in the sample were, in alphabetical order: Algeria, Botswana, Colombia, Egypt, France, Hungary, India, Ireland, Italy, Lebanon, New Zealand, Nigeria, Pakistan, Singapore, Spain, Sri Lanka, Sweden, Sudan, Tanzania, UK, US.
3. This work was sponsored by the ISBM/INTERMAN/EFMD and a report will be published in 1988.

REFERENCES

Balusubramanyam, V. N. (1980) *Multinational Enterprises and the Third World*, London: Trade Policy Research Centre.
Chase-Dunn, C. (1975) 'The effects of international economic dependence on development and inequality: a cross-national study', *American Sociological Review* **40**: 720–38.
Handy, C. B. (1975) 'The contrasting philosophies of management education', *Management Education and Development* **6**(2): 56–62.
Mangham, I. L. and Silver, M. S. (1986) Management and Training in the UK, A report produced for the ESRC (Report No. F.02400002) and the DTI.
Paul, K. and Barbato, R. (1985) 'The multinational corporation in the less developed country: The economic development model versus the North–South model', *Academy of Management Review* **10**(2): 8–13.
Rostow, W. W. (1960) *The Stages of Economic Growth*, Cambridge: Cambridge University Press.
Schlossman, S., Sedlak, M., and Wechsler, H. (1987) 'The "New Look": The Ford Foundation and the revolution in business education', *Selections* Winter: 11–27.

Part II

The challenges generated by cross-cultural transfer

In this section we have grouped together those chapters which question the practice of transferring approaches to management education and development from one country to another, from one culture to another. The chapters by Al Hashemi and Najjar, Dávila and Gupta all propose the development of approaches which are specific, and therefore relevant to, their own particular country and culture. These proposals arise out of a wish to prevent Western models and approaches being imposed when these are not necessarily always wholly appropriate. The chapters by Ghiat and Willey, Youker and Smith et al. all present research findings which suggest that cross-cultural transfer of approaches to education and development can be problematic – and even lead to provision which is quite irrelevant and inappropriate to the particular context.

Al Hashemi and Najjar offer an account of how Bahrain has developed its own management education system in a context in which expatriates had had a considerable influence. The key features of the Bahrainian initiative are the importance given to collaboration between education, industry, and government, and the integration of degree and diploma programmes in a single-track scheme. For the future they suggest the need to develop more variety in the programmes offered and to develop localized teaching materials. Fundamentally their approach is to develop educational programmes which are initially grounded in the local culture but which recognize that there is a relevant body of knowledge available from other parts of the world.

Dávila looks at the issues and needs of management education in Columbia, but set within the wider context of Latin America as a whole. Most developing countries are heavily dependent on Western, largely American, teaching materials. This is made worse by the acceptance of large-scale funded research as the right way to develop such materials, which makes it harder for countries to feel that their own 'home-grown' materials are respectable. Dávila feels this is particularly so in the materials for human resources in Latin America, where cultural differences are most evident. He argues strongly that the problem arises not only from the relative lack of resources in these countries, but also from the relative lack of power of educational institutions in these countries vis-à-vis the West. He proposes that local educational institutions should stand up more assertively for their own beliefs about their own particular needs, and should undertake locally focused research in order to develop appropriate teaching materials.

Gupta examines the question of cross-cultural transfer within the context of India. He discusses the importance of culture as an influence on people's attitudes and behaviours and suggests that unless management education in India is developed in such a way as to take account of the particular context then it will not only be inappropriate but also unsuccessful. Furthermore, adopting Western approaches to management education in India is likely to hinder the development of potentially rich and rewarding styles of management and organization which an Eastern approach would lead to. He identifies spirituality as an Eastern quality which could well be usefully brought into the arena of managing.

Ghiat and Willey present a study in which they investigated the ineffectiveness of particular Algerian organizations by looking at the influence of managers' personalities and styles on the organizations. Their findings suggest that the particular local culture in which the organization is set will influence the effectiveness of the managers on their organizations. They conclude that cross-cultural issues and the influence of culture on organizations is relevant not only at a national level but also locally within one country. The key point they make is that culture is influential.

Youker summarizes the findings from a number of evaluation studies of management development in Africa. All the programmes discussed were supported by some kind of outside funding institution. The key finding is that in most cases the training and development offered is neither appropriate for the particular person, the particular place or the particular time. The research gives us a picture of irrelevance and inappropriateness. The author's message is that management development needs to become more learner-centred and at the same time more aware of the external factors which can detrimentally influence the transfer of learning.

Smith et al. address the issue of leadership and the view that there is one best way to lead – a currently popular notion. In their paper they propose that although the 'what' of effective leadership may be substantially the same all over the world, the 'how' may vary. Their research examined differences between Britain, the United States, Hong Kong, and Japan and showed how for a quality such as 'being considerate', although held up across cultures as important for an effective manager, the practice in action may be quite different. This chapter warns that apparent similarities in the use of terms should be viewed warily as potential hazards until more research in different cultural contexts has

26

clarified and confirmed a common value or understanding.

All the chapters in this section point to the fundamental import-ance of considerations of relevance in management education. They point the way to learner-centred approaches which are grounded in the particular context of the relevant group of students and informed by locally conducted small-scale research. If management education does not tackle this challenge then provision is likely to be sterile.

2

Strategic choices in management education: the Bahrain experience

Ibrahim S. J. Al Hashemi and George K. Najjar
(Gulf Polytechnic, University of Bahrain)

INTRODUCTION

Perhaps one of the triumphs and failures of management education is its rampant pluralism. Scores of models continue to co-exist and compete with each other, offering different emphases and 'mixes'. Such plurality persists not only in between countries but equally vividly within different institutions in the same country. The last three decades have repeatedly witnessed the rise and fall of many a school of thought and an even greater number of fads. Management theory today is still in many ways no less of a 'jungle' than it was when it was first described as such in the early 1960s (McGuire, 1982).

Even with the wide array of options available, countries in transition like Bahrain have to make difficult choices in setting up their management education systems. Such choices can be made more rational to the extent that they are based on clear policy objectives and a thoughtful sense of the future. With its stratified manpower development policy, Bahrain is clearly in need of a type of management education that caters to para-professionals to a greater extent than to professionals, and which preserves the ratio that exists among them in actual work situations. A radically different system is a necessity in order to serve this purpose and simultaneously alleviate the inferiority stigma of non-degree programmes. What is required is a deviation from conventional models and to risk the uncertainties of innovation.[1]

Bahrain's experience suggests that there are more alternatives open to countries in transition than mere emulation of one or the other of the conventional models. This could perhaps be a beginning towards shifting focus, however modestly, in management education innovation, in favour of developing countries that have yet to derive some hard lessons in self-reliance. The disadvantages of being late-comers to the development process are perhaps all too clear to such countries. What should be equally evident are some of the advantages, particularly not having to repeat the same mistakes and not having a substantial stake in preserving the academic or professional status quo.

STRATEGIC CHOICES FOR MANAGEMENT EDUCATION AND DEVELOPMENT

This paper should not be understood as a call for a purely relativistic approach to management education. While its central argument is that systems choices should emanate from within rather than be superimposed from without, it appreciates fully the fact that international managerial professionalism requires a common body of knowledge and a core of shared perception. After all, a choice of management education system is partly a choice of format. This means, among other things, that differences of content may not be as radical as they sound (De Nisi et al., 1983; Schaeffer, 1985).

The central thesis of this paper is that no matter what the degree of openness or outside intellectual influences are, certain critical choices are bound to persist. Three such choices are particularly crucial: desired output of a management education system, the skills and values it is designed to inculcate, and its long-term manpower implications.

Bahrain's experience clearly suggests that such difficult decisions have to be settled decisively prior to launching a management education programme. Postponed choices are only likely to backfire at a later stage and create inertia, random incrementalism, and an unhealthy sense of drifting (Gulf Polytechnic, 1986).

It is equally imperative to create a collaborative framework within which academia, industry, and government come together in pursuit of a management education system that can be at once compatible with international norms, relevant to local needs, and capable of building bridges between the two. Nor should there be any question that making the difficult choices is an on-going living process, subject to continuous adjustment and sensitive to the dynamics of a rapidly changing world. Sound educational programmes are doomed constantly to re-define themselves and reach out to new horizons.

Against this conceptual backdrop we now turn to a brief discussion of the Bahrain experience in so far as it represents a non-conventional response to the challenges outlined above.

THE BAHRAIN EXPERIENCE

Educational planners in developing countries have had precious few unmitigated successes. Almost invariably, planners' efforts have been marred by a host of problems including inflated objectives, excessive traditionalism, and a degree mania that often fails to tie in with the requirements of economies undergoing rapid transition.

Nor are educational planners alone to blame for their problems. They usually find themselves faced with conflicting demands made by their varied constituencies and expected to swiftly redress serious imbalances in manpower supply and demand. At times it seemed that such imbalances were getting out of hand and threatening whatever progress has been made by way of socio-economic development.

This paper seeks to highlight the Gulf Polytechnic experience in management education with special reference to its objectives, scope, mode of operation, early results, future prospects, and conceptual implications. This latter part will centre around some cautious generalizations that may be derived from the Bahrain experience.

Historical antecedents

In its present form, the Gulf Polytechnic came to being in 1981 through an Amiri Decree issued in February of that year. From that early beginning, the institution developed a strong applied orientation and a philosophy of education that emphasized employability and a commitment to para-professional ranks. Time was to reinforce this policy further through the increasingly pressing needs for manpower at the technician and sub-professional levels in Bahrain and the rest of the Gulf region.

31

The winds of change: 1982 and its aftermath

The rapid socio-economic transformation of the 1970s fuelled by increasing oil revenues and Bahrain's ascent to a regional centre, started to have its full impact at the turn of the decade. The impact manifested itself in the rapidly growing demand for professional and sub-professional manpower, perhaps more than any other area. With trained Bahrainis in severely short supply, the ranks of expatriates swelled and the dependence of the country on their services increased. Simultaneously, pressure was building up from the business sector, Government, and the region for the newly established Gulf Polytechnic to take bolder steps towards the satisfaction of the dire need for a national management education and development centre. In response, the Board of Trustees of Gulf Polytechnic, chaired by His Excellency the Minister of Education, made a decision to revitalize the business and management programmes through establishing a fully-fledged Business and Management Department, introducing a considerably upgraded state-of-the-art curriculum with an expanded scope covering both the BSc degree, and, as a next step, an ambitious management development arm (Gulf Polytechnic, 1985).

It was specifically mandated by the trustees that the newly invigorated Business and Management Department was to transcend academic traditionalism and stress the diligent pursuit of relevance to local needs. An innovative one-track curriculum integrating diploma and degree in a four-year sequence was designed and officially introduced in the autumn of 1982 when external programmes were phased out. In the new programme, which has now graduated successive diploma and degree batches, incoming high-school leavers undergo a one-year orientation period covering English and Mathematics and designed with a remedial objective in mind. Upon successful completion of the orientation year, students are allowed to proceed to a 'core' semester covering five key subjects, namely microeconomics, accounting, introduction to business, english, and mathematics.

A final Grade Point Average (GPA) of 2.5 entitles the student to have his/her choice at one of two diploma/degree options. The first is the Associate Business Diploma – Bachelor of Science (ABD-BSc) programme and the second is the Associate Accounting Diploma – Bachelor of Science (AAD-BSc) programme. As may be surmised, the first of the two programmes offers a general business education with some grounding in each of the functional areas (accounting, finance, marketing, etc.), while the second is a specialized accounting course. Students require another three semesters to complete the diploma (ABD or AAD) thereby reaching their first destination two years after completion of the orientation programme. Those who pass the core semester but fail to attain the 2.5 GPA proceed to a watered-down practically-oriented two-year programme offering them a Commercial Studies Diploma (CSD).[2]

Associate Diploma graduates (AAD and ABD) may either join the labour force at para-professional levels, or, if academically qualified, continue on in the programme for two additional years and earn a BSc degree either in business and management or in accounting, depending on the track they follow.[3]

A major aspect of all these programmes, particularly at the diploma level, is their close ties to industry and their mandatory provision of extended attachment periods where students gain valuable industrial experience under closely monitored conditions and subject to detailed evaluation.

Objectives and scope

The integrated two-tier one track nature of the programme turned out to be an innovative formula for accomplishing the objectives and the scope assigned to the programme by policy-makers.

Since the very outset, two key objectives were to be actively pursued. First, introducing an upgraded, state-of-the-art pro-gramme on par with its international counterparts and fully integrated into international business education; and second, achieving that without sacrificing local relevance and maximum sensitivity to environmental factors. All along, the intention was to combine both rigour and relevance, and produce a type of graduate to fit employment requirements, yet general enough to allow for further growth and learning both formally and informally.

The curriculum is structured such that diploma courses are generally more operational in nature and more geared towards satisfying local employment conditions. The degree programme, on the other hand, is more heavily conceptual in nature and designed to inculcate in students a broader theoretical base. By the same token, diploma subjects are mostly mandatory in nature leaving students little leeway for further options within their chosen track (business or accounting) in order to offer them enough specialized exposure and enhance their employment chances. Further electives and room for individual choice are provided at the degree stage.

These and other aspects of the programme were decided upon in close collaboration between policy-makers, academic consultants, and industry. Programme designers from within the Gulf Polytechnic, as well as a select team from leading universities in the region, met extensively with industry and government representatives to discuss options at various stages. Hardly any institution of consequence in Bahrain was left out of this process and a number of joint seminars, brainstorming sessions and round tables were organized to ensure maximum feasible participation. This intensive dialogue also continued unabated after the new programme was launched and adjustments were made as often as necessary.[4]

Mode of operation

It should come as no surprise that a massive change on this scale was not without its problems. Some of these problems were of an *a priori* nature while others rose in the context of implementation.

The first source of anxiety was giving away the security of external programmes in favour of a new in-house scheme that was yet to gain recognition and whose credibility was something to be earned. Within a relatively short period all cushions of dependence were removed and the institution was suddenly on its own, experiencing the pangs of growth and the sobering fact that henceforth it had to rely on its own devices. There was no shortage of sceptics who questioned the ability of the budding institution to measure up to the enormity of the new challenge.

It should also be remembered that with the introduction of the new programmes the Department of Business and Management began operating on a different scale. The number of students more than doubled to reach a total of slightly above 1,000. Suddenly all the problems that are normally associated with size started to surface.

However, perhaps the most persistent problems faced by the new one-track two-tier business and management programme was managing the transition of students from one level to another. Such transitions include: orientation to core – core to ADD

(Associate Accounting Diploma) and ABD (Associate Business Diploma) – ABD/AAD to BSc, etc. in a manner that allows for maximum feasible flexibility without compromising quality control.[5]

The new programmes in action

It has been clear all along in the minds of the programme designers that some of the more serious problems were bound to surface only after the programme was made operational. The major challenge was to operationalize a programme unlike any other in the area combining diploma and degree. As such it does not subscribe to the argument that diploma programmes are inherently vocational and cannot be upgraded conceptually without compromising their applied nature. Nor is it constrained by the traditional view that degree programmes are supposed to be a 'cut above' for the élite who are being prepared for lucrative management careers.

No sooner had implementation of the new programme started than a few facts began to emerge:

(1) As a model, the new scheme was essentially sound and potentially capable of achieving its set objectives if properly managed, particularly in so far as channelling students from one stage to another was concerned.

(2) Although the very *raison d'être* of the one-track two-tier programme was to discourage the stampede towards degree programmes and improve the status of the diploma, it was apparent that, in fact, students continued on the whole to favour the attractions of the degree and many of them considered the diploma as just a transition along the way. Fortunately, however, the new system was better prepared to handle a situation like this by virtue of two important considerations:

(a) An integrated one-track programme naturally tended to remove the stigma of the diploma, since every student was a diploma student for the first two years.

(b) The possibility of exiting at the diploma stage, gaining some work experience, and then rejoining the college for a degree was very reassuring to many students, particularly at a time when jobs were

35

becoming relatively scarce and having one was no longer something that could be taken for granted.
(3) The novelty of the one-track system meant that its long-term viability would have to hinge on its continued ability to 'sell' itself to students and industry alike.

THE EARLY RESULTS

Four years after its launch, the one-track two-tier programme can be said to have established itself firmly in Bahrain and the region, and gained enough credibility to ensure its being accepted on a par with international undergraduate programmes in business management.

It is particularly noteworthy that two years following the introduction of the programme, Government and industry were satisfied enough with the early results to approach the Gulf Polytechnic with a view to starting a new management development programme to cater for the practising manager. As a result, and after eighteen months of preparation, the parallel Continuing Management Education Programme (COMEP) was introduced to offer diploma courses at five different levels: clerical skills, basic supervision, middle management, advanced management, and executive management.

In many ways, the Continuing Management Education Programme (COMEP) is a derivative of the one-track two-tier model described above. In the first place, COMEP, which has already graduated a few batches of managers, and enrolled some 200 others at present, was designed at the request of both Government and industry following their satisfaction with what they have seen of the one-track system. It was becoming evident to sponsor organizations that an institution which managed to put together a quality academic programme against considerable odds might be just as useful in satisfying their management development needs. Up to that point, such needs were mostly handled *ad hoc* either in-house or through short overseas programmes.

A particularly fortunate aspect of having both the one-track programme and COMEP offered by the same department developed more as a matter of serendipity than design. Within the first six months of COMEP's life, it became apparent that an active symbiosis had already started between the two programmes. By offering COMEP, the Department of Business and Management reaffirmed its commitment to corporate manpower planning and further reinforced its already strong corporate ties. This was soon to start paying off in terms of increased access to professional management circles on the island.

Transferability of management knowledge and skills from the classroom to the job context has always been a strategic priority for COMEP. The fact that many otherwise sound management development programmes failed because the transfer process was aborted, was all too clear in the minds of COMEP planners. As a result, an extensive monitoring and follow-up network was built into COMEP in order to link both ends of the management development process. The network provides for a full-time programme coordinator in charge of nomination, screening and admission of candidates; a full-time counsellor providing for career planning and review as well as handling obstacles to the learning process and its job applications. Furthermore, participating organizations were asked to appoint preceptors from among their line managers to coach, help, and facilitate the reintegration of trainees into their respective jobs. Preceptors were to be effective counterparts to COMEP faculty and play an effective role not only in facilitating participant learning but also in overcoming organizational barriers to the effective utilization of the acquired skills.[6]

Also part of the COMEP set-up is an elaborate programme evaluation mechanism that covers participants, instructors, materials, graduates and a host of other variables. The evaluation process is continuous throughout the academic year and it covers interviews, questionnaires, progress reports, and seminars.

Both the one-tier academic programme and COMEP converge around supporting a new wave of interest in managerial professionalism in Bahrain. This interest has so far yielded a series of exceptionally successful seminars touching on issues ranging from management education appropriate for Bahrain to the emerging corporate culture and the management profession in transition. Such seminars represented the culmination of a series involving a host of others dealing with technical topics. Dividends also came in the form of material support from industry to fit the micro-computer lab which opened in spring 1986.

37

FUTURE PROSPECTS

The one-track two-tier system has undoubtedly made significant strides within a phenomenally short period. However, for its long-term viability to be assured, it has yet to attain self-sustained growth. While it has gradually managed to shed its 'experimental' nature and project an image of stability and continuity, it is still in many ways experiencing the pangs of rapid development. While there is every indication that the programme is firmly set on solid ground, its future prospects will be considerably affected by its success in meeting the following challenges:

(1) The need for further re-structuring of the curriculum in the direction of greater specialization and a richer elective reserve.

(2) 'Bahrainizing' more of its teaching material through faculty-applied research that can be fed into classrooms and management development seminars.[7]

(3) Having gained solid local acceptance, the programme should intensify its efforts towards gaining greater regional visibility and international recognition. One important path to be further traversed in this direction is playing a greater role in working out with industry professional management standards.

In the ultimate analysis, the Bahrain management education and development experience stands out as a testimony to the dire need for collaborative approaches. If the much-sought interface between theory and practice is to continue, it is imperative to build frameworks that are structured enough to offer a clear sense of direction yet open-ended enough to allow for self-renewal.

NOTES

1. The move to confront 'degree inflation' and anchor management education around national manpower needs should be understood within the sociocultural context of Bahrain as indeed many other developing countries where degrees are indicators of social status. Fortunately, however, sobering economic realities and the new phenomenon of job scarcity are bound to reinforce the importance of para-professional education in management and other applied disciplines.

2. Based on experience it was found possible to allow those who complete the CSD Programme with a GPA of 3 to transfer back to the ABD/AAD-BSc track as second-year students.

3. The existence of a separate accounting programme was made necessary by the mounting demand in the labour market for qualified accountants. Graduates are hired immediately upon graduation and move on either towards an MBA or a professional certification as part of their career plan.

4. The dynamics of industry–university interface created as a result continue to gain momentum and have created an active management forum for the first time in Bahrain.

5. Most of the difficulties in managing the various transitions were due to the novelty of the programmes and the relatively wide range of academic variables related to transition decisions. Following some mixed lessons of experience the system is now fully operational.

6. Some organizations were reluctant to go ahead with the preceptor idea as it implied commitment to programme evaluation perhaps beyond what was feasible at the moment. As a result, a new attempt is now being made to revitalize this avenue through the broader strategy of assessing skill transfers from COMEP to job context.

7. A major track in this direction is the development of Bahrain-based case studies.

REFERENCES

De Nisi (ed.) (1983) 'Management in transition: a study of management style in Saudi Arabia', Academy of Management Meeting, Dallas, USA.

Gulf Polytechnic (1985) 'Strategy for continuing management education in Bahrain', Seminar Proceedings.

Gulf Polytechnic (1986) 'The Bahrain management profession in transition', Seminar Proceedings.

McGuire, J. W. (1982) 'Management theory: Retreat to the academy', *Business Horizons*, July–August.

Schaeffer, W. G. (1985) 'The formation of managers in developing countries: The need for a research agenda', *International Review of Administrative Sciences* 1(3).

3

Grounding management education in local research: a Latin American experience

Carlos Dávila
(Universidad Javeriana, Bogota, Colombia)

BACKGROUND ON MANAGEMENT EDUCATION IN LATIN AMERICA AND COLOMBIA

Latin American management schools

To set a ground for the issues discussed in this chapter, I will start by presenting some basic information on management education in Latin America.

For the most part, Latin American university programmes in management go back to the post World War 2 period. Concurrent with an expansion of the university system since the 1960s, the number of institutions as well as the number of students has risen spectacularly in the last twenty years. Presently, one out of ten university students attend programmes in management, amounting to nearly 600,000 students (Tedesco, 1983; quoted by Gómez and Pérez, 1985). During the same decades, professional schools of management in the United States went through a period of ascendancy: the number of students in undergraduate programmes amounted to 230,000 in 1982 and MBA graduates increased from 4,600 in 1960 to more than 62,000 in 1983 (Rehder, 1982, quoted by Harris, 1984).

In Latin America these rising numbers of students are primarily undergraduates. A recent survey of fifty-eight institutions in thirteen countries of the region indicated that 78.5% of the student body is engaged in a four- to five-year professional degree programme in management (roughly equivalent to the US Bachelor's degree in management) (Cruz *et al.*, 1984). Perhaps the most striking data refer to Brazil: in 1979, more than 150,000 undergraduate students were enrolled in 250 programmes, representing 9.3% of Brazilian university students.

The number of graduate programmes has also been rising steadily. According to Cladea (Latin American Council of Graduate Management Schools), an association of graduate programmes established in the mid-1960s, there exist fifty graduate programmes: forty-six MBA and four doctoral-level programmes in five countries (Brazil, Colombia, Chile, Peru, and Venezuela) (Gómez and Pérez, 1985). Some of them are organized as part of university departments or schools; the rest are management schools separate from the university, generally the result of private-sector initiatives.

This explosive growth in management education has resulted in a critical situation in terms of academic standards. The inadequacy in number, dedication and training of the faculty is at the crux of the problem. In fact, as the above-mentioned study shows, about 60% of the faculty have a part-time dedication, i.e. teaching one or two courses concurrently with a full-time career in professional management. Full-time faculty can be found in only one out of three schools; and in those cases they generally amount to a small proportion of the faculty. Altogether, they only represent 15% of the 3,464 faculty members reported. Only one out of three holds a master's degree (for the most part the MBA degree), and only 16% hold a PhD (Cruz et al., 1984).

The consequence of this shortage and inadequacy of faculty are obvious: poor teaching, aggravated by a cult for pragmatism and 'how-to-do-it' training; disregard for and lack of research and, consequently, extreme scarcity of local intellectual production; and weakness and inadequacy of links with the environment (Dávila, 1980). These consequences mutually reinforce and result in a grim picture regarding the quality of management education in Latin America. This becomes a counterpoint to the optimism that a glance at the expansion of educational opportunities and enrolment figures could leave. In terms of the international division of labour, this situation is closely related to a passive, dependent role on the part of Latin American management schools in the transfer of management theories, models, and technologies developed in the industrialized world.

It is important to mention that the general features of management education in this area of the world are better understood by pointing out its unequal development across countries; and within each country, across regions, and schools. Consequently, there is an increasing gap between those countries ranking high in management education, e.g. Brazil, and those at the bottom of the scale; or within a particular country, between a handful of top management schools and the rest.

Management schools in Colombia

As will be shown later, these imbalances can also be seen in the case of Colombia. This country of 28 million people, located in the north-west corner of South America, is best known for its coffee-based economy, the strong inequalities in income distribution, an urban network departing from the primate-city pattern, a well-entrenched dominant class, a lasting bi-partisan coalition, thirty years of guerrilla warfare, and, more recently, a burgeoning narcotics business. According to the general Latin American pattern, figures on the growth of management education are startling. Although management courses were part of the curriculum in one of its best-known engineering schools since the 1910s as well as in a school of economics created in the early 1940s, the first management school established as such goes back to 1959. Ten years later, in 1970, their numbers increased to sixteen, doubled by 1976 and reached forty-three in 1980 (perhaps a number higher than in many European countries of similar size) (Scarpetta et al., 1986). The majority of these programmes offered only undergraduate degrees; in 1980, the number of graduate programmes (MBA as well as specialization programmes) was fourteen (Icfes, 1980). Out of these, only four are not part of universities.

Concomitantly, the number of management students has risen dramatically. Whilst they represented 0.2% of the country's university students in 1960, by 1972 the proportion had increased to 4.0%, 4.3% in 1976, 10.6% in 1980 and 17.7% in 1984. In absolute terms, this means that the small group of 64 students in 1960 had increased to 1,600 in 1976, 25,300 in 1980 and 48,500 in 1984 (Scarpetta et al., 1986). This 'uncontrollable explosion' has led to a crisis in management education in the country (Dávila, 1980).

In addition to the chronic problems of low academic quality in the field of management, a poor academic image vis-à-vis other disciplines, as well as increasing unemployment and underemployment for management graduates must be considered.

Under these circumstances, the pattern of unequal development and increasing gaps among schools should be kept in mind. In fact, while in many of the schools academic standards have remained consistently low since their beginning, there exist a few schools with high performance standards. Low standards are the result of attachment to routine and massive teaching, recitation of either old-fashioned or recent best-selling textbooks, almost total reliance upon part-time faculty with poor academic credentials, lack of any research activity, absence of management development events for executives and lack of curriculum planning.

In contrast, the other schools are concerned with improvement. This is carried out in a variety of ways: development of their faculty, starting research activities, recruiting the best students, experimenting with new teaching methodologies and the like. As a result, each category of schools seems to adjust to its status and its role in the country: the top, élite schools tend to reinforce their leading role whereas those in the lower echelons gradually weaken. As in the case of the industrialized world vis-à-vis underdeveloped nations, the gap between the two groups has increased over the years. In the early 1970s the differences were not so remarkable.

A good example of the imbalances between the two groups may be seen by analysing the papers presented at the annual meetings on management research since 1982 (Dávila, 1984). In the 1982–84 period, private schools were responsible for twenty-three (70%) of the thirty-three papers presented. In regional terms, schools located in the capital of the country contributed with nearly half of the papers. Despite the fact that the existing schools are located all over the country, those in the three largest industrial cities were responsible for 75% of the papers. Most striking, two private schools located in the capital of the country contributed eight (or 25%) of the works presented by the twelve participating schools (Dávila, 1984).

Finally, it should be mentioned that some inter-institutional efforts have been started in the past few years revealing a growing consciousness of the situation presented here. Besides the annual meetings on management research, other national and international events have taken place to address some critical issues. These include a meeting of Latin American management researchers held in Colombia in 1984, a national conference on the nature of management carried out in 1982, and a recent international conference on strategic planning and diagnosis of management schools, sponsored by, among others, INTERMAN

– an ILO, Geneva-based, international co-operation programme among management education institutions, the Colombian Association of Management Schools (Ascolfa), the Latin American Council of Graduate Management Schools (Cladea), and a private Belgian Foundation (Fon Leon A. Bekaert).

This paper maintains that prospects for the future are good even though the pattern of unequal development is likely to continue. In other words, such prospects do not seem to be evenly distributed among schools, perhaps reflecting the underlying inequality of a highly stratified society. To be sure, these prospects are not linked exclusively to funding and financial considerations. Matters related to management educational philosophy and academic policies also acquire importance in Latin American countries.

DOMINANT VALUES IN MANAGEMENT EDUCATION: SOME REMARKS

A number of long-held values and assumptions underly management education, the validity of which should be scrutinized both in the industrialized world as well as in developing nations. Without attempting to discuss them in length in this chapter, some issues should be raised. The following are especially important:

(1) The idea of management as the basic, dominant institution in contemporary society (Drucker, 1954) underrates the role of other institutions of society, such as the State and Labour.

(2) Conceiving underdevelopment in the Third World as a 'management problem' is a gross over-simplification.

(3) Management theory and techniques are not culture-free but deeply culture-bound.

(4) Management theory and practice as well as management education should not be seen any longer as 'neutral' or 'objective'. Power, class, and inequality are at the core of management, in spite of the fact that conventional management theories are not concerned about them.

(5) Management education cannot be limited to the development of 'practical' skills at the expense of solid theoretical background and social responsibility. The overemphasis on 'practice' has led to an anti-intellectual atmosphere in management schools.

(6) Dominant management and organizational theories lack a historical and critical perspective; they also tend to be ethnocentric, unilateral and reductionist.

(7) Top US business schools have had an enduring influence on management education around the world. The adoption of their paradigm in Europe as well as in Third World countries has shown some of the shortcomings of inappropriate technology transfer.

(8) The adherence to private business ideology narrows the scope of management education. The growing role of the State in the development process is a fact of life to be taken into account in order to maintain the relevance of management studies.

(9) Under structural poverty conditions prevalent in developing countries, the 'management of poverty' seems to be as relevant as the 'management of affluence' in the industrialized world. The delivery of social services, the performance of the 'informal sector' of the economy, and the emergence of new organizational structures different from the conventional ones based upon private property are definitely posing a challenge to management schools.

EXPERIENCES IN MANAGEMENT RESEARCH IN COLOMBIA

The remainder of this chapter is based upon the premise that the prospect for management education in less developed countries (LDCs) in general, and in Latin America in particular, rests upon the concern for and priority given to research in their management problems and practice, i.e. their 'management reality'. For this purpose, a re-focusing in educational and academic policies on the part of management schools in these countries is advocated.

Undoubtedly, strategy and policy choices are not made between polar opposites (as 'either/or' questions). Many options for policy-making in management school strategies count on midway positions, those that involve some of the 'theoretical' and 'practical' paradigms. However, in order to contrast the position held in this paper and the one currently found in business schools, it may be useful to portray them in terms of four dichotomies, as follows:

45

(1) A concern for knowledge *vis-à-vis* the anti-intellectual orientation of 'practical' training.
(2) An active role in adapting management theories and techniques to LDCs' development potential and problems *vis-à-vis* a passive, dependent posture towards transfer of management technology.
(3) An independent, critical position about private business, particularly multi-national corporations and big money *vis-à-vis* management schools as the bastions of managerial ideologies.
(4) A concern for public, semi-public, and private management and administration *vis-à-vis* the exclusive private business focus.

The setting

The pursuit of research in the management schools of Latin America is related to the experience of two top management schools in Colombia.

From the early 1970s they have been engaged in various research efforts that have already provided experiences to shed light on the policy issues raised in this section. I shall describe below the main features of two of these projects.

The two schools involved are private institutions and are located in Bogotá, the capital city of Colombia. The first of them, the School of Management at Universidad de los Andes, became one of the university's seven divisions in 1973 after fifteen years of being part of the School of Economics. Universidad de los Andes is a private, non-denominational university founded in 1948 by a group of local élite members interested in departing completely from the traditional university model inherited from Spain, and is patterned after the North American model. Los Andes has gained a reputation for its high academic standards and a strong quest for innovation. Its enrolment is 4,000 students, with about 500 belonging to the School of Management. At present it has five programmes:

(1) The undergraduate, five-year programme leading to a professional degree in Management.
(2) The MBA, a one-year full-time programme.
(3) The specialization, postgraduate programme in finance,

human resources and marketing, started in 1984 with part-time students and an eighteen-month duration.

(4) Top management programme established in 1967 for senior executives.

(5) Management development seminars: a variety of short courses in the functional areas of management initiated in 1973.

In its peak years, the school's full-time faculty have numbered up to fifteen, in the downward periods the numbers dropped to three full-time professors. Consequently, the number and role of part-time faculty have fluctuated a great deal.

The second institution, Universidad Javeriana, is a private, Roman Catholic, Jesuit University founded in the seventeenth century. Presently it has 12,000 students. Its School of Interdisciplinary Studies (FEI) was established in 1973 as an academic unit for postgraduate education as well as for intensive research. Its organization contrasts with the rest of the traditional, unidisciplinary schools into which the university is divided. FEI is organized into eight programmes: economics, educational technology, health and hospital administration, demography and population, political studies, rural development, food and nutrition, and social systems administration. All of these programmes and the school as a whole are directly engaged in research in development-related areas.

Even though none of its programmes deal specifically with management as such, in several of them, namely economics, health administration, and management of social systems, a variety of management-related activities are conducted. What is relevant to point out in this chapter is the programme in economics. It has a master's degree programme (enrolment of eighty students) whose participants for the most part are engaged in managerial rather than professional careers in economics. It has also become active in short courses in management development, even though on a smaller scale, if compared to Universidad de los Andes' School of Management. Since 1981 the programme in economics has sponsored both regular courses and research in business history and labour relations, both of which will be dealt with in the next section.

The programme's faculty has remained small, ranging between two and five full-time professors, all of them holding a PhD; there are six part-time professors. The projects mentioned next in

47

this chapter have been the responsibility of one of the full-time professors.

The labour relations and trade unionism in contemporary Colombia project

This project, initiated in 1978 at Universidad de los Andes, is still in operation. In 1983 it became a joint effort with Universidad Javeriana. It has been developed in the context of courses on contemporary labour relations and trade unionism in Colombia offered at the undergraduate, master's and specialization level. Its main objective has been to develop course materials and a methodology for teaching these courses. It stemmed from the uneasiness with the current orientations of teaching of industrial relations in Colombia which has either a personnel administration focus or a legal orientation. None of them permits the understanding of growing labour conflict and new trends in labour relations.

In order to alter this situation, the two faculty members in charge of the project designed an alternative course in 1978. Its main feature was to involve the participants directly in carrying out small empirical studies (case studies for the most part) on labour conflicts and/or on trades unions under the supervision of the staff. The idea elicited a positive response from students. In the 1978–82 period the course was offered regularly as an elective subject for undergraduates. The number of research monographs done by the students increased steadily at the same time that sixteen of them completed additional work on these topics for their bachelor's theses. A selection of the best of these monographs and theses was gradually included as part of the course materials, and since 1980 they have been regularly examined, tested, and further revised. In 1982 the course was introduced into the MBA programme; in 1983 it became an elective course in the MA programme in economics at Universidad Javeriana, and in 1985 it was included in the specialization in human resources programme. Union leaders have been invited to participate in the course since 1983.

A book containing a selection of these materials is in preparation (Rodríguez and Dávila). Each piece has a study guide for the student as well as a teacher's guide.

The book is intended as the basis for training faculty of several regions in the country. Its methodology is distinctively active and heavily empirically-based. Its chapters deal principally with research studies on the following topics:

(1) The social organization of strikes, both urban and rural, and in the public and private sectors.
(2) Labour and management strategies in specific labour negotiations both in the private and public sector.
(3) Ideological orientations of labour confederations.
(4) Labour relations in public services agencies.

This project has not received any external funding apart from that of the two universities. They have sponsored it as a part of their current activities.

The Colombian business history project

This ongoing project was started at Universidad Javeriana's School of Interdisciplinary Studies (FEI) in 1981. Its main objective is to promote and develop business history as a relevant field in economics and business schools in Colombia. For that purpose research and teaching activities began simultaneously.

Three research studies have been conducted: (1) an inventory of sources and existing literature on business history in Columbia, and its further critical review; (2) a study on the origins and formation of industrial entrepreneurship in two Colombian regions; and (3) an ongoing history of a public regional development corporation. Parallel to these, a postgraduate seminar in Colombian business history has been developed; up to the present it has been offered on six occasions.

The prospects for the near future are promising: requests have been made from several management schools in other cities of the country to assist them in the training of faculty for the future inclusion of a course on this subject in the curriculum and the formation of research capability.

A book recently published (Dávila, 1986), an annotated bibliography under preparation, and the development of teaching materials for the above seminar are the by-products of this project.

The guiding principle for the seminar has been the usefulness of approaching critical issues in the study of entrepreneurship by means of an historical perspective. Histories of firms, biographies of entrepreneurs, histories of particular economic sectors and the like contain, among others, important lessons on management strategies and practice that reflect the conditions of the economic, social, and political environment. In our viewpoint, management schools should be the 'natural audience' for this specialized field of economic history.

49

However, business history generally seems to be a rather strange subject in management schools. A good example of this may be seen in the neglect of historical perspective that has been characteristic of the renewed interest in entrepreneurship that has flourished in the United States in the past few years.

Finally, it should be mentioned that the project has been supported from its beginning by funds from Universidad Javeriana. A recent contract granted to the university to write a history of a public agency (1961–86) may be an indication of better prospects for funding in the future.

THE NEED FOR MANAGEMENT RESEARCH IN LATIN AMERICA: A PROPOSAL FOR REFORM

On the basis of these experiences, it is proposed that work begin towards a re-formulation of academic policies in Latin American management schools in order to promote research on their management problems and practice.

Policies to be re-defined should cover a number of critical issues. Among them, the following deserve particular attention: the role of business schools in the transfer of management theories and techniques originating in the industrialized world; strengthening of research capabilities by means of improving faculty recruitment strategies and development, formulating research agendas, linking research and teaching, and organizing proper diffusion of research work.

A new role for management schools in the transfer of management technology

Management theories and techniques originated with the advent of capitalist development and became salient as Western countries furthered their industrialization. Gradually they have become one of the most important 'soft' (or human-embodied) technologies that are transferred from advanced capitalist countries (the United States for the most part) toward the less-developed areas of the world.

Universities and educational institutions in LDCs are one of the leading channels or institutional vehicles of technology transfer. As such, they utilize a variety of mechanisms: training of faculty at selected business schools in Europe and the United States; utilization of their books and teaching materials; replication of programmes (for example the standard MBA programme) and courses used in those schools; and hiring management education consultants.

Generally the schools in LDCs play a rather passive role reflected in the adoption of concepts, methodologies, orientations, and techniques embodied in the above and other mechanisms without a critical screening. The lack of experience and tradition in Third World countries in the management field, the growing opportunities and demands to which they have to respond, the scarcity of books and teaching materials developed in LDCs, and the lack of an adequate and stable number of full-time faculty are some of the factors reinforcing dependency and passiveness on the part of management schools as vehicles for the transfer of technology.

The consequences of this situation are very serious for LDCs. The contribution of management to development tasks both in the public and private sectors is frequently hindered by the inappropriateness of the technologies transferred without due attention to the circumstances of the recipient countries. It is common that technologies respond to problems that are culturally-bounded: they may be a priority in the United States, for example, where they were developed but may be irrelevant in LDCs. This has been the case, for example, with some of the approaches and techniques in the field of human resources management.

Moreover, there are additional high costs of inappropriate import of technology: students coming out of management schools are ill-equipped and as a result they lose prestige and credibility. This is reflected in the diminishing role of management schools in LDCs vis-à-vis transnational corporations as channels of technology transfer in the fields of marketing, finance, human resources, and business policy.

In order to deal with the problem of management schools as mechanisms of inappropriate transfer of technology it should be kept in mind that it is necessary to peel away the mystique of management schools to lay bare the reality of their passivity in the process. In fact, it is common for them to portray themselves, instead, as leading agents for change highly concerned with national development strategies and trainers of entrepreneurial leaders and the like. It is not in this rhetoric that the problem is to be found but in the policies and strategies they follow.

51

Despite these serious shortcomings, there is a basis for a different set of policies and strategies to be attempted. As the experiences illustrated in this paper point out, it is possible to define an active role for management schools confronted with management theories and techniques coming from developed countries. In general, the prospects for this role depend on the prospects for four sorts of change in management schools' proclivities. First, an understanding of the different levels of management knowledge is needed. Teaching theories with an explanatory power, i.e. some theories of organizations, is different from lecturing on conventional administrative proverbs; at the same time, working with concepts and categories useful to describe aspects of management reality implies different skills from those required to implement a particular technique. Generally there does not exist any concern for the implications of these differences. As a result, management school faculty may pretend to be working simultaneously at all levels – theory, proverbs, practice, and applications of techniques. Since the resources of our schools are so restricted this is a mere illusion leading to poor teaching at any level. It would seem more appropriate for management schools in Latin America to concentrate on the level(s) of knowledge at which they are most proficient. To be sure, this cannot be done by adhering to the common-sense dichotomy between 'theory' and 'practice'.

Second, there is a need for understanding the inevitability of adapting management techniques to the conditions of developing countries in order to increase the probability of their successful implementation. For this purpose a comprehension of the local context is required and it depends greatly, if not exclusively, on empirical research. This is not aimed exclusively at the level of theory testing and explanatory purposes; good empirical descriptions of the local setting may be very useful in dealing with adaptation of technology. In any case, for the pursuit of a more fundamental understanding of local conditions, empirical research of one kind or another is indispensable. Solely 'practical experience' of managers and the advice of consultants are by no means sufficient. Doubtless, engaging in research is a rather complex task, especially if compared to the mechanical transmission, copying, and dissemination of techniques that are so tempting, especially as packaged programmes in the functional areas of management have flourished.

Third, a willingness and openness towards 'alternative'

management technologies in some selected fields is required. As in the case of agriculture and industrial technology there seems to be room in LDCs to develop some cheaper, simpler, and small-scale management technologies along the lines of Schumacher's Intermediate Technology Group. Small-size industry and to some extent the informal sector of LDC economies represent a vast field in need of attention regarding marketing, organization, human resources, and finance. To be sure, this should be an option open not to all schools but particularly relevant to some of them, depending on their location and the socio-economic characteristics of their immediate audience.

Fourth, a stronger stance on the part of Latin American institutions concerned with management education in their relationships with North American and European Universities, governments, transnational corporations, and foundations is needed. Exchange and international co-operation programmes should be based on mutual respect and understanding of the cultural, ideological, and political differences of the parties involved. Mutual reciprocity and the understanding that co-operation programmes benefit both parties – not merely the LDCs – should remove any traces of paternalism or imposition of attitudes.

The different role for management schools in Latin America being proposed is quite different from isolationism or neglect of contemporary political and economic realities. The leadership and pre-eminence of Western countries in the field of management is a fact of life. Confronted with this, an active, creative role is considered a better option than the passive, dependent role corresponding to the 'supplier–recipient of technology' model.

Strengthening of research capabilities

A new role for management schools in Latin America regarding the transfer of management technology is only possible if local research capability is developed. In spite of the scarcity of resources germane to management education in this region of the world, it is argued that funds channelled for building up a research basis will render fruitful results, and will significantly improve management education. In other words, in the light of limited resources, research, rather than a teaching and/or consulting focus, will render greater benefits in terms of the quality of education as well as of institutional consolidation. In this view, management research is not a luxury affordable only to industrialized countries. The future for management education in developing Latin American nations rests upon their concern for understanding their management reality and problems. This can be reached only through empirical research.

The experiences discussed previously suggest that there are ample grounds and opportunities for developing new research capabilities and strengthening the existing ones in Latin American institutions concerned with management education. Academic policies and strategies on a number of issues might contribute to this by the following means:

Faculty recruiting and development

(1) Increasing the number of faculty with PhD research training in the basic disciplines on which management is founded (sociology, economics, applied mathematics, psychology, etc.), rather than resting mostly upon MBAs.

(2) Providing faculty with greater stability and better opportunities for an academic career and decreasing the emphasis upon 'practical' experience and managerial careers as the desirable goal for faculty.

(3) Increasing the proportion of full-time faculty *vis-à-vis* part-time faculty.

(4) Planning advanced training for faculty by using selective criteria regarding the countries, schools, and type of programme most appropriate.

(5) Pooling high-level human resources already existing in the region, in specialized training events for faculty of several Latin American countries.

(6) Recognizing the need for local faculty to keep strong links to the international academic community in its respective field of specialization.

(7) Encouraging faculty to commit themselves to the promotion and legitimacy of research in those schools circumscribed to teaching and consulting.

(8) Promoting the formation of interdisciplinary research teams under the leadership of project directors.

(9) Abandoning the idea that promotion of researchers towards administrative positions is *the* way to strengthen research capabilities.

Research feasibility and priorities

Abandoning the idea that large-scale, multi-million dollar, internationally sponsored research projects are the best strategy for management research in Latin America; and de-emphasizing financial limitations as the single obstacle for engaging in research. In brief, de-escalating the model of research activity prevalent in the developed nations, in particular the United States.

(1) Recognizing the possibility of a variety of arrangements for organizing research activities; decreasing the emphasis on the research centre as the key for building a research capability.

(2) Recognizing that in management research the cost of laboratories, equipment, materials and the like is lower than in many other fields; consequently, funds should be channelled principally towards strengthening of faculty.

(3) Elaborating a long-term research agenda which sets priorities, depending not only on available funding but on strategic needs for each school according to its public or private nature; the socio-economic profile of the student body; the type of link with other institutional sectors; the interests and composition of faculty, etc.

(4) Developing research areas instead of mosaic-type research projects.

(5) Promoting comparative research projects among Latin American countries.

(6) Understanding the nature and risks of research work, e.g. long-run productivity; contradictory, non-linear evolution; high risk of getting into new research topics; impossibility of value-free research.

Linkages between research and teaching; use and diffusion of research

(1) Emphasizing the need for a close interrelationship between teaching and research; stressing the shortcomings of teaching divorced from a rigorous approach to reality.

(2) Encouraging students, either at the undergraduate or postgraduate level, to become directly involved in research projects under the supervision of faculty with the understanding that this is a valuable experience for future managers.

(3) Teaching respect for management research and research careers, challenging the cult for practical experience.

(4) Encouraging the production of teaching materials as a by-product of research on Latin American management reality.

(5) Promoting the diffusion at an international level of the results of research carried out in the region.

(6) Identifying the qualitative differences between research and consulting especially in terms of their usefulness for teaching.

REFERENCES

Cruz, F., Escobar, W., and Galarza, J. (1984) 'Estado actual de la investigación en Administración en las escuelas de Administración Latinoamericanas', paper presented at the First Meeting of Latin American Management Researchers, Universidad del Valle, Cali, Colombia, 21–24 November.

Dávila, C. (1980) 'La crisis de la educación en Administración en Colombia', *Revista Universidad Eafit – Temas Administrativos* **39** (Julio–Agosto–Septiembre): 20–35.

Dávila, C. (1984) 'La investigación en Administración: anotaciones sobre la experiencia colombiana y políticas para su promoción a nivel nacional y latinoamericano', paper presented at the First Meeting of Latin American Management Researchers, Universidad del Valle, Cali, Colombia, 21–24 November (Published 1986 in *Cátedra* 1(April–June) 13–27.)

Dávila, C. (1986) *El Empresariado Colombiano. Una Perspectiva Histórica*, Bogotá: Universidad Javeriana (FEI, Programa de Postgrado en Economía). Editográfica.

Drucker, P. (1954) *The Practice of Management*, New York: Harper & Row.

Gómez, H. and Pérez, C. (1985) 'Estudios de administración en América Latina', Cladea, mimeo.

Harris, R. (1984) 'The values of economic theory in management education', *American Economic Review* **74**(2): 122–6.

Icfes, 'Estadísticas de la educación superior, 1980', Bogotá.

Rehder, R. (1982) 'American business education: Is it too late to change?', *Sloan Management Review* **23**(Winter): 63–71.

Rodríguez, M. and Dávila, C. 'Relaciones Laborales en Colombia: Estudio de Caso', Bogotá: Universidad de los Andes (to be published in 1989).

Scarpetta, R., Alvarez, A., Echeverry, R.D., and Pabón, R. (1986) 'Diagnóstico sobre las Facultades de Administración en Colombia. Informe preliminar', paper presented at the Seminar on Diagnosis and Formulation of Strategies for Colombian Management Schools, Universidad del Valle, Cali, Colombia, 20–22 August.

Tedesco, J. C. (1983) *Tendencias y Perspectivas en el Desarrollo de la Educación Superior en América Latina y el Caribe*, París: Unesco.

4

Cultural dynamics and management development

N.S. Gupta
(*University of Jammu, India*)

MAN – THE CRITICAL FACTOR

Management consists of ten letters which together make one word meaning one body. One may be stated as perfect, on top, flawless, absolute or the ultimate. Without entering into a metaphysical or spiritual interpretation, the basic objective of management is to achieve perfection by removing deficiencies in man and his environment.

The focal point of management is MAN – the first three letters of the word management. The remaining seven letters, connoting (i) authority, (ii) government, (iii) environment, (iv) material, (v) ethics, (vi) nation or society, and (vii) technology, are the satellites of the epicentre MAN. Though they derive power from the epicentre by revolving round it they also emanate radiation in the process and influence the centre.

Man is the nerve centre of the organization and society. The principles, practices and techniques of management help man to be as perfect as possible by making up for deficiencies by reducing the incidence of wastage in human and material resources through the actualization of his purposes.

Man lives with others. To achieve his objectives, he requires *authority* to guide and direct the actions of others and to structure relationships in such a manner that each one accomplishes his object without impinging on others' rights and privileges. He must also make motivational dynamics work and be meaningful. Authority is the source of both ambivalence and conflict. Equity in distribution forges unity but the reverse causes conflict in organizations and society.

Man and government are inter-dependent. The behaviour of

government is determined by the will of its people and peoples' conduct is regulated by the writ of government. If man's behaviour and conduct are less deviant, government's plans and policies will be more humane and dynamic. The government's regulatory and developmental role should reflect the thinking of its people. Harmony should exist between policy formulation by the government and policy implementation by the people.

Behaviour is the function of man and environment. His attitudes, value system, and perceptions insulated by his social beliefs and customs are reflected in his personality composition and behaviour. What are virtues and vices, or supportive and obstructive behaviour are defined by the social system. Social ethos and components of culture in the form of social beliefs, customs, and values should not be perceived as barriers but as pay-offs for better organizational behaviour.

Man's behaviour also depends on the quantity and quality of material he gets for consumption and production. If he does not get the proper quality and quantity of material in the form of consumables, he may, at some stage, snatch from those who have in abundance, and thus portray abnormal behaviour. Similarly he needs material for keeping the wheels of production in motion.

Ethics provides sanctions for the various roles played by man in society. In the event of deviation, corrective devices are set in motion.

Social institutions influence man as man influences society. It is a two-way system which establishes durability in the relations between man and society. Similarly technology and man's behaviour are inter-connected.

Technological development results in weaker social relationships, much less loyalty and commitment to organizations, and a greater materialistic outlook due to perceived alienation.

CULTURAL DYNAMICS

In this section, I will discuss the role of culture in personality development, the socializing function of culture, and the role of culture in individual and social behaviour.

Culture, the components of environment, engraves an indelible mark on the personality development of man. The behaviour of people is determined by their cultures which are manifested in the terms of ideologies, values, and social roles. In the same manner a number of research studies suggest that sociocultural beliefs have a profound influence on organizations and values (Argyris, 1957; Abegglen, 1958; Dowling and Pfeffer, 1975). Those leaders and organizations which are capable of working in time with the sociological environment will prove to be more receptive to personnel and better equipped to realize organizational objectives with efficiency (Kaufman, 1967).

Culture dictates 'dos' and 'don'ts'. For instance, kissing is socially acceptable in American society but it is not permissible in many Eastern cultures. It is culture which develops traits of independence, aggression, competitiveness, and co-operation. These attributes then determine the behaviour pattern of individuals in organizations. Nystrom and Starbuck (1981) summarize a number of studies in the following words:

> Employees from cultures that emphasize independence are likely to be most comfortable with personnel policies and organisational structures that allow them to act as individuals, autonomously and with little dependence on others. By contrast, employees from cultures that emphasize conformity will be more satisfied if the social environment of the organization is highly structured. Employees from cultures where independence is valued would find agreeable those job environments in which inter-dependence is required for successful performance.

Culture becomes social ethos through the writ of family and society. This is a process of socialization. It is the socialization process which indoctrinates individuals with cultural dynamics which, in turn, dictate the pattern of behaviour. The family, social groups, and other social forces all contribute to cultural socialization which gives direction to the behaviour of individuals and groups

Studies on cultural socialization reveal interesting results. Sawyer and Levine (1966) describe contrasts between agricultural–pastoral and hunting–fishing cultures. They identify nine factors of cultural variation. Similar studies have been made by Dawson (1973) and Berry (1976). 'Hunting cultures socialise children to behave independently and self-reliantly; their personalities are reticent . . . and they do not conform to social norms in experiments testing such behaviour' (Berry, 1976: 415). Whereas 'children in agricultural cultures are taught to value the company of others and rewards are dispensed to those who conform and obey' (Berry, 1976: 415).

A number of other studies on cultural socialization reveal contrasts within culture. Kohn (1969) for example, reveals that in the United States and Italy children belonging to the upper class are taught creativity and independence whereas lower-class children are taught obedience and conformity. In this way children belonging to the lower class are socialized for positions as subordinates and followers and those belonging to the upper class for professional and business success.

Cultural socialization radiates social ethos and insulates individual and social behaviour. Man's behaviour gets attuned to the attributes and values around him. Consequently, a sharp difference is noticeable in the behaviour patterns of people living in different areas. For instance, people brought up in a Western culture develop traits of independence, autonomy, a materialistic or pragmatic outlook, and a less emotional attachment to the organization in which they are working. Conversely, people brought up in an Oriental culture are found to be dependent, obedient, and emotionally committed to organizations and their work place. The main reason for this difference derives from the development of the personality in a particular cultural environment with determines the behaviour of man.

MANAGEMENT DEVELOPMENT AND ORGANIZATIONAL EFFECTIVENESS

Management development is a systematic process used for the training and growth of managers and supervisors so as to improve their management of organizations. In other words, management development may be stated as a formal training programme to develop managerial skills. It became popular in the post-World War 2 era. A management development programme, which might involve on-the-job or off-the-job techniques, passes through five stages according to Heyel (1963):

(i)   awareness of the problem area and dissatisfaction with the status quo;
(ii) recognition of alternative solutions;
(iii) selection and practice of a new behaviour;
(iv) feedback from a reliable source, and
(v)   generalisation and integration of the new behaviour pattern into an established frame of reference.

(Heyel, 1963: 470)

However, the processes and the techniques of management development programmes which are designed to improve organizational effectiveness, often fail to realize their objectives because of standardization of format which has resulted in all management programmes throughout the world, even today, containing the following elements: (i) background information about the company; (ii) present management principles and techniques; (iii) human relations; (iv) technical knowledge and skills; (v) economic, social, and political environments; and (vi) personal skills. Human relations and environmental settings are prescribed (Stone, 1969; Goodman and Moore, 1972) but their utility becomes minimized when they are focused through standardized management principles, techniques, and processes.

Management development programmes ought to be structured in micro and macro perspectives. The micro perspective has an important bearing on organizational effectiveness. The management development programme should be tailored to suit the internal environment of the organization. The micro perspective takes account of three levels: individuals, departments, and re-organization. Duncan (1972) outlines the parameters of the macro perspective as (i) customers, (ii) suppliers, (iii) competitors, (iv) sociopolitical context, (v) social forces including government policy, and (vi) the technological context. The micro and macro perspectives focus on man as a being whose behaviour is determined by the cultural dynamics around him. Consequently, management styles may be considered as a dependent variable, rather than as an independent variable because of the differences between cultures of the East and the West (Negandhi and Reimann, 1973; Pfeffer, 1973).

A management development programme based on a standardized package of management techniques and processes cannot but touch the fringes of change and development. Consequently managers exposed to such programmes find themselves helpless in introducing the desired behaviours for achieving the goal of organizational effectiveness. The tools of management development are incapable of exerting much impact on the behaviour modification of employees working therein.

A CULTURAL MODEL OF MANAGEMENT DEVELOPMENT

The standardized package for management development has not

achieved the goal of organizational effectiveness. Managers and supervisors, even after thorough exposure to the latest tools and techniques of management, cannot persuade people in their organizations to commit themselves unreservedly to realize organizational goals with efficiency. Behaviour interventions adopted by them perpetuate the forces of tension, acrimony, and even conflict. These tensions sometimes assume an explosive shape when they come out of the four walls of the organizations and engulf a sizeable proportion of the population.

The reason for this malfunctioning is that the package of management development evolved in the Western environment of greater autonomy, aggressiveness, lesser emotional attachment to organizations, and competitiveness, are alien to Oriental culture. Technology has further transformed Western behaviour. Most people have developed a sense of isolation, powerlessness, normlessness, and self-estrangement which results in the formation of a materialistic outlook with less reliance on the effectiveness of social bonds which prove too weak to tide over economic and other problems. In Western culture, the child is brought up in an environment of practically no 'dos' and 'don'ts' which results in greater autonomy, independence in work and decision making, and selective commitment to organizations and their purposes. Consequently, a job for life is discounted on the principle of efficiency of the individual and the organization. There is a greater decentralization of power and authority through the upholding of the norms of individuality and competitiveness; and greater credence is given to a rational and objective outlook than to emotional commitment to organizations and people.

Managers exposed to a development programme based on such an ethos and such a system should realize the inappropriateness and ineffectiveness for people brought up in a different sociocultural environment. A child in the East is brought up in an environment of 'dos' and 'don'ts' which develops in him dependence, respect for authority, a sense of corporate spirit, a commitment to team work through submerging individuality, and a greater emotional commitment to work and organizations. Since technology and urbanization are less advanced, people living in villages or towns are still attached to the principles of corporate life, social interdependence, unquestionable commitment to social norms and institutions, and unbound respect to the status of elders and the tenets of religion. Even in the Oriental culture one can find differences in the behaviour patterns of people living in advanced urban centres like Bombay and the less-developed areas of Uttar Pradesh and Madya Pradesh in India. A Bombayite is comparatively less social, more materialistic, less dependent, more aggressive and competitive compared to his counterpart living in other parts of the country where the level of urbanization is lower.

Managers and supervisors fresh from a training programme seek to socialize the behaviour of others with the attributes of an alien culture. Such incompatability negates the value of the programme of change and development initiated by the managers. Even the technique of reinforcement or interventions to transform behaviour prove ineffective. Consequently a management philosophy for the East should be based on the principles of interdependence, limited delegation of authority, reasonable centralization in decision-making, the development of team work, and the encouragement of an emotional commitment to work and organizations. If managers attempt to drive people with practices and techniques which are alien to their culture, they will encounter yet more problems in their efforts to achieve organizational effectiveness. A living example of such maladjustment is the behaviour of coal miners in the Bihar region of India. By and large, the coal miners were docile and committed to work and their organization before nationalization. After nationalization a new pattern of aggressiveness and deviant behaviour has emerged which is posing a serious threat to the coal-mining industry. The reason for this change was the reckless application of the tools and techniques of management by managers having had exposure at Harvard or MIT or their satellite institutions like the Indian Institutes of Management to Western management styles.

CONCLUSION

A cultural model of management development may be summarized as follows:

(1) Culture is an important variable in human behaviour. Man's perceptions, attitudes, and values are cast in the mould of cultural dynamics.
(2) Managers cannot easily transform indelible cultural influences. They are so deep-seated in the personality that the desired behaviour modifications are not possible

63

within the standard paradigm of management development.

(3) Social beliefs, customs, and values and their concomitant patterns of behaviour should not be perceived as barriers but as pay-offs for better organizational behaviour. Some of the contributions of Oriental culture which are different and traditional from the West are: respect for authority, an emphasis on work groups and team spirit, and an emotional commitment to the organization. The emphasis on spiritualism reduces the incidence of frustration, and individual and group conflict and tensions.

(4) A management development programme, instead of being standardized should be designed so as to capitalize on the particular social ethos in order to achieve the management objective of organizational efficiency.

REFERENCES

Abegglen, J. C. (1958) *The Japanese Factory*, Glencoe, Illinois: Free Press.

Argyris, C. (1957) *Personality and Organisation*, New York: Harper & Row.

Berry, J. W. (1976) *Human Ecology and Cognitive Style*, Beverley Hills: Sage/Halsted.

Dawson, J. L. M. (1973) 'Effects of ecology and subjective culture on individual traditional–modern attitude achievement motivation and potential for economic development in the Japanese and Eskimo Societies', *International Journal of Psychology* 8: 215–25.

Dowling, J. and Pfeffer, J. (1978) 'Organisational legitimacy: Social values and organisational behaviour', *Pacific Sociological Review* 18: 122–36.

Duncan, R. D. (1972) 'Characteristics of organisational environments and perceived environmental uncertainty', *Administrative Science Quarterly* 17(2): 313–27.

Goodman, R. S. and Moore, B. M. (1972) 'Cross cultural management research', *Human Organisation* 31: 39–45.

Heyel, C. (ed.) (1963) *The Encyclopedia of Management*, New York: Reinhold Publishing Corporation. p. 470.

Kaufman, H. (1967) *The Forest Ranger* (2nd edn), Baltimore: Johns Hopkins Press. pp. 222–3.

Kohn, M. L. (1969) *Class and Conformity*, Homewoods, Illinois: Dorsey.

Negandhi, A. R. and Reimann, B. C. (1973) 'Task environment decentralisation and organisation effectiveness', *Human Relations* 26(2): 203–14.

Nystrom, P. C. and Starbuck, W. H. (1981) *Handbook of Organisation Design*, vol. 2, Oxford: Oxford University Press, p.187.

Pfeffer, J. (1973) 'Canonical analysis of the relationships between an

organisation's environment and managerial attitude toward subordinates and workers', *Human Relations* **26**(3): 325–57.
Sawyer, J. and Levine, R. R. (1966) 'Cultural dimensions: A factor
analysis of the world enthnographic sample', *American Anthropologist*
68: 708–33.
Stone, D. (1969) 'Bridging cultural barriers in international management', *Advanced Management Journal* **34**: 59–62.

5

The impact of local culture and attitudes on organizational effectiveness in Algeria

Boufeldja Ghiat and Phillip C.T. Willey
(*University of Nottingham*)

INTRODUCTION

When I (B.G.) first became interested in the effectiveness of Algerian organizations, and was told about the impact that culture and attitudes had on organizational effectiveness, I was sceptical. Production systems which have been imported from Western developed countries are amongst the most sophisticated available. The associated managerial styles were copied (with a few subtle changes) from the Eastern socialist countries, and workers were allowed to participate in the management of their organizations. I thought that culture would not influence working life but would really only be concerned with religion including patterns of worship, and relationships between people, their families, and friends. The work of organizations, I thought, would be independent of cultural factors. The facts, however, were otherwise. Organizations which should have worked efficiently, stayed ineffective and inefficient. Many had high rates of absenteeism, labour turn-over, and accidents. Most of them ran at a loss, despite the investment in facilities, despite the freedom from pressures of competition, and despite continual financial and advisory support from central government.

The factories were modern and the management techniques and styles were sophisticated. Only one factor remained to investigate: the broader environment in which these organizations operated. This broader environment includes the national and organizational infrastructures together with the political, economic, social, and cultural aspects, most of which are transitional by nature.

Algeria has a socialist political system. Political policies, it should be realized, influence management styles and organizational

66

structures. Yet, at the same time, industrial organizations influence the national infrastructure and the economic environment. The combined effect is that these influences bring about continual change and development.

In contrast, a more persistent factor, and one which may take a generation or more to change, is social attitude and the cultural setting. Knowledge of the culture is fundamental to the understanding of human attitudes and reactions to different managerial styles and techniques.

Several papers and books (Negandhi and Estafen, 1965; Mansfield and Poole, 1981; Schipers and Fijardo, 1983; Cool and Lengrick-Hall, 1985) have tackled the relationship between culture and management. Tom Lupton points out that 'the state of technical, economic and socio-cultural environment in which an organization lives and has its being is the significant factor that determines the pattern of relationships and the style of behaviour' (Lupton, 1971: 18).

Karl Deutsh (1980) divides the world's people into those having a 'proto-industrial culture' and those living in a 'counter-industrial tradition'. The two concepts are explained in Deutsh's own terms as follows:

By proto-industrial, I mean a culture that has already taught people the value of saving and thrift; the benefit of working for distant goals; the need for accuracy, precision and reliability; the use of time; and in particular, the maintenance of contracts – both a certain flexibility in making contracts and a certain dependability in keeping them.

He also found that

Counter-industrial cultural traditions were present . . . where industry grows more slowly, where industrial habits take a longer time to root, where there is much trade and little manufacture, and where on the whole there is much interest in laws and little in science.

Peter Blunt focuses on the effect of culture on organizations. He points out that 'an individual's perception of his job and work in general is substantially determined by the stock of cultural values and norms he has acquired from his living environment' (Blunt, 1983: 54).

67

As a result of our inability to explain the persistent shortfalls in effectiveness in Algerian organizations, we felt it essential to carry out studies on the personalities of managers, their styles of management, and the effects these had on their organizations. These studies were part of a broader investigation of the effectiveness of Algerian organizations.

This paper explains some aspects of workers' reactions to the managerial styles and behaviour of their managers by examining the cultural environments of the organizations which we studied.

METHODOLOGY

The study was carried out in three textile units:

(1) Unit one is a cloth-making unit, situated on the outskirts of a big city, Oran.
(2) Unit two is a clothes-making unit and situated in a small city, Maghnia.
(3) Unit three is a cloth-making unit and situated in a town, Sebdou, in which most of the inhabitants are from rural backgrounds.

We describe below the findings from each case unit and we then outline further cultural factors, identified from our broader study, which may have an impact on organizational effectiveness in Algeria.

All three units are State-owned and are organized according to the Socialist Management of Enterprises which is an Algerian participative model, in which workers contribute to the management of their organizations through five committees and a management council. Within the management council, the manager and his close assistants sit with workers' representatives in order to discuss and make all the important decisions.

An average of fifty workers from each unit were interviewed by the researchers. The informants were from different departments and different hierarchical levels.

THE THREE CASES

An authoritative management style

The manager of the first unit was a former production manager. He knew the work process and most production workers knew him. He had been promoted to manager of the unit and he enjoyed exercising his authority within it. He respected the hierarchical structure of the unit. For example, if he saw any abnormality while observing working operations, he talked to the worker's supervisor and never to the worker himself. He was inaccessible to workers from the shopfloor and, if there were complaints, workers had to make them through the formal hierarchy.

This manager was asked about the necessity of getting agreement from workers' representatives before taking important decisions. He was also asked about the delays in carrying out these decisions. He replied that, as manager and as the person principally responsible, he himself would take urgent decisions, if necessary, without consulting workers' representatives. He would inform them later on. 'I have to make them accept my decisions' he said. He carried out his duties without trying to be nice to people. Disciplinary sanctions were taken immediately after any trouble, whether caused by the worker or by middle managers.

The result was that everyone within the unit carried out their duties as they should. The researchers expected to find hatred for the manager and a good deal of stress amongst the workers, but the fact was that the manager was respected, though this respect was mixed with fear. Fear was manifested by the fact that in this production unit, as compared to the practice in others, workers were in constant attendance at their place of work and dared not leave their machines for unofficial reasons such as going to talk to friends in other departments.

An open management style

The second unit was smaller than the first. As in the case of the first unit, the manager had previously worked in the production department. But in this case the manager had a different personality, in that he was open to people. There were no restrictions on anyone visiting him in his office or talking to him outside his office. That was mainly because of his familiarity with workers, and the small size of the unit. He did not do anything without meeting workers' representatives in order to get them to accept any proposals or decisions. A workers' representative, who had been elected at both unit and enterprise levels, was asked by us if the manager of the unit created problems for workers' representatives. He replied that it was the unit manager who, in meetings at the enterprise level, needed help from the representatives in order to defend the manager's point of view. As a result, compared with the manager in the first unit, this manager, at least in the opinion of the workers' representative, was less respected. The manager's openness thus led to his authority being undermined by the workers' representative as well as by some middle managers. So, the cohesion of the management group was adversely affected. In attempting to operate an open style of management, as required by the model for Socialist Management of Enterprise, the unit manager's position had appeared so inconsistent and weak that his immediate subordinates did not identify him as a focus.

A rural community

The third unit was situated in a small town in a rural area. In this unit the workers' complaints about their manager were about his personal behaviour, both within and outside work. He was well known, in the Muslim community, as a drinker of alcohol and as a womanizer, both of which received much disapproval from within this conservative rural environment.

The manager's personal behaviour, of course, had nothing to do with his work nor with his abilities and managerial skills. Nevertheless, as a result of the local culture he was not seen as a good manager. In their eyes a 'good manager', whether well-educated or not, should be someone who sets a good example, both within and outside the work setting.

OTHER CULTURAL FACTORS

Kinship

What was also noticed in many of the other organizations in

which the broader research study was carried out was the strong feeling of kinship amongst the workers. This affected the organizations at several levels. First, recruitment officers found it difficult to select the most suitable people for particular jobs. I (B.G.) was previously a training officer, and I had been directed to recruit new workers. Many of my own and my father's relatives and friends used to come to see me at home on behalf of their sons or relatives, instead of coming to the office where I work. This is an example of the deeply ingrained cultural belief that you can be more easily accepted for a job if you have a friend or a relative who is able to influence the organization on your behalf. So, the kinship or friendship ties of prospective employees become more important than their abilities and qualifications. Psychological testing for selection and appointment is, therefore, useless in these situations. Second, these strong kinship ties and loyalties in developing countries can cause conflict and mutual dislike between members of different tribes when employed in the same organization.

Elders/Respect for the old

Organizational effectiveness is also affected by the belief that older people should be respected. So, conflicts arise between people who are older and have experience within an organization and those who are younger and have qualifications. One senior worker argued against educated people saying that 'when they were studying I was working and taking care of production, so why should they be promoted and not me?'. This problem leads to mutual mistrust between the types of managers who are experienced but have few, if any, qualifications and those who are qualified but younger. The result is a high turn-over of educated people to the extent that some organizations run without a single engineer.

Female attitudes

Female attitudes towards work and the cultural attitude towards working women are other burdens on all Algerian organizations employing female workers. In Algerian society, most women who work in jobs which are low paid, give up working when they

71

marry or, if not then, when they are expecting their first child. These conditions were present in all the units we studied, but were more crucial in the units located in rural areas or small towns. Two examples illustrate this. Unit two, the sewing unit, always had about ten female operators in training, in order to replace the ones who would be leaving. Unit three found it very difficult to recruit female operators from the rural environment in which it was sited, even for those jobs which were more suitable for females.

DISCUSSION

If we look at the three cases from the point of view of Western culture and managerial know-how, we would have expected to find in the first unit a conflict between workers and their representatives on the one side and management on the other, caused by the rigidity and strong authority of the unit manager. However, the reality was that, despite poor working conditions caused by old machinery and workplace noise, the unit was doing well and workers were happy with their unit manager.

In contrast, the openness of the manager of the second unit, which might have been expected, according to Western culture, to create a better organizational climate and greater workers' satisfaction, led to a conflict mainly within the managerial group. It also led, in some cases, to the undermining of the manager's authority.

In the third unit, the effect of culture is clear. The manager was expected to behave outside work according to his workers' culture and traditions. Yet, in the West, a manager's out-of-work behaviour would usually be regarded as irrelevant, his managerial reputation being based entirely on his performance at work.

We can see the effects of culture when we compare the first and third units. The first unit is in a big city, where workers have industrial work experience and attitudes. Workers find satisfaction and self-respect in their high productivity and the good performance of the unit. The personal behaviour and private life of the manager is not considered.

In contrast, the rural people in the third unit spend much of their time outside work talking about work problems and the private life of their manager. In rural areas, work is not taken as seriously as it is in city contexts. The personnel manager reports higher absentee rates when there is a good film, a serial, or an international football match on the television. Also, there is more absence on market days than on other working days.

In units two and three, management is obliged to allow some workers a break of an hour or two in order to go into the town centre. When the personnel manager was asked about this, he replied that management was obliged to allow them that break, as otherwise they might take the whole day off.

Another conclusion reached from observations of the first and second units, is the fact that the autocratic leadership style was more successful in running the first organization than the democratic style of running the second unit. Although we cannot generalize this finding because of the small sample, further research is needed concerning the most appropriate style of management in developing countries in general and in Algeria in particular.

Cultural values and norms are dynamic and not static. They influence peoples' behaviour and judgements about different aspects of life. Culture is also influenced by changes in politics, levels of development, and educational standards. But these changes take decades to evolve, and often have to await the passing of several generations.

One thing is undeniable, cultural differences cannot be ignored. Even among the industrially advanced countries there are differences in culture and characteristics. When deciding about managerial styles and techniques in different countries there is no optimum system which can be prescribed in advance. We must be prepared to seek and modify systems so that they are appropriate. It is much easier to change the way people are managed, in order to be compatible with the cultural environment, than to change attitudes and cultures. Schipers and Fijardo point out that 'where success has been experienced, modern management has been adapted to mesh with local culture, social and political environment' (Schipers and Fijardo, 1983: 1).

We believe that this study indicates that cultural and environmental factors have to be taken into consideration when deciding the managerial styles and techniques to be applied in different environments even within a single country. We further suggest that the curriculum of training managers ought to include consideration of the cultural aspects of different environments.

CONCLUSION

The structure and organization of Algerian manufacturing units have developed in that they now allow workers to participate in the management of their units. However, most of the techniques and managerial know-how are copied from the East or the West, and much still remains to be done by local managers, social scientists, and organization theorists in order to develop management styles which are more appropriate to the local culture. This is a strong lesson to learn and one which also applies to organizations in other developing countries.

REFERENCES

Blunt, P. (1983) *Organizational Theory and Perspective: An African Perspective*, New York: Longman.

Cool, K. and Lengnick-Hall, C. A. (1985) 'Second thoughts on the transferability of Japanese management style', *Organization Studies* 6/1.

Deutsh, K. (1980) 'Theory of imperialism and neocolonialism', in S. Rosen and J. Kurth, (eds) *Testing Theories of Economic Imperialism*, Toronto: Lexington Books.

Lupton, T. (1971) *Management and the Social Sciences*, Harmondsworth: Penguin.

Mansfield, R. and Poole, M. (1981) *International Perspectives on Management and Organization*, Aldershot, UK: Gower.

Negandhi, A. R. and Estafen, B. D. (1965) 'A research model to determine the applicability of American management know-how in differing cultures and/or environments', *Academy of Management*, December, pp. 309–18.

Schipers, F. and Fijardo, H. R. (1983) *Appropriate Management for Small and Medium Size Industries in Developing Countries*, Singapore: Technonet Asia.

6

Lessons from evaluation in Africa for external funding bodies

Robert Youker

THE PROBLEM

Many resources are spent each year on management training for Sub-Saharan Africa. For example, in the fiscal years 1984 and 1985, the World Bank alone committed an average of US$25 million per year for management training. The overall figure, combining all countries and donors, would be much higher. Worldwide, the Bank committed US$240 million for all types of training in 1985. These funds are used for fellowships, hardware, local training, study tours, and expatriate experts.

Training in the developing world is big business and the effectiveness of that training in improving organizational performance is important. The efficiency and effectiveness of management training is important for reasons beyond simple return on these large investments.

Almost all parties in Africa now agree that finance, the policy framework and effective management are the missing keystones in African economies today. Report after report pinpoints management as the key problem from the logistics of drought relief to the management of management training institutes. If management training is not effective in improving organizational performance, then Africa will not be filling this gap.

A large number of studies by different agencies in the last few years have all indicated that technology transfer via training in Africa has not been as effective and efficient as necessary or possible. Within the World Bank, there has been concern about the relatively weak performance of the training components it has financed. We should note, however, that with extensive effort in the last ten years (the Bank only started financing training components systematically since about 1972), the quality of training components has increased substantially. Specific problems identified by the Bank include the lack of borrower commitment; the lack of overall human resource plans; poor preparation of training; the lack of relevant training; and the poor timing of training.

The problem can be summarized by saying that too often the wrong person gets the wrong training at the wrong time and in the wrong place. Once again, the problem is relative. There is a great deal of very effective training in Africa, but not enough training meets the high standards we must set.

This paper will reference some of the recent major evaluations of training and training needs in Africa and summarize the main findings. In addition to broad studies, there have also been a number of specific evaluation studies of individual courses or country programmes. The paper will summarize the conclusions from some of these studies and present a series of 'principles' for effective training which logically follow from the above evaluations of negative and positive results. The essence of the principles is that training must be aimed at changing specific on-the-job behaviour.

These 'principles' will not be surprising. As you read them, you will say that they sound like common sense or that you have known them for many years. But the evaluation studies show that some members of the training profession are not always following these well-known rules in our work in Africa today.

I will start with a list of principles. Then I will go back to the various evaluation studies to present evidence to support the principles.

PRINCIPLES FOR TRAINING

(1) The basic purpose of training is to improve organizational performance by changing individual behaviour back on the job. Behaviour includes thinking and attitude change and can be an objective of training.

(2) The objectives of training may be, and in fact often are, different for the organization, the individual, the training institution, and the trainer. Differences must be recognized and dealt with.

(3) Many organizational performance problems and human

resource development problems are not amenable to solution by training or by training alone.

(4) Some of these problems are beyond the organization and are general to the environment.

(5) Training and the evaluation of training start with the definition of objectives.

(6) These objectives must be expressed in terms of required behaviour on the job.

(7) The definition of training needs and the management of training should be a regular part of an organization's staff development plan and personnel management system.

(8) In addition to the capability and motivation of the trainee, behaviour on the job, after training, will be almost totally influenced by the systems on the job and the reinforcement behaviour of the supervisor and the job environment.

(9) Trainees will not continue to perform the new behaviour, back on the job, unless they feel confident that they have the skill and that they will be rewarded (or not punished) for performing the behaviour.

(10) Training needs should be jointly defined by the superior and the subordinate.

(11) The actual training should be based on job needs, not the teacher's knowledge and skills. There is a dilemma here because teachers will also perform what they feel confident to do and what they get rewarded for and that may not be what the trainee needs.

(12) Confidence to perform requires the trainee to practise in realistic job conditions.

(13) Training institutions should also offer consulting services to actually help organizations to improve performance, if these services are not available elsewhere.

(14) The top management of the client organization must be interested in improvement and be active in an overall institutional development programme of which training is only one part.

(15) Managers have to learn how to manage scarcity (get work done by people who are hardly paid, have no operating budget, lack foreign exchange resources, etc.), a subject about which few expatriate trainers or managers know anything.

(16) Most management training for Africa needs to be performed at local institutions for reasons of relevance, national aspirations, and cost.

FINDINGS FROM MAJOR STUDIES

Let us now look at the findings of several recent studies of management training in Africa. There are nine in all: many of them are quite forthright about the problems and successes that they have discovered.

NASPAA

In 1984 and 1985, the United States Agency for International Development (USAID) financed a report by the National Association of Schools of Public Affairs and Administration (NASPAA) on the management training needs for the Southern African Development Co-ordination Conference (SADCC). A large international team studied more than 3,000 critical events as well as interviewing officials in ten countries. Their findings on the performance of African training institutions showed that in many cases, examinations and other evaluation materials derived from advanced industrial countries are utilized without any regard to their appropriateness in Southern Africa.

Despite a few happy exceptions, teaching methods used are overwhelmingly didactic, they involve memorization of theoretical concepts and provide few opportunities for participative learning or gaining experience through doing. These methodologies are of little value in training senior managers and provide almost no opportunity to learn motivational skills, inter-personal skills, or negotiation skills. In other words, they do not address some of the most critical training needs. There are also major resource problems. The lack of finance makes necessary a heavy stress on giving formal courses as contrasted with in-house and organization development training approaches. These, although more costly to conduct, are likely to have greater impact on organizational performance. The heavy work loads and teaching loads of the international training institutions leave little time or energy for research or consulting work. Furthermore, many faculty have had little experience in consulting and would be reluctant to undertake such assignments.

There is clear evidence here that the training is not focused on job-related behaviours but on the capabilities of the training institution.

IFAD

For the past three years, the International Fund for Agricultural Development (IFAD) has conducted a major training programme for managers of African agriculture projects in association with the African Development Bank (AfDB) and the Economic Development Institute of the World Bank (EDI). The first phase was for Southern and Central African countries and was completed in December of 1985. The training design involved a series of seminars for several different members of project teams from IFAD and AfDB projects held at local training institutions. An extensive evaluation of results is about to be completed by IFAD. The preliminary results show that although the seminars were rated highly for usefulness, mastery of subject, and importance of team work in improving project management, their impact would be increased if more emphasis had been placed on the job site and the project team rather than on general training sessions.

One positive outcome was that the approach of having each team prepare a performance improvement plan, assisted greatly in influencing behaviour change back on the job. However, it was clear that this approach needs continued follow-up. In addition to project managers, it is important that senior management be aware of the training and be prepared to make changes in the overall situation to make the training more effective.

This evaluation, with both negative and positive results, supports the need to focus on the actual job situation of the trainee.

USAID

The United States Agency for International Development (USAID) Center for Development Information and Evaluation recently analyzed 277 agricultural projects in Africa. The report supported the use of clearly defined work assignments on the grounds that they challenge an individual's skills and can serve as an incentive or motivator. There was also evidence that on-the-job learning from role models was effective in leadership training.

Recommendations for change were made in three areas. First, it was felt important that management development should include assertiveness training to help managers learn how to take the initiative, to plan ahead, and have confidence in his/her decisions.

79

Second, it was pointed out that training in general skills was of limited value and that hands-on or job-related training would be more useful. Training that is closely related to the tasks that staff are asked to do has always been more successful than general skill training. Such training should be offered on-site, should join teams of people from the same organization to focus on their tasks, and should relate the training and technical assistance to problems in the immediate local setting. Third, it was recognized that trainees need follow-up support rather than a single exposure to training. This could be a second round of training, but ideally it would take the form of on-the-job visits and consultations. Without such follow-up, the initial investment in training can be lost.

EDI

For the last five years, the Economic Development Institute of the World Bank has jointly conducted a course on National Economic Management with the training centre of the Central bank of the West African States (BCEAO–COFEB). Recently, questionnaires were sent to participants, followed up by interviews with supervisors and participants. Forty-five of seventy-two participants returned questionnaires and twenty-eight were interviewed. The participants and supervisors expressed a level of satisfaction with the course. The supervisors said, however, that students need to be taught not just mechanical techniques, but how to communicate and to work with others to introduce change. Seventy-five per cent of the participants made some use of what they were taught; however, only a minority said they made much use of the specific technique of economic analysis they had been taught in the course. The reason was that the French 'effects' method dominates the procedures in French-speaking countries.

It was felt that the training should have started with a needs analysis looking at the local systems for project appraisal. Then it should have used a module that included the 'effects' method. EDI has learned a lesson here and a recent evaluation of results in Zambia included recommendations that Project Analysis Training Courses which teach project techniques to middle-level officials are important but should be more effectively integrated with 'on-the-job training in project work'.

EDI/ESAMI

For several years the EDI has assisted the Eastern and Southern Africa Management Institute (ESAMI) of Arusha, Tanzania, with a course on promoting small businesses. Recently, during an evaluation, ex-participants from a local bank were interviewed. The finding demonstrated the importance of the commitment of the organization. In this case the potential value of the training was largely relegated because a high percentage of trainees had been transferred to a totally different job shortly after their return from training. Among those who were not transferred, returning participants found a lack of interest of their supervisors in the training and none of them had been required to submit a report. Moreover, when participants tried to introduce small improvements learned from training, they were rebuffed by bureaucratic obstacles and resistance from their superiors.

EEC

A few years ago, the European Economic Commission (EEC) conducted an evaluation of the extensive training they had financed in Malawi. Three of their key findings were as follows: first there were problems at the selection stage. The lack of a systematic process leads to poor selection of participants with little relation between course design and job needs (individuals organized their own training with overseas institutions without reference to supervisors). It was also apparent that specific technical courses had been more successful than broad courses. The reason for this was felt to be that in the latter case the objectives were unclear and were not sufficiently related to organizational problems. They were also critical of the instructors who did not tailor teaching materials to the local environment nor did they consult with local managers.

This evaluation again demonstrates the need to relate course objectives and teaching materials to the actual job situation.

EDI/UNDP programme

The EDI, in association with UNDP and other donors, held a round-table discussion of African Management Training Institutions in Kenya in June of 1986. Small groups discussed various topics which were then reviewed in general sessions on how to improve training in Africa. The following conclusions from this review support the thesis of this paper: first they agreed that greater attention is needed to assess local problems and to identify the skill gaps which limit performance; second they felt there was a high priority need for the production of local training materials.

World Bank

In 1985, the Education Department of the World Bank conducted an evaluation of the results of the institution building components of education projects in Africa in association with UNESCO and ILO. One of the key findings was the need to train trainers in defining training needs, and to help clients to implement change.

CDC

The Commonwealth Development Corporation (CDC) has developed a management training centre for agriculture at Mananga in Swaziland (MAMC). The CDC plans to 'localize' and 'internationalize' the centre and asked the World Bank to perform an evaluation. With a mail questionnaire, the Bank mission received back 82 questionnaires from 280 course members and interviewed more than 75 participants and supervisors in nine countries. The overwhelming conclusion was that the Mananga training was very effective.

The training style includes extensive reliance on small-group work shaped to the professional concerns of the individual course members. Over and over again in conversations with those who had sent staff to MAMC, the mission heard that the course members gained 'confidence' or were much better able to work with their staffs. Characteristically, course members are individuals with technical training in agriculture who have recently been promoted to middle-level management positions. Generally, their training at MAMC is the first they have received in management techniques. The very personalized small group tutorials allowed each participant to work out specific solutions to human relations problems in his/her work.

CONCLUSIONS AND RECOMMENDATIONS

In summary, the above evaluation studies in Africa tell us that too often training needs are poorly defined or the wrong participants are selected; that courses and materials are not relevant to local needs; that training is not combined with on-the-job support and follow-up; and that local training institutions are poorly financed and suffer from low status and lack of contact with the job place.

The positive evaluation of the CDC-sponsored Mananga Agricultural Management Training Center in Swaziland proves that good training can be effective in changing on-the-job behaviour. The challenge for trainers is clear. We must obtain sufficient time and resources to find out, in some detail, the specific local training needs. We then need to work closely with the management of the client organization to prepare courses and materials that match their needs. It is important to work with trainees for long enough so that they feel confident to apply new approaches back on the job, and this also needs to be accompanied by follow-up consulting services on the job. At the same time one should be alert to the external factors that may affect performance and make sure that the training will help managers recognize – and possibly deal with – these external factors. It is essential to evaluate our performance continually to see that we are really accomplishing improved organizational performance.

This requires a learner-centred approach, not a teacher-centred approach. This is the major challenge for teachers, for course-givers, and for donors. A learner-centred approach takes much more money and time than just offering general courses. Will donors and countries provide this type of long-term support to a well-designed staff development programme?

Such a long-term programme may provide opportunities for twinning arrangements between training institutions in the developed and developing world to work together to help Third World organizations to improve performance.

REFERENCES

Ali, Kebede, Pope, G., and Streydio, J. M. Consultants, PF (1986) Agricultural Management Training Programme for Africa (AMTA), Draft Mid-Term Review Report, International Fund for Agricultural Development (IFAD), Rome, Restricted Distribution.

Auerhan, J., Ramakrishnan, S., Romain, R., Stoikov, G., Tiburcio, L., and Torres, P. (1985) Institutional Development in Education and Training in Sub-Saharan African Countries, Report No. EDT22, Discussion Paper, Education and Training Series, Operations Policy Staff, Education and Training Department, The World Bank, Washington, D.C.

Economic Development Institute (1986) Mananga Agricultural Management Centre Review Mission, The World Bank, Washington, D.C.

National Association of Schools of Public Affairs and Administration (NASPAA) under sponsorship of USAID (1985) Improving Management in Southern Africa, Washington, D.C.

Rosenthal, Irving, Tuthill, Janet, Bury, Robert, and Frazier, Michael (1986) 'Signposts in development management: A computer-based analysis of 277 projects in Africa', *Aid Evaluation Occasional Paper* No. 10, US Agency for International Development (USAID), Washington, D.C.

Shields, N., Davies, H., Lynn, R., Roberts, and Langseth, P. (1986) Botswana, Lesotho, and Swaziland (BLS) Study of Public Administration Management: Issues and Training Needs, Volume I: The Main Report, Report No. 5948, The World Bank, Washington, D.C., 21 April, Restricted Distribution.

World Bank Operations Policy Staff, Education and Training Department (1986) Analysis of Lending Operations in Training in Bank/IDA Financed Projects – FY85, The World Bank, Washington D.C., Restricted Distribution.

The views reported here are those of the author and they should not be interpreted as reflecting those of relevant funding bodies.

7

The cultural context of leadership actions: a cross-cultural analysis

Peter B. Smith (*University of Sussex*)
Monir Tayeb (*Heriot-Watt University*)
Mark F. Peterson (*Texas Tech. University*)

Anyone who tries to evaluate the diverse range of research findings concerning managerial leadership is likely to find it a bewildering task. The temptation is strong to accept one view or another as holding most promise and to reject or ignore other views. For instance, over the past several decades there has been a continuing debate between those who maintain that it is possible to specify in some detail a single style of management which will be effective in a wide variety of settings; and others who see effective managerial style as something which is tightly bounded by function, by level in the organization, and by the culture of that particular organization. This particular debate has evolved to the point where the second of these schools of thought has now become the dominant one.

Debates of this kind do little to help us forward because they confuse important issues in the study of leadership. They treat as alternatives approaches which are both needed if we are to understand why a particular leader behaviour is required in a certain setting. We shall first of all argue what is the nature of this confusion and then show how the findings of a research programme conducted by ourselves and other colleagues in several countries supports our argument.

Those who first developed the notion of 'One Best Way' of leadership most usually saw two components of leadership as being required. These were first, some attention to the structuring of the task and second, some attention to the maintenance of good relationships within the work team. Such emphases are found, for instance, in the Ohio State leadership research programme (Stogdill and Coons, 1957), in the Managerial Grid theory (Blake and Mouton, 1978), and in the earlier work of researchers at the

University of Michigan (Likert, 1961). We need not be concerned here with differences of opinion between these authors as to how these two dimensions may interact with one another. What is important is that those who argued for this view were attempting to make general statements as to what effective leaders need to do. They had much less to say about how, in practice, a manager should carry through this style of behaviour.

Most recent commentators (e.g. Bryman, 1986) agree that these formulators of the 'One Best Way' have not stood the test of time. This is partly because they were so vaguely phrased and partly because those research studies which were carried out failed to give them uniform support. None the less, one has only to note the phenomenal attention currently commanded by, for instance, the 'Excellence' books (Peters and Waterman, 1982; Peters and Austin, 1985) to see how much continuing interest there is in a 'One Best Way' formulation. What is interesting about the work of Peters and his colleagues is the way in which the leader behaviours he advocates are much less vague and much more specific than are the older models. For example, when he advocates MBWA or 'Managing By Wandering Around', he is no longer directly addressing the concerns of the older theorists as to what goals the leader must have; he is speaking instead about how those goals might be accomplished. The difference between the 'what' and the 'how' of leadership is illustrated in Fig. 7.1. Supervisors target their actions (the 'how') toward achieving such immediate goals as having their action experienced as considerate or as having made the subordinate's task more easily accomplished (the 'what'). More generally, supervisors act in the expectation that dealing with their subordinates' immediate situations will contribute to desired outcomes for their subordinates, for the work group, and for the organization. The actions which the supervisor chooses (the 'how') must be adapted to both the immediate work context and the larger organizational and cultural context. It may well prove that the Peters' model, like so many before it, is oversold and has value only within certain settings. What is important, however, is the switch from talking about the 'what' of leadership to the 'how'. That in itself is enough to justify its current popularity.

We can now state the main burden of our argument. The 'what' which effective managers need to do may well prove to be substantially the same all over the world. However, the 'how' of accomplishing these goals will vary greatly between different

Figure 7.1 The 'what' and 'how' of leadership: a circular model

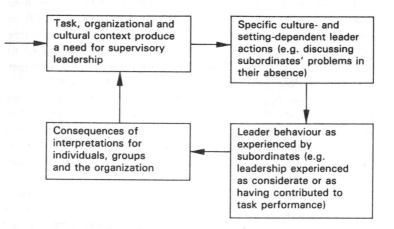

cultures and settings. One obstacle which has hindered US researchers' search for consistent aspects of perceived leadership is that the measures most widely used have been static and invariant. The use of identical questions has often been mistakenly equated with assuring equivalent measurement, even when the questions are applied in very diverse settings.

An alternative approach followed by Misumi (1985) has succeeded in documenting a consistent basic leadership pattern, which can be discerned despite contextual variablity. His work over the past thirty years has covered many diverse work and non-work settings in Japan. The laboratory and field studies consistently show that high performance and effective group functioning are achieved where the same two aspects of leadership are present. These consistent results are due in part to this avoidance of fixed and static measures in his field research. Where circumstances warrant, such as in studies of engineering leadership compared to manufacturing leadership, new measures have been devised, thus allowing a greater proportion of the 'how' to creep into the measures as well as the 'what'.

Our own interest in this field of work was triggered by the arrival in Britain of a substantial presence of Japanese electronics firms. The policies pursued by these firms are by no means as uniform as is implied by the myth that there is a single standardized Japanese management style. None the less, on the whole these firms, and those in other industries who have followed

87

them, have been remarkably successful. Some firms started with green-field sites, while others operated for a while as joint ventures. In one electronics plant we have studied in the traditionally inward-looking coal-mining area of South Wales, the workforce jumped onto the canteen table and cheered when it was announced that the joint venture was to cease and the Japanese firm was to take over single ownership. Instances such as this provide a clear opportunity to examine the relationship between the what and the how of leadership. The 'what' should be the same as that required in identical plants in the US and Japan, but in which manner would it be necessary for management to adapt the 'how'? We soon started to come upon instances of initial misunderstanding.

As is widely known, many Japanese firms have a strong concern for the welfare of their employees. One way in which this was at first expressed in another Japanese plant in Britain was by supervisors making visits to the homes of workers who were off sick. This was strongly resented by the workforce who felt that supervisors were actually checking up to see whether they were indeed sick. Thus a behaviour which the Japanese supervisor intended as considerate and friendly was interpreted as intrusive and controlling. The practice was discontinued. When firms establish plants in new locations it is inevitable that some such misunderstandings shall occur. The success of Japanese firms in Britain has derived from their willingness to learn from such mistakes. They have a clear conception of what they wish their supervisors to accomplish, just as they do of their overall task, but they are open to change as to how best to accomplish these goals.

If we are to anticipate the difficulties that will arise when plants are established in new locations, it is important that studies be done which identify the relation between the 'what' and the 'how' of leadership in a variety of organizations and countries. A series of such studies is in progress, in collaboration with colleagues in several countries (Smith *et al.*, 1986; Smith and Peterson, 1987). In the first study a comparison was made between samples of middle managers attending training courses in Britain, the United States, and Hong Kong. In each case the manager was asked to answer a range of relatively general questions which are used to provide a description of their own boss's leader style. A further thirty-six questions followed which asked much more specific 'how'-type questions about the boss's day-to-day actions. By comparing the leader style measures with the answers to the more specific questions, we could quickly see for how many items a particular leader style implied the same behaviour in all three countries. The overall pattern of findings did give a clear picture. This can be illustrated, for example, by looking at the manner in which the boss conveys to subordinates that he or she is considerate toward them.

Out of the thirty-six behaviours we found nine which were seen as being part of a considerate leader style in all three countries. These included such behaviours as discussing subordinates' personal difficulties sympathetically, arranging for co-workers to help when personal difficulties make this necessary, and sharing information concerning the organization's plans and performance with subordinates. Thus we found that at least between these three countries there was a common core of considerate behaviours. However, we also found a further fourteen behaviours which were related to consideration in one or two of the countries but not in all three. The most interesting are those which were found to be unique to each country. In Hong Kong we found that it would be seen as considerate to discuss a subordinate's personal difficulties in their absence. In sharp contrast this was found to be inconsiderate in both the British and American samples. What we presumably have here is an expression of Chinese culture whereby it is thought more tactful and less embarrassing if a personal difficulty can be resolved without discussion that is open and public (Bond, 1986). A similar finding has emerged from our subsequent studies in Japan. In Anglo-American cultures on the other hand, we have norms favouring openness and directness.

It was by no means the case that all the differences which we found were those which distinguished Hong Kong from the Western samples. In the British sample a series of task behaviours were seen as more considerate than in other countries. For instance, instructing subordinates in how to increase job skills was seen in this way. Most probably the explanation for this would lie in what Americans might think of as the relatively impersonal quality of British culture compared to the United States. In Britain, friendliness may well be conveyed by talking about task-related issues to a greater extent than in the United States.

No behaviours were found which were distinctively linked to considerate behaviour in the US but not in the other countries. Thus the overall pattern found was of a common core of considerate behaviours which obtained everywhere, plus distinctive ones in both Hong Kong and Britain. Possibly this is because the concept of consideration as a dimension of leader behaviour was first distinguished from task behaviour by researchers in the US. Whether that is the reason or not, the findings indicate that the 'how' of considerate behaviour does start to diverge as one moves into other cultures. The finding of a common core does not provide much reassurance for managers operating in different cultural contexts. If the manager carries through five behaviours which are considerate and one which is judged not to be so, subordinates' overall view of them is likely to be that they are not considerate.

In a further study along related lines we have been undertaking surveys of shop-floor workers in electronics plants in Britain, the US, Hong Kong, and Japan. Here we are concerned with whether or not an organization can change the meaning of particular supervisory behaviours. For instance, can a Japanese plant in Britain change the meaning attached to good timekeeping? Or can a US plant in Hong Kong change the meaning attached to open, face-to-face communication? Our results to date show that the meanings attached to considerate and to task-centred supervisor behaviours have much more to do with where the plant is than with who owns it. This is true not only for plants which have opened or been acquired relatively recently, but also for other Japanese plants in the West, which have been operating for several years, and which have a substantial number of Japanese supervisors. Studies within these plants show a pattern of relations between supervisor style and performance measures which is quite like that found by other researchers in Western organizations.

We can now summarize the conclusions emerging from our project. It has been found useful to distinguish between what supervisors are trying to accomplish and how they go about doing it. The goals which supervisors seek to attain may well be similar whether they be Japanese, Chinese, American, or whatever. The behaviours they need to employ to accomplish those goals turn out to vary quite sharply, even when one is comparing firms within the same industry and countries as similar as the USA and Britain. An instance was quoted earlier of how one Japanese firm adopted a particular supervisory behaviour so that it should not convey an unintended message to the workforce. This may well illustrate the basis upon which Japanese success in other countries has been built. Many Japanese firms have not sought to impose

Japanese practice upon their foreign plants in a wholesale manner, but have thought carefully about which elements will or will not fit the cultural context. (Trevor, 1983; White and Trevor, 1983). Where they have, none the less, miscalculated, they often have been willing to learn from mistakes. Inevitably some of the more traditionalist Japanese firms have been less able to do this, particularly in the finance sector, as is illustrated by the considerable difficulties encountered by the C. Itoh company in the US (Sethi *et al.*, 1984).

For Japanese companies able to adapt to their circumstance, the answer is not likely to be the same, for instance, in southern California with its substantial Japanese–American population, as it is in the mining valleys of South Wales or in the banks of the City of London. Some elements of Japanese practice, such as the emphasis on product quality and the elimination of status barriers in dress and eating places turn out to be readily compatible within many other cultures. Others, such as the singing of the company song, and regular after-hours socializing with one's workgroup are much more rarely encountered in Western countries. Yet others, which are alleged by some researchers (Takezawa and Whitehill, 1981) to be still widespread in Japan, such as asking one's boss for advice on who to marry, are unlikely to make much progress elsewhere.

It is pragmatic attention by the more successful companies to such issues as the 'how' aspects of a supervisor's work behaviour which has sustained their successes. Such a strategy makes sense whether one is speaking of cultures from different parts of the world, or of cultures created over time within one particular organization. This type of pragmatism will also best reward all of our attempts to manage plants in a manner which fits the culture within which each one is embedded.

REFERENCES

Blake, R. R. and Mouton, J. S. (1978) *The New Managerial Grid*, Houston, Texas: Gulf.

Bond, M. H. (ed.) (1986) *The Psychology of the Chinese People*, Hong Kong: Oxford University Press.

Bryman, A. (1986) *Leadership and Organizations*, London: Routledge, Kegan Paul.

Likert, R. (1961) *New Patterns of Management*, New York: McGraw-Hill.

Misumi, J. (1985) *The Behavioural Science of Leadership*, Ann Arbor, Michigan: University of Michigan Press.

Peters, T. J. and Austin, N. K. (1985) *A Passion for Excellence*, New York: Random House.

Peters, T. J. and Waterman, R. H. (1982) *In Search of Excellence: Lessons from America's Best-Run Companies*, New York: Harper & Row.

Sethi, S. P., Namiki, N., and Swanson, C. L. (1984) *The False Promise of the Japanese Miracle*, Boston: Pitman.

Smith, P. B. and Peterson, M. F. (1987) *Leadership in Context*, London: Sage.

Smith, P. B., Misumi, J., Tayeb, M. H., Peterson, M. F., and Bond, M. H. (1986) 'On the generality of leadership style measures across cultures. Unpublished manuscript'.

Stogdill, R. M. and Coons, A. E. (1957) *Leader Behavior*, Colombus, Ohio: Bureau of Business Research, Ohio State University, Monograph 88.

Takezawa, S. and Whitehill, A. M. (1981) *Workways: Japan and America*, Tokyo: Japan Institute of Labour.

Trevor, M. (1983) *Japan's Reluctant Multinationals*, London: Pinter.

White, M. and Trevor, M. (1983) *Under Japanese Management*, London: Heinemann.

Part III

The challenges generated by social and political change

In China, Hong Kong, Turkey, and Hungary important changes have been taking place. These are changes which affect national, political and social issues. The challenge which the five papers in this part raise is how can management education help to ensure that the outcomes of these internal changes achieve successful objectives. The authors are asking how, whether, and what the 'discipline' of management education is able to contribute. A major issue raised by several of the authors in this section is whether a significant lead can be made by management educators in bringing about effective change or whether the discipline simply should accept that its role is to follow in the wake of change.

The section starts with a chapter by Chen Wen Ya who describes the economic responsibility system which is currently being introduced in China to replace the 'backward' management system with one 'more suited to a socialist and public ownership economy'. The key themes of this new system are responsibility, authority, and profit. Enterprises will now be responsible for producing wealth for the State but they will be able to retain any profits made over an established limit. This requires an amount of authority to be given and the relationship between responsibility and profit is passed down to the individual worker in such a way that hard work is rewarded and commitment to success is ensured.

Although this chapter does not itself deal directly with management education within China it points to the fact that such a major innovation will require significant contribution from management education in order to develop the appropriate attitudes, skills, and knowledge and it provides the context for the chapter which follows.

The chapter by Qiu, Yu and Xu starts with the recognition of a fundamental change in the approach of managers to management in China – that they need to take management more seriously. The authors believe that the key task of management education is to ensure rapid change in the way management is both perceived and practised in China from a view of management as an art (which cannot therefore be taught because it depends on experience and insight) to management as a science. As well as this conceptual shift, management education must provide new managers with the necessary skills to carry out this scientific management.

Esin Ergin's chapter from Turkey describes the rapid economic change caused by policies adopted after 1980 which not only required public sector companies to be run more efficiently with a profit objective, but also included the opening up of relations with other countries. This politically fairly stable country is now faced with the presence of multi-national corporations and a growth in population which is due to workers returning from Germany. All of these factors combine to create a major cultural challenge. Should different programmes be developed for the different cultural perspectives within Turkey or should an attempt be made by management education to match the dominant characteristics of the business world?

The chapter from Hungary describes the social change which is taking place as the centrally planned economy which has existed for twenty years is replaced by decentralization. Managers who have been trained to implement externally devised plans now have to adapt to new industrial structures. Decentralization creates the need not only for more trained managers but a different kind of manager, one who will innovate, think strategically, and act like an entrepreneur. Those who have been managers since the reform in 1968, and those who will now be trained will have different needs and different problems. Csath suggests that action learning and distance learning are possible ways of training this disparate body of managers, but the bottleneck of training required is going to create a major challenge for business schools in Hungary.

The final chapter in this section proposes that management education should concern itself with the ethical issues arising from the practices of corporations in a free enterprise system. Tam sets his argument in the context of Hong Kong which operates within a free enterprise system which works according to 'family' commitments. He implies that the transition to Chinese rule in 1997 makes it imperative for management education in Hong Kong to influence the social awareness and responsibility of managers, if the free enterprise system is to survive.

8

Incentives for management in China: the economic responsibility system

Chen Wen Ya
(*Beijing Economics College, China*)

The 'economic responsibility system' is a new way to operate a socialist enterprise. About 80% of the industrial enterprises in China have already begun to adopt this.

The system was first developed as the 'production responsibility system' in the agricultural sector. In recent years, great changes have taken place on the farms as a result of the new system, and the majority of the Chinese peasants are now well clad and well fed. For example, Pinglu county of the Shangsi province was one of the poorest counties in our country; for over twenty years, its grain supply was dependent on other counties. But after making each family unit responsible for production the county has become self-supporting in grain, and has even had some surplus. The average income per person doubled within a year after the introduction of the system. Although there are some differences between agriculture and industry, it is felt in China that the principles of the responsibility system can also be applied to industry. This paper describes the new economic responsibility system and discusses its implication for enterprises and managers.

The economic responsibility system is a type of management system, under the guidance of the State plan, which combines responsibility, authority, and profit together. The system has two components: the first concerns the economic relationship between the State and the enterprise. The basic principle here is that if the enterprise contributes more profit to the State, it will be allowed to retain a larger portion of this in order to develop production and to increase welfare facilities and workers' income. The second component concerns the regulation of the economic relationship within the enterprise. The principle here is that when the enterprise distributes its production tasks and its technological and economic objectives to every unit (workshop, group. etc.) and every worker, their responsibilities, tasks, rewards, and/or punishments should be clearly fixed. The enterprise should reward the diligent workers and punish the lazy ones. The more the worker contributes, the more income she/he will get. This idea represents a significant shift in policy within China. It is intended to overcome the widespread phenomenon of egalitarianism with 'everybody sharing food from the same big pot', and to develop the initiative of enterprises and of their workers and staff.

In past years, the main problem in socialist enterprises has been lack of invigoration, or lack of activity, flexibility, initiative, and responsibility. It is believed that this is not because of the socialist system or the public ownership system itself, but because of the backward management system, in which power and egalitarianism were over-concentrated in distribution, neglecting commodity production and the role of the market. Consequently, responsibility, authority, and profit were not closely related. These problems dampened the enthusiasm of workers and staff for increased economic performance.

One example of the successful use of the economic responsibility system is the Capital Iron and Steel Company which introduced the system in 1981. In 1981 iron output was 290,000 tons less and steel output 70,000 tons less than the year before. However, profit increased from 290 million yuan to 316 million yuan, that is, increased 9.07%. At the same time, there were three main changes in management:

(1) from grasping for production only, to grasping for production and marketing together;
(2) from emphasizing the building of new factories, to emphasizing technical transformation aimed at expanding production; and
(3) from fulfilling narrow production objectives, to improving the economic performance of the whole enterprise.

The above changes are fundamental and had not taken place in the past thirty years. The system is an outcome of reform. It is a system with Chinese characteristics. In the remainder of the chapter I shall discuss the economic responsibility system in terms of how it functions in the relationship between the enterprise and the State, and its main features within the enterprise. I conclude with some observations about the future development of the system and the management ideas underlying it.

THE ECONOMIC RESPONSIBILITY OF THE ENTERPRISE TO THE STATE

Relationships

The relationship between the enterprise and the State is defined as follows: first with regard to economic activities, the State is the leader and enterprise is the follower. Second, it is accepted that the State owns the means of production, the enterprise is the user of these means. Third, in terms of economic benefit it is a relationship of whole interest and partial interest. This is the basic economic relationship. Because it remains the State's responsibility to finance major projects, the State gets the largest share of the profits, enterprises get a considerable share, and individuals get the rest.

Responsibility, authority and profits

The enterprise has the responsibility to produce readily marketable goods according to the State plan and to market demand; to gain profit only through better management and higher economic efficiency, and to render profit or tax to the State; to abide by the law and policy of the State; to protect State properties; to care for the safety and livelihood of workers and staff; and to prevent and cure pollution.

In order to implement the above responsibilities, the enterprise has to be granted a measure of economic authority. This is given in four mains areas: production, finance, buying and selling, and organizational structure and personnel. In the production area it means that after fulfilling the mandatory plan assigned by the State, the enterprise is allowed to accept production orders according to market demand. Financial authority means that the enterprise can use fixed assets and circulating funds. Idle assets can also be rented out or sold by the enterprise. The shared profit can then be used for bonus, welfare, and production development. The enterprise can make external investments with its unused funds. The third area of authority is that – under the general guidance of the State plan – the enterprise can buy raw materials or equipment and can sell its products. It can also set the price of its products within the limits prescribed by the State. Fourth, the enterprise has the authority to decide its organizational structure and personnel. It can appoint, remove, employ, or elect its own personnel according to relevant regulations. It can decide on how to recruit and use its workforce, and it can also determine appropriate wage levels and rewards.

The potential profits to the enterprise are defined quite simply. It shares its profit with the State according to its performance: if the enterprise performs well, it will get more profit.

Thus, responsibility, authority, and profit are closely combined. It is also recognized that responsibility should be appropriate to authority. If the enterprise is not going to be given full guarantees on production or marketing by the State, then its power of decision in these areas needs to be enlarged.

Forms of profit-sharing

Previously the profit of State-owned enterprises was turned over entirely to the State. This source of income has formed the bulk of China's State revenue over the years. Conversely, the State subsidized all the losses of State-owned enterprises, and virtually all their outlays had to be appropriated out of the national budget. There was no incentive under such a fiscal system for enterprises to improve economic management, because profit or loss was of no concern to the individual enterprises. After 1979, a profit-sharing system was tried, whereby individual enterprises could retain a portion of their profit to use at their own discretion. There are three main forms of profit sharing that have been introduced for different enterprises in China.

Sharing a percentage of profit

This can take two forms: (i) sharing according to one fixed rate, for example, 87% for the State and 13% for the enterprise; or (ii) sharing according to two rates, one lower rate for the base profit and another higher rate for the excess profit (Table 8.1).

Contracting for profit delivery quotas on an increasing basis

First a profit delivery quota is set up as a base figure. The enterprise must then deliver this amount of profit to the State (e.g. 360,000 yuan). If it fails to reach this sum, it has to fill up the deficit with its own funds. If the actual profit exceeds the quota (e.g. 400,000 yuan) the excess part (40,000 yuan) now all belongs to the enterprise.

Table 8.1 Example of sharing profit according to two rates

Enterprise	Annual output (000 yuan)	Profit rate on output	Base profit	Share of base profit (at 8%)	Increased output	Increased profit	Total profit	Profit share by one rate (at 13%)	Share of increased profit (at 50%)	Profit share by two rates
A	1000	30%	300	24	200	60	360	46.8	30	54
B	1000	15%	150	12	200	30	180	23.4	15	27
C	1000	15%	150	12	100	15	165	21.4	7.5	19.5

For a period of three or five years, we can set a profit quota in the first year, then set an annual increasing rate for the coming years. The increasing rate is fixed within a certain period of time. If the increasing rate is 5%, then the profit quota for the second year will be 378,000 yuan [360 + (360 × 5%)].

This form of profit sharing can guarantee the income of the State and promote the improvement of enterprise management at the same time. However, setting the right profit quota for each enterprise is very complicated indeed.

The profit-taxing or taxation system

On 1 June 1983, a new profit-taxing system was introduced. In this system the State-owned enterprises pay taxes instead of delivering their profits to the State. In order to avoid an immediate changeover, the new system was implemented in two steps. For the first step, all large and medium-sized enterprises have to pay income tax at a rate of 55% of profit realized, and the after-tax profit is shared by the State and the enterprises, either by fixing quotas or according to fixed proportions. For example, if an enterprise realized a profit amounting to 1,000,000 yuan in 1983, its after-tax profit would be 450,000 yuan [1,000,000 − (1,000,000 × 55%)], and if the sharing proportion for the enterprise is 20%, then the enterprise will get 90,000 yuan (450,000 × 20%) remaining for its own use.

From 1 October 1984 the second step, characterized by full taxation, began. That is to say, after paying all kinds of taxes, the remaining part of the profit belongs to the enterprise. The main taxes levied are of two types: one is income tax at a rate of 55% as before; the other is an adjusted tax at various rates. The adjusted tax can be levied on those enterprises that gain more profit owing to external factors beyond their control, such as irrationalities in the price structure or the quality of plant equipment. This is intended to ensure that competition between enterprises is fair. One of the main advantages of this system is that it helps to eliminate bargaining between the State and enterprises over profit sharing. For example, enterprises may demand that their profit delivery quotas be cut when cost of production goes up, or when workers' wages increase. Under the new system, enterprises pay income taxes at fixed rates, and so no bargaining is possible.

The taxation system provides the enterprises with more decision-making power and gives them more incentive to improve management and operations. This is expected to be of great significance in ensuring a steady growth in State revenue and in further strengthening control and supervision by the State over financing and accounting.

Finally, the taxation system can fix the distribution relationship between the State and the enterprise in the form of taxes. It thus makes the enterprise more independent of the State, and hence responsible for its own profit and loss.

THE ECONOMIC RESPONSIBILITY SYSTEM WITHIN THE ENTERPRISE

The economic responsibility system within the enterprise is the foundation of the economic responsibility between the enterprise and the State. Its expression in the enterprise reflects a combination of responsibility, authority, and profit in relation to every post and unit within the enterprise. It includes the assignment of economic responsibility, the giving of economic authority, the conducting of performance evaluation, and the distribution of profit.

The assignment of economic responsibility

There are two kinds of economic responsibility to be assigned. One is in a vertical fashion, from the top to the bottom of the organization. In this case it is necessary to break down the overall objectives (economic responsibility of the enterprise to the State) into small parts and to assign them to plants, workshops, groups, and workers. For example, the overall objectives of the Capital Iron and Steel Company in 1981 were defined in terms of: profit to be rendered, output in variety and quality, energy used, and bonuses for the workers and staff. At the lower level of a plant, the objectives are broken down into a greater number, such as: profit, output, variety, quality, energy used, cost, number of workers and staff, safety, protection of environment, and so on. As the number of units at a particular level increase, the number of objectives increases, as shown in Figure 8.1.

The second kind of economic responsibility follows a horizontal line, that is, all units within the company are closely related, so every unit has the responsibility to offer conditions to related

Figure 8.1 Example showing how the number of objectives increases as the number of units increases

No. of units	company	No. of objectives
28	plant	325
646	workshop	10,773
3,112	group	30,730
7,173	post or working place	60,417

units. For instance, when the rolling steel plant wants to fulfil its energy use objective, the energy plant must provide gas at a certain pressure and calorie.

It is important that the economic objectives are defined at a reasonable level, that is, it must be possible for the majority of the workers to attain them, through effort.

The setting of economic objectives needs to consider the characteristics of the unit. The practice of the Capital Iron and Steel Company is as follows:

(1) For plants or workshops that produce profits directly for sale, the key objective is to make a profit.

(2) For plants or workshops that produce semi-products, the key objective is cost-reduction. If the cost of the semi-product can be reduced, the profit of the whole enterprise will be increased. But if you put a profit objective to these plants, it tends to cause blindness in production which disregards the market demand.

(3) For subsidiary production units such as energy and transportation, only the reduction of total expense is considered relevant. This should make these units develop better co-ordination with production plants.

Economic authority within the enterprise

Though most authority is concentrated at company level, there is still some authority given to units within the company, corresponding to their economic responsibilities. These include the power to deal with production and technology matters, and some financial and personnel power within defined limits.

Performance evaluation

Performance evaluation is an important aspect of the economic responsibility system. Units or persons doing good work need to be given rewards. The criteria and techniques for evaluation and the evaluators must be decided carefully, and the evaluation itself should be performed rigorously. The executives and workers should care only for the results of evaluation. The practice of handing out bonuses indiscriminately must be avoided. As we are looking forward to enterprises turning out products of higher quality and lower cost, the key criteria for evaluation must be improvements in quality and economies in materials.

The distribution of profit

The distribution of profit among units and workers is mainly based on their performance. But the role of the unit, and the difficulty or ease with which they can increase income or reduce expense also needs to be taken into account. The Capital Iron and Steel Company has set up bonus coefficients for different plants and workers (Table 8.2). The bonus coefficient for a subsidiary worker is 1.0, but the bonus coefficient for a worker in a key post that will determine the quality of the product should be higher, e.g. 2.2. The higher the coefficient, the greater the bonus that the unit or worker will be able to get.

There are two commonly used forms of profit distribution:

Table 8.2 Bonus coefficients set up by the Capital Iron and Steel Company

	Iron and steel plant	Welding plant	Transportation department	Machinery plant	Timber plant
Bonus coeffient	1.9	1.7	1.4	1.3	1.0

Table 8.3 Example of marks put on sub-objectives assigned to plant

Sub-objective	Marks
Output	20
Quality	25
Use of material and energy	25
Attendance	5
Safety	10
Management	15
Total	100

bonuses and floating wages. The bonus is paid according to marks gained from work performance. As previously noted, the company breaks down its overall objectives into many small parts which are assigned to plants. In order to monitor results, different marks are put on each sub-objective assigned to the plant, as shown in Table 8.3. If the plant is able to fulfil its output target, it will get 20 marks for that sub-objective. The more marks gained, the more bonus will be earned.

For a long time we have had a problem known as the 'iron bowl' in the wage system. In recent years, more money has been allocated in the form of bonuses than in promotions. The difference between bonus grades is small, and some bonuses were dealt out regardless of work performance. After implementing the taxation system, the enterprise has the possibility of trying the floating wage, which is intended to keep the economic results of the enterprise and the performance of the worker directly connected.

The floating wage usually means that a small part of the basic wage and the bonus are floating together. They are distributed according to economic results and work performance. It was first tried by the Beijing Optical Instrument Factory in 1982. They took out 11 yuan (20% of the average monthly wage per person from each person's monthly wage, together with bonus (about 8 yuan for the average monthly bonus per person) to be floated. This sum was to be distributed according to economic results and work performance. Meanwhile, 80% of the basic wage or salary would remain fixed and guaranteed, thus putting a 20% break into the 'iron bowl'.

In order for fair distribution among staff and indirect workers,

Table 8.4 Percentages of average floating wage distributed to five categories of staff and indirect workers

Post	Percentage earned
1	95
2	90
3	85
4	75
5	65

they divided all the work posts into five categories according to the responsibility, volume, difficulty or ease, and labour-intensity of the work. For example, the director and the department chief were placed in the first category or Post 1; the watchman and the parking-lot worker were placed in the fifth category or Post 5. When the staff and the indirect workers have fulfilled their work, they can get a certain percentage of the average floating wage of the production workers in the workshop, according to their post (Table 8.4). Thus the floating wage of the staff and the indirect workers is closely related to that of the direct production workers.

It is not yet clear how much of the basic wage should be assigned to the floating part but it is believed that a figure in the range 10 to 30% may be reasonable. This is because if the floating part is too small, e.g. below 10%, it would not really provide an incentive, and if it is too large, e.g. above 30%, there is the danger that low ratings could affect the standard of living of workers and staff.

Since the nature of trades and the size and production conditions of enterprises differ from one another, we are still trying to work out other forms of the responsibility system within enterprises which would be suited to their specific conditions.

THE FUTURE DEVELOPMENT OF THE SYSTEM

As mentioned above, the basic principles of the economic responsibility system include a combination of responsibility, authority, and profit; the unity of the interests of the State, the collective, and the individual; and the linking of the income of workers and staff with their job performance. After introducing the system, both the enterprise and its workers and staff will be motivated to run the enterprise well and achieve its strategic goal. This is a key to the successful running of socialist enterprises. This system has been treated as one of the three basic management systems in large and medium-sized enterprises owned by the State. The other two systems are where the director or manager assumes full responsibility as in a leadership system, and where congresses of workers and staff assume full responsibility, as in a democratic system.

Why it works

One might ask why this economic responsibility system is proving to be effective. I think there are three main reasons for this:

(1) It is based upon the socialist theory regarding ownership and the control of operations. When a State-owned enterprise adopts the system, the workers and staff of the enterprise obtain certain powers over the operation, even though ownership still remains with the State and the People. One of the main reasons why the State exercised excessive and rigid control over enterprises in the past was because it equated the concept of ownership by the People with the concept of direct control by State institutions. Since social demand is very complex and in a state of constant flux, since the conditions in enterprises differ in a thousand and one ways, and since the economic links between enterprises are complicated, no State institution can know the whole situation fully and cope with everything in good time. If State instructions were to directly administer and manage all kinds of enterprises owned by the State, it would be very hard to avoid serious subjectivism and bureaucratism, with a subsequent suppression of enterprise vitality. So the conclusion is that ownership can be duly separated from the power of operation.

(2) It reflects the ancient management thinking of China. Sun Wu, a famous Chinese military strategist, pointed out over 2,000 years ago: 'If the general wants to win the war, he must treat his soldiers as brothers and take every care of them, then in return they will fight bravely for the attainment of the common goal set by the general.' This is also true in business management. In the development of the economic responsibility system, it is important to handle correctly the relationship of the workers and staff to their enterprise so that they are its real masters and can work as

such at their jobs. This will arouse their deep interest in the operation and in the effectiveness of their enterprise and enable their performance to be closely linked with their own special prestige and material benefits.

(3) It meets the basic principles of scientific management. Fayol, an early pioneer of scientific management, said that responsibility and authority must be identical. Two well-known economists in recent times, Barnard and Simon, have said that contribution and profit must be connected and appropriate. These two principles are also appropriate for socialist enterprises when adopting the economic responsibility system.

The role of ideological and political work

The new system is able to overcome the phenomenon of egalitarianism. In order to apply fully the principle of rewarding the diligent and good and punishing the lazy and bad, and of giving more pay for more work and less pay for less work, the differences between the wages of various trades and jobs was widened. In this way some people will become better off earlier. This is quite a change. In the past, if someone earned much money, he or she would be recognized as a person lacking socialist consciousness. Now we say if you earn money by hard work it is wholly proper and honourable. On the other hand, we must avoid such unhealthy tendencies and practices as benefiting oneself at the expense of others, pursuing private interests at the expense of public interests, and putting money first in everything.

Also, in the case of enterprises, improper ways of gaining profit, such as reducing quality, raising prices, or cutting services, must be prevented too. A foreign passenger in Beijing complained about the taxi drivers who refused to drive him to a nearby destination. He said 'I had heard that according to the new responsibility system, taxi drivers were earning extra money for any distance they drove beyond a fixed quota. This is highly praiseworthy and represents a step forward. But I never imagined that the new system would result in drivers acting irresponsibly by refusing to serve their customers' needs.'

The core of cultural development, ideological and political work is considered very important because it can educate people to make money in a proper way. In the work of socialist modernization we must strive for a high level of both material and cultural development. The two are inseparable. Only by so doing can we ensure the sustained growth of the national economy and the socialist orientation of material development.

Therefore, while we are in the process of adopting the economic responsibility system, ideological and political work must be strengthened at the same time.

CONCLUSION

The implementation of the economic responsibility system is likely to lead to major developments. Through the relationship of the enterprise to the State we can see the development from profit-sharing to a full taxation system. Within the enterprise, the development may be represented as three stages:

Distribution ⟶ Management ⟶ Participation

Distribution indicates the first stage of the system. Its main aim is to solve the distribution problem, to implement the principle of distribution according to work. Most Chinese firms are at this stage.

A few firms have come into the second stage – management. The main aim of this stage is to raise the level of management. The Capital Iron and Steel Company in Beijing has delegated its managerial functions such as planning, financing, technical, personnel, equipment, and so on, from the company level down to the plants, the workshops and eventually to the relevant person. This was done in the same way as the assigning of production objectives. Each managerial task has been clarified by criterion, responsibility, procedure, co-ordination, and evaluation. By doing this, it makes the application of computers in management much easier, and managerial work can then be conducted more efficiently.

Participation will encourage the interests of the workers and staff in the field of participation or democratic management. The main aim of this stage is to stabilize the status of the working people as masters of their own enterprise. In this case, workers will have some decision-making power over such things as setting objectives or evaluating performance, and this may coincide with the MBO of the Western experience. When MBO was first introduced in 1954, only executives had the authority to set

110

objectives for their subordinates. Since the widespread development of this movement, the workers now play an important role in the practice of MBO. In general, the future development of the economic responsibility system in China will meet the requirements of reform and the overall tendency towards modernization and democratization through maintaining an awareness of the important role of the human factor.

9

An evolutionary account of management and the role of management development in China

Qiu Xu-Yao, Yu Ke-Chun, and Xu Chan-Min
(*Beijing University of Iron and Steel Technology, China*)

RECENT DEVELOPMENT OF BUSINESS MANAGEMENT IN CHINA'S INDUSTRIAL ENTERPRISES

China has achieved a great measure of success in the search for economic growth since the founding of the People's Republic in 1949. The process of development, however, has not been smooth; it has had its successes and failures. After ten years of turmoil prior to 1976, China has begun to realize that her fundamental task should be to develop the economy and gradually improve the living standards and the cultural life of the people.

The nation's primary task has been set as the realization of a socialist modernization of industry, agriculture, national defence, and science and technology. The specific goal is to quadruple the value of the national gross annual industrial and agricultural production by the end of this century and to approach the level of developed countries in another thirty or fifty years. To attain such a goal, it is imperative to modernize and increase industrial production very rapidly.

The experience of industrialization in other countries shows that the acceleration of the process of industrial development depends not only on advanced technology in production but also on improved management. China's industries are still suffering from backward technology and management. Advanced technology and equipment can be imported in a short period, but the improvement of management needs time. It involves changing concepts, attitudes, and habits and recruiting new managers, managing staff, and workers. Below we give a brief review of changes in China's business management in industrial enterprises, an analysis of the causes of slow development, and the measures to be taken for rapid change.

112

The historical evolution of management

From the history of management in most industrialized countries, it can be seen that the process of development usually consists of three stages:

A long period of conventional management

In this period, industrial production was chiefly operated by manual workers and the scale of production was small. The distinguishing feature of management is that decisions were made by managers based on personal experience or past practices.

Scientific management

As industries expanded rapidly and factories grew into large enterprises, more complicated machines were used and conventional methods of management were not adequate for the changing conditions. A few pioneering engineers and managers began to inquire into the causes of inefficiency which existed in production. They carried out experiments using scientific methods to determine work standards, wage rates, etc. The concept of scientific management was gradually introduced and developed in the first decades of this century.

The distinguishing feature of scientific management is that all managerial problems are solved with the resources of science and not merely through the judgement of an experienced manager.

Modern management

Along with technological advances and the continuing mechanization and automation of the process of production, new ideas and techniques, such as systems analysis, operations research, value engineering, computers, etc. have been used in designing, planning, running, and maintaining a production and operation system with the aim of minimizing costs and optimizing profits. The application of modern management methods requires accurate information and a proper environment shaped by the fundamental work of scientific management.

The development of business management in China's industries, 1949–85

An attempt is made here to analyse and assess the development of

113

business management in China's industries according to the criteria of scientific management.

The period under investigation is divided into the following stages according to economic and political events:

1949–57: *Rehabilitation and the first five-year plan*

China entered a new economic era during which large-scale construction of industrial projects was accompanied by the introduction of scientific management. These projects, 156 in all, were all State-owned and operated on a planned basis. A planned system was set up and scientific methods were used to determine work standards, quotas, operation schedules, piece rate and time rate wage systems, etc. The managerial staff had been partly trained abroad or within China. The economic results of these enterprises during this period were the highest throughout the whole period from 1949 to 1985.

1958–66: *The great leap forward and the second five-year plan*

The drive for a 'great leap forward' was launched in the first three years and resulted in large investment in heavy industries, especially the iron and steel industry, and a serious imbalance in the economy. Both agricultural and light industries production dropped in the following years. From 1963, there was a period of re-adjustment and consolidation in the following three years and the economy recovered quickly in 1965 and 1966.

During the first three years, business management in large enterprises was adversely affected because most of the rules and regulations were criticized as not conforming to the doctrine of socialism and were stopped *en masse*. In many newly built medium- and small-sized factories, managers and staff were appointed without specialized training. Most of the workers came from agriculture without specialized skills. Management was chaotic and most of these new enterprises ran at a loss, subsidized by local government. This condition improved from 1963, when there was a return to scientific management.

1966–76: *The 'Cultural Revolution'*

The national economy was disrupted in these ten years. The value of industrial production dropped rapidly in 1967. After 1970, many industrial enterprises stopped production. The entire national economy was brought to the brink of collapse in 1976.

114

Business management was even worse. The established system of scientific management, recovered from 1963 to 1966, was again brought to a stop through the 'Cultural Revolution'.

1977–86

Relieved from the ten years of disruption, China began to improve its economy after 1976. The modernization of industrial production was foremost in the four modernizations of the nation. However, inefficiency was serious in most industrial enterprises in 1976.

Measures have been taken to establish a normal order of production for all enterprises. Emphasis has been put on the fundamental work of scientific management, such as the setting up of primary records of production and quotas for work, in order to improve efficiency. Industrial production has returned to normal and developed rapidly again. The annual percentage rate of increase in the value of industrial production was 18% for 1985.

In the meantime, theories and practices of modern management have been introduced into China through contacts with managers and scholars from industrialized countries. Modern methods of management have been gradually adopted in some of the enterprises.

The present situation

The fundamental work of scientific management is essential to the application of modern methods of management and the successful operation of industrial production. We can therefore evaluate the present management situation of China's industrial enterprises by examining the state of their fundamental work. We can divide them into three groups according to the state they are in.

(1) Enterprises with relatively complete and exact primary records of production; advanced quotas and standards for work; complete measuring instruments for inputs and outputs of production; better information systems; complete responsibility systems; and complete rules and regulations for all production teams. These enterprises all have a relatively long experience of scientific management and have a trained staff. Newly built enterprises with advanced

technological equipment also belong to this group, although their level of management may be much higher than that of other, older enterprises in this group.

(2) Most of these enterprises have primary records of production but quotas, standards, and measuring instruments are incomplete. They have established a set of rules and regulations for production but they are not strictly put into force.

(3) These enterprises are chiefly in a state of conventional management. Their production is usually not normal. Primary records of production are incomplete and inexact; measuring instruments are deficient; quotas and standards for work and consumption of materials are both incomplete and at low levels.

An investigation of more than 1,300 enterprises in Shanghai in 1983 revealed the following results:

(1) only 28.92% of them had complete primary records;
(2) only 26.75% of them had good measuring instruments;
(3) only 30.50% of them had responsibility systems for staff and workers;
(4) only 30.95% of them had quotas for the consumption of raw materials; and
(5) only 27.39% of them had better information systems.

The investigation shows that in the most industrialized city in China, Shanghai, only one fourth of industrial enterprises reached a level of scientific management with completed fundamental work. One would expect the percentage to be much lower in other parts of China.

Our investigation of several medium- and small-sized steel plants has also shown that most of the management staff in their workshops did not know how to do time study and work measurement in the process of production. After an analysis carried out by our consultancy service, they were finally convinced that there existed great potential for an increase in production after measures were taken to eliminate the waste of time which existed.

It is obvious from the above that the potential for an increase in productivity is great if scientific methods are applied in all enterprises in China.

116

Obstacles to be overcome

After many years of investigation and recent consultancy we have come to the conclusion that the causes of slow development are the conceptual problem, the lack of specialized training of management staff, and the low level of education of workers. The most important is the conceptual problem.

The importance of management to the successful operation of an industrial enterprise has been overlooked for many years, especially during the 'Cultural Revolution'. After 1978, it was emphasized by the Government that measures should be taken to strengthen the role of management both in the macro-economic control of the national economy and in the management of individual enterprises. After several years most of the large enterprises have improved successfully, but there are a number of medium- and small-scale enterprises which still remain at the conventional stage of management. This is because their concept of management has not changed.

The recognition by managers of the importance of management does not imply their recognition of management as a 'science'. This concept of management has not really been recognized and accepted by leading executives, managers, engineers, and various levels of management staff in China.

In most of the enterprises, managers and management staff were appointed without special training in management. Managers carried on their work chiefly based on their technological knowledge. They were accustomed to and quite satisfied with their management methods. They could not see that there was any necessity for frequent management training, because they did not recognize management as a science. Instead they regarded management as an art which should not be taught at school at all. This is one of the reasons why management education has not been popular in China for a long time.

There is no doubt that a qualified manager needs management experience and personal characteristics which cannot be learned from universities, but she/he also requires a systematic and fundamental knowledge of general management and technical skills which can be learned from specialized programmes, and if applied, can improve industrial production tremendously.

Moreover, the importance of an acceptance of management as a science should not only be associated with the need for special training, but should also be emphasized as the scientific approach

117

to solving managerial problems which are essential to the rationalization of industrial production and the application of modern management methods.

The acceptance of the concept of management as a science needs a complete change of thinking on the part of society as a whole. Until there is a real change in conception, the transition from conventional management to scientific management cannot be accelerated.

However, a change in thinking does not mean that scientific management can be achieved in all enterprises in a short time. China also has to face the task of training and recruiting thousands of management staff to get the capacity and skills for establishing a system of scientific management and proceeding to the application of modern management methods in due time. We also need to undertake the task of training and recruiting thousands of technical workers, quite a number of whom in small factories are still illiterate.

Prospects for the future

The prospect for change is optimistic for the following reasons:

(1) Conceptual change will be rapid in the coming years because of government policy emphasizing the importance of management, the gradual release of power to individual enterprises making it imperative for management to increase efficiency, and the introduction of modern management methods from other countries.

(2) There is an increasing demand for trained management graduates all over the country. Many universities and technical schools have established programmes on various management subjects. Many medium- and small-sized enterprises have begun to search for consultancy services on management problems. Many kinds of training programmes, from one month to two years, have been carried on since 1978. Undergraduate and graduate students from universities are gradually welcomed and employed by enterprises. This will help in the implementation of scientific management.

(3) Training and recruitment of technical workers has been carried on in all industrial enterprises to raise their level of education and technical skills.

These tasks may be arduous and cannot be fulfilled in a short period, but the direction of development cannot be changed.

RECENT DEVELOPMENTS IN MANAGEMENT EDUCATION IN CHINA'S UNIVERSITIES[1]

The modernization of China's economy described above demands a rapid advance in science and technology and also a rapid improvement in management, especially in industrial enterprises. The number of industrial enterprises has increased from 380,000 in 1981 to 392,000 in 1983, and a further increase is expected by the end of this century. This expansion creates a rising demand for management staff.

How to meet this demand is an urgent problem that cannot be overlooked in the near future. Here we analyse the present change in management education in universities and institutes, and envisage problems to be solved that might help explore possible developments for the future.

The development of management education, 1949–77

A brief review of the development up to 1977 will be given as background to the changes since 1977.

In 1947–48, of 207 universities and institutes 80 had established departments of economics, finance, and management. The number of students in these fields of study accounted for 31.4% of the total number of 155,000 students enrolled in all universities and institutes of the country. The percentage of students was small in engineering, only 17.7%. This reflected the fact that industrial production in old China was too limited to create enough jobs for graduates of applied science and technology.

After 1949, in order to meet the increasing demand for technicians and engineers from a big expansion in industry, there was a planned re-adjustment of the universities in 1952 and 1953, which resulted in an increase in applied science and engineering and a reduction in the number of institutes and university departments of economics, finance, and management. Students admitted to these fields dropped by 70% from 1951 to 1953, the percentage in total enrolment of students dropped from 15% in 1951 to 2.9% in 1953.

119

In 1954, a national conference on economics and finance in higher education discussed and emphasized the importance of higher education for training specialists in economic theory and business management. The role of three kinds of institutions should be distinguished: institutes of economics and finance which trained specialists for government administration and large-scale enterprises; faculties of economics and management in universities which trained theoretical workers for research institutes and teaching staff for universities; and faculties of management in universities of technology which trained specialists in engineering economy. As a result, there was a gradual and planned increase of students in these fields from 1953 to 1956. In 1957, there were thirty-five institutes with departments in economics, finance, and business management: six of these were institutes of economics and finance (including management), eleven were established in universities, and eighteen were established in universities of technology.

In 1958, along with the large increase in industrial investment and the expansion of industrial production, there appeared a large increase in newly established universities all over the country. The number of universities increased from 229 in 1957 to 1,289 in 1960 and the number of students more than doubled. However, the number of students specializing in economics, finance, and management increased by only a small amount. The number of universities then dropped to 407 in 1963.

All the higher institutions were prevented from admitting students in the first three years of the 'Cultural Revolution', and recovered admissions thereafter. Most subjects related to economics, finance, and management, as well as other social science subjects, could not admit students until 1978.

From statistics of management education and from the above analysis, we can draw the following conclusions for this period:

(1) The development of management education was more rapid than in old China if we compare the number of students graduated from departments of economics, finance, and management. The average annual number of graduates was 4,194 for 1949–65 and 1,972 for 1966–76, compared with 950 for 1928–47 (Table 9.1). However, the development of management education was slow compared with the increase in graduates from engineering.

Table 9.1 Comparison of graduates specializing in economics, finance, and management

	Graduates 1928–47 (19 years)	Graduates 1949–85			
		1949–65 (17 years)	1966–76 (11 years)	1977–85 (9 years)	Total (37 years)
Total number of graduates, in 10,000	18.5	155.44	103.29	242.62	471.35
Graduates of economics, finance, and management, in 10,000	1.9	7.13	2.17	7.68	16.98
Percentage of economics, finance, and management graduates in total (%)	10.3	4.6	2.1	3.6	3.6
Average number of graduates per annum	950	4,194	1,972	8,533	4,589

(2) The increase in numbers of students specializing in economics, finance, and management was small compared with the rapid increase in the gross value of industrial production.

(3) Because the number of students admitted to different departments of specialized subjects were planned by the Ministry of Education, the slow development of management during this period is a reflection of state policy towards the importance of management. There was a general belief that economics and management were not so important to the development of the national economy as were science and engineering. Management could be learned through practice and experience. In other words, the importance of economics, finance, and management to the improvement of economic development was overlooked during this period.

121

Drastic changes in management education, 1978–85

It can be seen that after 1977 there was the beginning of an era of unprecedented expansion in higher education. The number of students admitted into universities greatly increased. The increase was remarkable for students specializing in economics, finance, and management. The main changes which appeared in this period may be summarized as follows:

(1) The rate of increase in numbers of students enrolled in economics, finance, and management was the highest compared with those years before 1978. The number of students enrolled in 1976 was 2,453 and increased to 67,017 in 1985.

(2) Institutes of economics and finance have re-opened after ten years of being closed. The total number of such institutes increased to 22 in 1979 and to 62 in 1985.

(3) Departments of management have been established in many universities of technology and have expanded into schools of management recently.

(4) New fields of specialization, such as systems engineering, engineering economy, management information, decision science, operational research, forecasting, marketing, and technical-economic analysis, have been gradually introduced. The growing number of staff permits greater specialization and a wider range of teaching and research. The universities exhibit greater independence than before 1978.

(5) Postgraduate studies in these fields have been established in many universities and research institutes. The number of postgraduate students increased from 49 in 1978 to more than 2,700 in 1985.

(6) There is also an increase in colleges specializing in recruiting staff for industrial enterprises. In 1985, the number of such colleges was about 100 with 40,000 students enrolled. In addition, there is also an increase in evening schools and correspondence divisions in many universities. Besides, many employees have attended various kinds of short-duration classes in specialized subjects offered by schools of management.

(7) There has been an increasing number of students sent abroad for graduate studies although the number of

students specializing in economics and management is much less than those specializing in science and engineering.

The above changes in educational provision indicate that government policy and social opinion have gradually recognized the importance of economics and management to the achievement of the modernization of the national economy.

New problems

The mushrooming of higher education institutions of economics, finance, and management in recent years, has led to new problems:

(1) Although there has been a planned increase in the number of students admitted, it is far from meeting the growing demand for management staff from industrial enterprises. The number of graduates from universities was 8,533 for 1977–85 (Table 9.1).

(2) At present, there is an urgent and increasing demand for management teaching staff from these newly established institutions. In 1985, the total number of teaching staff for economics and management was under 13,000, with enrolled undergraduate students about 14,700, the ratio of teachers to students being 1 : 11.4, compared with 1 : 4.9 for science and engineering. The situation is more serious in that there is a shortage of middle-aged teachers because of the lack of management education in the ten years before 1978.

(3) There is also a problem with the quality of the present teaching staff. In general, they need new knowledge and practical experience of management. At the same time, experienced managers lack a systematic knowledge of modern management and the capacity to generalize their own experience into organized knowledge. The suggestion to exchange management staff and teaching staff between universities and enterprises has not yet been put in force.

(4) The structure and content of courses properly adjusted to meet China's economic conditions are still under discussion.

(5) It is necessary to reform traditional teaching methods. New methods with an emphasis on developing one's capacity instead of just getting knowledge from lecturing and reading are needed.

In spite of many problems to be resolved, it is encouraging that after thirty years of slow development, there is finally a beginning to the change of thinking which is a pre-requisite for the improvement of management and management education.

NOTE

1. Management education is used here in a broad sense, including subjects related to macro-economic control of the national economy, and to the business management of an enterprise.

BIBLIOGRAPHY

Achievement of Education in China, Statistics, 1949–1983, People's Education Press, 1985.
Contemporary Economic Management in China, Beijing: The Social Science Press, 1985.
Modernisation of Management (monthly) 1984–85.
Xu Dixin (1982) *China's Search for Economic Growth*, New World Press.

10

Reconciling the East and the West: management and management education in Turkey

Esin Ergin (Ahmet)
(Istanbul University, Turkey)

INTRODUCTION

Turkey is one of the very few countries in the world situated between the Eastern and Western cultures. Turkey's geographic place, its level of economic development, and the present economic policies give rise to a clash rather than a synthesis of these two cultures on most issues. Management is one of these areas where there is a considerable amount of clash and a substantial effort for synthesis as well.

Turkey is a country undergoing very rapid economic change. The economic policies adopted after 1980 have opened up the country to the outside world. Economic and political relations with the external environment have increased. The country is trying to join the EEC as soon as possible; has straightened out its relations with the IMF; and has increased its trade with the USA, EEC countries, and Arab countries as well as African countries and China. Turkey's guest-workers in the Federal Republic of Germany and the ones who returned have brought about considerable social and economic change to the country.

The Turkish population has characteristics different from the developed world. It increases at a rate of 2.7% every year; 60% of the population is under the age of 25; the literacy rate is 64%; and the portion of the annual budget allocated to education is small compared to the countries of the developed world.

With all the facts stated above, it is felt that there is a need to catch up with the technological change of the outside world. But, technologies cannot be brought into the country as much as is necessary because of economic constraints.

Turkey has a developed public sector. Outdated technologies, inefficient management, and overemployment because of political reasons are some of the characteristics seen in public-sector companies. Even with these characteristics, the first ten places among the 500 largest Turkish companies are taken up by State-owned companies. These firms take up the first places with their turnover, invested capital, and the number of employees. On the other hand, the private-sector companies in Turkey are run relatively more efficiently and tend to be open to new technologies.

Companies from both sectors appear among Fortune's 500 largest companies in the world.

THE ROLE OF MANAGEMENT AND MANAGEMENT EDUCATION IN A RAPIDLY CHANGING ENVIRONMENT

Management styles of private-sector companies are different from those of public-sector companies, and the prevalent cultures of the two sectors are also dissimilar. After 1980, the economic policies required public-sector companies to be run more efficiently with a profit objective, more like a private firm. Implementation of such a policy required new managers with a different outlook who had to operate in an established culture.

In private-sector companies the managers and owners set up the prevailing culture. Even then, the employees come from diverse educational, social, and cultural backgrounds. Sometimes it is not easy to find a fit among these differences of culture and education of employees and managers. Therefore, in both sectors, it is not very surprising to find more behavioural problems than technical problems facing managers.

So, in this very unique situation Turkish managers have to operate in a cross-cultural setting within the country as well as dealing with foreign or international companies with their increased interaction through increased trade and financial deals. Some managers are able to deal very successfully with this situation, while others find it extremely stressful.

Furthermore, managers of both sectors are in close contact with institutions in their environment. Relations with the central Government and the municipalities, as well as relations with society in general have to be dealt with by managers. There is increasing demand from society for environmental control, for more contributions to the community, and there is increasing pressure to create employment opportunities. There is also a fundamental change in the nature of demand and values of the society as a whole which needs to be scanned continuously if firms are to remain viable within this changing environment. And, in a developing country, managers also have the role of a catalyst in bringing about change with their strategic choices.

In this context, the role of management education in Turkey is critical in the sense of preparing future business managers, and developing practising ones in both the public sector and the private sector. The quality and direction of management education will decide the future of economic and social development in Turkey. Therefore, the content of management education should equip managers with tools to predict or sense changes in the environment and their likely effect on the economy, on the firm, and on the country. These tools should also enable managers to prepare viable strategies for the future. Within the organization, managers are the strategists who bring in technological change. With these special circumstances in mind, management education in Turkey should equip managers with the know-how to adapt to the different cultural demands they face. It should also help to modify behaviour models to deal with diverse cultures within the firm, in the country, and in the international environment.

THE PRESENT CONDITION OF MANAGEMENT EDUCATION IN TURKEY

In Turkey, the need for a separate higher education institution for management education was felt in the changing economic conditions of the 1950s. Up to that date the School of Economics of Istanbul University and other social science programmes at major universities met the demand for educating managers. From 1960 onwards the number of business schools increased. A number of students were sent to the Harvard Business School to be trained as the future lecturers in these business schools. Statistics show that only 50% of them stayed on at the university to continue an academic career. A research report published in 1973 states that management education is developing in the opposite direction of the economic development of the country (Aysan and Kurtulus, 1973).

There are several points which are important in understanding the present situation of management education in Turkey. There are twenty-seven established universities in the country with one or more business schools attached to them. The core programmes of these schools are decided upon by the Higher Education Council (YÖK). Each school builds its curricula around the core programme.

In these business schools the problem lies more with the quality of teaching rather than with the length of the programmes or the curricula. The number of students per instructor, the number of students per course, and the number of students per school are very high. In the large and established universities the teaching staff do not have the financial means to follow up current developments in their areas through books or journals because of budgetary constraints. The situation is better in smaller and newly set up institutions, but in these schools, the foremost problem is inexperienced teaching staff and lack of training programmes for them.

Second, there is the problem of teaching materials. The books in Turkish are few and most of them are outdated. It is very expensive for an instructor to publish a book, and there is very little in the system that would motivate people to publish books or articles.

A set of case materials was developed during the 1960s and 1970s. This is already very much outdated because of the fast economic and social change undergone by the country. So, any instructor who wants to use a case has to develop his own case or translate from foreign sources. Usually the cases can only be used in the MBA programmes rather than the undergraduate programmes because of the large size of classes. At the School of Economics the undergraduate class on business policy had 360 students enrolled during the 1986 spring semester. Classes cannot be divided up because of the lack of teaching staff.

Some schools are better off because they have new technologies and skilled teaching staff. Universities in Ankara and Istanbul have management development programmes for managers in the private sector and the public sector. Some Government institutions, like the TÜSSIDE (Turkish Institute of Industrial Management), also have programmes for managers in industry. Mostly multi-national companies operating in Turkey, some industrial firms, and banks have their own management development programmes within the firm.

In the last two years the German Government has started financing management training programmes for Turkish students educated in Germany and coming back to Turkey to work.

There are various reasons for having so many management development programmes for experienced managers at the university level and within firms. The university can have a more efficient system in a management development programme by controlling the number of students enrolled and by choosing more efficient teaching staff. These programmes have the advantage of enrolling motivated students. In the firms, management development programmes are mostly required by the headquarters of the foreign affiliated firms. These programmes orient managers with the management system of the headquarters. In a very few Turkish firms the management development programmes have been started by a strategist at the top who believed in the benefits of training and education at all levels of the company. These programmes are usually planned and run by a top-level manager. The teaching staff are drawn from managers of affiliated firms as well as universities.

The German Government-sponsored programme draws teaching staff from among the experienced managers in industry and from the universities in Istanbul.

EXPERIENCE OF THREE DIFFERENT MANAGEMENT PROGRAMMES

In this section details of three different programmes will be given. One reason for choosing these programmes was to emphasize the cultural differences among them. Second, it is easier to assess programmes with which one is involved. These programmes cater for different segments in the market for management development programmes. Therefore, the problems faced by the programmes are substantially different from each other.

The management development programmes run by the School of Economics of Istanbul University

There are four different programmes run by the School of Economics of Istanbul University.

The first one is the MBA programme which is designed to equip recently graduated students, without any work experience, with tools to deal with the international environment. It is a

129

one-and-a-half year programme at the end of which the students
have to submit a thesis. The students are usually graduates of
universities other than Istanbul University. It is a very popular
programme. The courses offered in this programme are on basic
management, finance, accounting, and marketing in the international context.

The second programme, the Business Administration Program
is for managers or for people who will become managers. It
requires four evenings attendance each week. Its formal aim is to
change outdated management practices in firms and help
managers develop their skills. The subversive aim is to bring
about a change in values, practices, and behaviour. In this
programme, the participants are oriented to the use of new
technologies, amongst other things. It is attended mainly by young
people from the public sector and by small-business owners. The
curriculum provides the basics of business administration with
related courses in general economics, business law, labour law,
and public finance.

The other two programmes on salesmanship and accounting are
highly technical, specific, and of short duration. The accounting
programme has the subversive aim of setting standard accounting
practices for the small-business owners and public employees.

The limitations of all the programmes are the limited number
of teaching staff and inadequate technological equipment. With
more funds these shortcomings can be overcome.

KOGEM – programmes of the management training centre of Koç Holding

Koç Holding is one of the oldest group of companies in Turkey
and was founded sixty years ago. Some of the companies in the
group appear among the 500 largest firms in the Fortune's list.
KOGEM is the management training centre for Koç Holding, set
up in 1982. In the first years the seminars offered were few in
number. The programmes were formed on the informally
expressed demands of firms and managers in the group.

The teaching staff were also asked to submit their offers for
seminars and courses according to their area of specialization. Of
the courses offered in KOGEM, 40% are on general management
subjects and 20% are related to finance and accounting subjects.
The rest of the courses are on marketing and production

management subjects. There are also four courses for secretaries. In 1982 only two subjects were offered in the KOGEM programme. In 1986 this number had increased to forty subjects. The statistical figures related to KOGEM show that the programmes are more popular among the first and middle-level managers rather than the top ones. The reason for this may be the nature of the subjects offered as well as the timing of the seminars.

In 1985, questionnaires were sent to top and middle managers asking for management development needs for themselves and their subordinates. In 1986, new programmes were introduced according to the results of the questionnaire. When the seminars offered in 1986 are examined, it can be seen at first hand that the subjects demanded are not all offered in the 1986 programme. It is also significant that there is a substantial demand for courses on behavioural subjects rather than technical subjects. This fact may arise from the particular characteristics of the companies.

In KOGEM, the top managers primarily demanded courses on technical subjects like decision-making techniques or financial analysis or financial planning. From their demands it is evident that they are performance-oriented rather than people-oriented. In their demands for their subordinates it is significant that their first choice is for courses on human relations in organizations. The technical subjects are listed after this first choice as the perceived needs of their subordinates.

The middle managers' choices for themselves are more on the practical side. They are performance-oriented too. For their subordinates they want 'line relationships' to be clarified as the perceived most important need.

The choices of the top and middle managers for themselves and their subordinates are significant in describing the leadership style of the Koç group of companies. Also, the method of asking the managers rather than the employees for their own needs for development reflects the more authoritarian and traditional values of the Koç group. These cultural characteristics are also a reflection of Turkish society. One study on the characteristics of managers and subordinates states that 'the Turkish subordinates value an expert and nurturant leadership style. They expect their leaders to be more knowledgeable and expert than themselves. They also expect him to plan and structure their tasks' (Aldemir, 1986: 9).

The main limiting factor of the KOGEM programme is the

very conservative outlook of the company. This conservative attitude is reflected in the choice of teaching staff. The teaching staff come from among managers in the Koç group and from universities in Istanbul. The second problem lies with inadequate premises for teaching purposes.

KOGEM is a unique institution in Turkey and its experience will ensure that it remains the leader in its field.

AMT – Angewandtes management training and DIA

This is a programme designed to train technically oriented graduates of German universities who will be coming back to Turkey to work. The programme is organized by Deutschen Gesellschaft für Technische Zusammenarbeit, Centrum für Internationale Migration und Entwicklung, Kübel Stiftung (Riedenburg, München), and DIA which is a private research, consulting, and training firm. This is a partly Government-sponsored programme which was started in 1985. The first half of the programme is run in Germany. It is an eight-month programme in which the participants spend three months working in various firms in Turkey.

Most of the participants have work experience in Germany rather than in Turkey. The main aim of the programme is to introduce the trainees to the present economic, business, and social conditions in Turkey. The courses offered try to give the participants the basics of business management.

The curriculum has been changed after the first programme with the feedback received from the participants. The curriculum is now more practical rather than theoretical, and the points of emphasis are more on legal matters and regulations and on the use of computers. This is different from the initial German emphasis.

The teaching staff is at present drawn half from the universities and half from industry. The tendency is towards more people from industry.

CULTURAL DIMENSIONS OF THE THREE PROGRAMMES

The programmes run by the three different institutions cater to the demands of different groups of managers and management trainees with diverse cultural backgrounds.

Programmes of the School of Economics

Some of the students coming to these programmes are educated in Turkish schools which have more of an authoritarian educational system. They are not used to class discussions and they take at least three months to get used to conferring with the instructor on more or less equal terms. The dominant attitudes tend to be on the conservative side with a fatalistic view of the world. The motivating factors for their attendance to the programmes are mainly for economic gain rather than for personal development.

Also, there are participants who are graduates of foreign secondary schools in Turkey. It is inevitable that they carry some of the characteristics of a traditional Turkish educational system. They also have a more questioning attitude in class. They tend to be active in discussions and more likely to demand democratic relationships. Knowledge of at least one foreign language and awareness of different values and cultures give them a different, more analytical outlook than their classmates. At times these programmes are attended by Iraqis, Iranians, Cypriots, and West Thracian Turks which raises additional language and cultural problems.

Most of the problems due to different cultural backgrounds come up during class discussions, on cases, and during games. Different cultures lead to different perceptions of the problems leading to different solutions. Especially during games on behavioural subjects the resulting friction may become difficult to manage. The dominant culture is not used to experiential learning or cases which seem to be unrealistic and superficial. Participants are more willing to accept the vast generalizations uttered by a person of authority who is the instructor in this case. In some cases, the instructors are also more likely to stick to lectures rather than leading class discussions or analysing cases which would need extra effort on their part too.

It is a big question whether Anglo-Saxon teaching materials and methods used in these programmes lead to learning or behaviour modification among the participants as intended. It will be some time before feedback is received on these issues.

KOGEM programmes

The participants in the KOGEM programmes are distinctly different culturally from the participants in the university programmes. The dominant culture is the company culture. The few top managers who attend the seminars choose the subjects they know something about. They exist in a very competitive world and are very aggressive. They are critical of the ideas presented. The middle managers, who form the majority of the participants, look and sound very competent in their specialized subjects. They also exist in a very competitive world, but they are more open to new ideas, experiential learning, cases, and games. They are also very questioning.

The KOGEM participants are, on the whole, aware that any educational programme is an asset for their personal development. The company culture has started to accept the KOGEM seminars as prestigious gatherings, perhaps a step on the way to the top. These seminars also create an opportunity to meet others in the group.

If the people working in the group companies were to decide on their training and development needs, perhaps different and more innovative subjects would come up.

AMT–DIA programme

The participants in this programme have a synthesis of the Turkish and German cultures in their backgrounds. They realize that two different cultures are separately dominant in some of their attitudes when they are in Turkey. They behave like a German in Germany, but it is hard for them to behave like a German in Turkey. Their thinking is systems-oriented and they have an analytical and questioning mind, so at first they feel frustrated and helpless in an oriental culture with outright resentment. It generally takes them some time to accept the realities of their new environment. Some have language problems. The teaching material and the teaching staff are mainly Anglo-Saxon-oriented and so in these programmes there is the clash of three different cultures. Usually at the end of the eight months the atmosphere of the programme becomes lively and friendly.

It will also take some time until we receive some feedback on how the participants have benefited from this programme.

134

POLICY ISSUES OF MANAGEMENT EDUCATION IN TURKEY

If we evaluate the three programmes described in this paper, we can say that all of them have different 'customers' coming from different cultures with different needs and different perceptual sets.

The university programmes seem to be slow in meeting the demand and diagnosing the change in the environment. Also, these programmes have not yet developed an approach which synthesizes the Western and Eastern cultural characteristics. The main constraints of the university programmes are lack of adequate teaching staff, materials, and technology because of a shortage of funds and educational policy. Being a teacher at the university is no longer an attractive job. Therefore, the system suffers from lack of qualified personnel.

It is these limitations and inadequacies of university management education that lead other institutions like KOGEM and DIA to fill the gap in the market for management development programmes.

The KOGEM programmes are tailored to the needs of the Koç Holdings group of companies, mainly reflecting their own ethics and outlook. The programmes are very conservatively planned and implemented with little expert knowledge on the design of such programmes. The level of development of the Koç group necessitates new approaches and new dimensions in their management thinking. KOGEM seems to be too closed a system to be able to develop a new perspective at the moment, although the need for change is felt at the top managerial level.

The AMT–DIA programme has stressed the technical aspects of management learning rather than emphasizing the human sides of management. This limitation arises because of the dominant ideas of the sponsors of the programme. It will be more beneficial if this programme tries to synthesize the best of three cultures and give more importance to the orientation of the participants into Turkish society.

CONCLUSION

The above evaluation of the three programmes raises a few questions about the policy issues of management education in Turkey:

(1) Do we need to develop programmes oriented to different cultures in a country? Or should we try to change the dominant culture to cater to the dominant characteristics of the business world?

(2) Should the institutions offering management development programmes focus on the demand or on what is thought to be essential academically?

(3) Should the management development programmes be planned and run by closed separate institutions catering to the needs of their own clients only, rather than bringing different outlooks to participants who will be change agents in a fast developing country?

Whatever the answers or policy choices for the above questions turn out to be, there is a definite need to train teachers for more awareness of cultural differences in the participants of management development programmes in Turkey. Or as Aldemir says 'the assessment of cultural values must be incorporated into management education programs' (Aldemir, 1986: 13).

BIBLIOGRAPHY

Aldemir, C. (1986) 'The impact of cultural values upon managers' choice of social power base', paper presented at the International Management Development: Challenges and Alternatives Conference, 16–19 September, University of Lancaster, Lancaster.

Aysan, A. and Kurtulus, K. (1973) *Project Managers: Research Report on the State of Management Education in Turkey and Opportunities for Development*, Management Education Foundation, Istanbul, October; Vols I–III.

KOGEM Seminar Catalogue, Koç Holding Education and Development Center, Istanbul, 1983, 1984, 1985, 1986.

Research Report on the Educational Needs of the Koç Group, Koç Holding Education and Development Center, Istanbul, 1987.

11

Management education for developing entrepreneurship in Hungary

Magdolna Csath
(*Karl Marx University of Economics, Budapest, Hungary*)

INTRODUCTION

Management methods and consequently the needs for management development are closely connected to the economic, social, and political situation of a country. Therefore, before saying anything about the possible ways and methods and the institutional problems of management education in Hungary we have to summarize the history of the economy, the major changes, especially the most recent ones, and put together these inner changes with the most characteristic environmental changes to show the basic problems Hungarian managers have to face and have to solve. This approach will help us to understand the specialities which characterize the needs for management development in Hungary.

Hungary has been a centrally planned country for more than twenty years. This has meant that structural changes in the economy basically have been carried out, for more than twenty years, through centralized decision-making without any role given to market forces. This time the managers were not really managers. They were directors, appointed by central agencies, more or less on the basis of their political reliability. These directors had no real responsibilities, they were not independent in deciding about strategic questions. They even had no chance to select their own deputies. All they were allowed to do was to fulfil the plans which were formulated outside the companies, in the national planning office and in the branch ministries. This situation created a generation of managers who were not really able to change their attitudes, to become more flexible, more independent, to take risks when the time had come for these changes. On the other hand, they tried to do their best, so it was not easy to get rid of them by giving them the chance of an honest withdrawal. This has been one of the greatest problems to solve after introducing the economic reform in 1968.

During the twenty years of central planning, the environment has changed a lot around Hungary. It turned out to be more and more clear that centralized decision-making is slow, extremely inefficient, and unable to manage the adaptation of the economy to the rapidly changing environment.

More and more problems have accumulated:

(1) decreasing competitiveness, because of poor quality, low productivity, high costs;
(2) inadequate industrial structure: big, inflexible companies, with highly hierarchical structures, huge, energy-demanding industries in a country with poor energy sources and raw material availability;
(3) bureaucracy, rigidity in the decision-making systems;
(4) poor knowledge of modern management methods in companies;
(5) low labour mobility; and
(6) lack of interest in better performance.

Companies became more and more vulnerable to outside forces and pressures as the environment grew increasingly unstable and accelerative, and straight-line growth in an equilibrial environment became the nostalgia of the peaceful past. It became urgent to change ways of managing the economic system, to delegate more responsibility to the corporate level and to develop new kinds of leadership for the survival of the economy.

REFORMS: 1968, 1982

The initial economic reform was introduced in 1968. The basic idea of the reform was to increase the role of market forces, to decentralize the decision-making process, to delegate decision-making responsibilities to a lower level, nearer to the market; and to make it possible to develop independent corporate strategies. However, at least two serious problems remained unsolved. First, the 1968 reform did not alter the ownership by the State of means of production, since social ownership continued to be interpreted as meaning ownership by the State bureaucracy. The other important problem was that company management remained overly tied to administrative hierarchies, basically because top executives were still appointed by the branch ministries.

The second stage of the reform which started in 1982 introduced:

(1) further development of enterprise management autonomy;
(2) development of the institutional structure of the economy and the organizational structure of the companies; and
(3) a break in the hierarchical link between organs of state administration and the enterprises.

Many companies, especially in the basic industries, had outgrown their organizational structures. These represented a significant obstacle to efficiency and effective development and hence the Government authorities intervened: during four years many big companies became decentralized, and were cut into smaller, independent parts. Affiliated companies were formed all over the industry. Around 100 new medium-size companies were established and approximately 28,000 new, small enterprises of different types came to life, including private businesses.

Concerning the ownership of the companies, four basic groups of companies can be formed now:

(1) Public service enterprises, e.g. those providing utilities, and some large-scale enterprises. In this group the management system of the companies has not been changed: the top executives are still appointed by branch ministries.
(2) Small, local companies, where the management devolves solely to the collective of the enterprise.
(3) The mainstream of all public manufacturing enterprises, where the management is elected by the 'corporate council' consisting of representation from the enterprise collective and from the management. From 1,200 companies belonging to the industrial branch ministries 800 were already working in the new system in 1986.
(4) Private enterprises: there were already approximately 250,000 around in every sector of the economy in 1986.

In a much more complex system of management and ownership it is very important to be clear about who the managers are now, and what kind of problems they are encountering recently. It is important to note the year here. Since the system is developing continuously, the figures mentioned will probably be out of date by the time of publication.

MANAGERS IN PUBLIC INDUSTRY

What are the main characteristics of managers in public industry? On the basis of research done in the industry I found the following characteristics:

First of all looking at age, the majority of managers are over fifty. Basically these are the managers from the time before the economic reform in 1968. Some of them are rather conservative, risk-averse and dependent, which is understandable as they have spent the majority of their managerial careers in a totally different environment, in a strict, centrally planned system. And naturally it would be unreasonable to believe that it is enough just to declare that after having more autonomy in decision-making these managers will be able and want to behave quite differently. Behaviour does not change automatically and especially not within a short period of time. People cannot change rapidly. Managerial cultures and behaviour are long-lasting phenomena, which are deeply rooted. These managers need new types of knowledge, new attitudes, and skills. They need to change from the day-to-day type of management to the strategic type of management. On the other hand it would not be very efficient to put these managers into classes for several weeks or months and try to cram the new knowledge they really need into their heads. The only promising approach to management development in this group is a mixture of action learning, distance learning, and self-development.

The other characteristic group of managers is the so-called 'reform-generation'. They were deeply involved in initiating the economic reforms in 1968. They were for more independence in decision-making at the corporate level, for financial and economic regulation of the economy rather than for direct, tight control. They were more creative and entrepreneurial by nature, but as the reform process has advanced and companies have started to be more and more profit-oriented and independent from the authorities, they too have started to feel the need for more up-to-date knowledge and skills, especially in adapting to the rapidly changing environment. But the question has to be raised again:

where and how? They prefer the learning-by-doing approach. The most common solution is in-house training, and what is more, in several cases the establishment of company training centres. Sometimes they try to combine the training process with consultancy on real problems assisted by prestigious home and foreign consulting firms.

The other emerging group of managers consists of young, mostly newly elected ones who are near the age of 40, and who keep abreast of the times. They are progressive and try to do everything to push the economic reforms ahead, and to struggle for greater enterprise autonomy. They are already well equipped with the most up-to-date theories and practices of management and are eager to apply them. They also try to keep informed about achievements in management development abroad. Naturally they too need continuous training which can be solved with the help of distance learning and planned self-development. The other aspect worth mentioning is the professional background of managers. This is a very interesting area which is closely connected to the history and traditions of industry in a country. In Hungary, for decades production was the most emphasized area in industry. The economic and marketing aspects of production were basically rejected. Even R&D activity had had no real contact with the market. The efficiency and effectiveness of production and R&D activity were seen as non-essential. In this period of time it was natural that the majority of managers were engineers. However, nowadays it causes more and more trouble if the top manager is a so-called 'pure technical specialist' and has no inclination toward the marketing, economic, and financial aspects of the business. These people need urgent development of their thinking, otherwise they can very easily lead the company towards bankruptcy. They can best use action learning methods but what is more important is that they need a new type of attitude towards how to manage a business which is not working very well in a rapidly changing, competitive environment.

The size and the organizational structures of companies also have an effect on the needs for management development. For example, in large enterprises it is an especially important top management task to discover how to make the organization more flexible, how to communicate, how to motivate people to be more creative, and how to create a small-business climate within the company. Another aspect is the type of management and the type of ownership in which a company is operating. Does it have an elected or an appointed management? Is it a public, a private or a co-operative firm, and in what concrete form is it operating? Depending on the management and ownership form, the companies are working in different hierarchical, social, and power structures, and therefore they have different strategic objectives and policies, which need management methods fitting to the specialities of the businesses. Concerning management development needs it is very probable that special topics can be especially important, like team-building, participative management, risk-taking, human research management, etc., besides general management development. Universities and business schools can provide this kind of education and distance-learning methods can be easily adapted, too.

To sum up my findings I would say that three aspects of management are urgently needed to strengthen public companies:

(1) strategic thinking,
(2) more inclination to innovation, and
(3) more entrepreneurship.

We need more strategists in management who have the ability to see and evaluate business opportunities and to take advantage of them. Innovations can be the result of actions by those strategists who know there are are two ways to go broke: do nothing or do something, and the latter is greater fun. Naturally more freedom is needed to create more strategists, innovators, and entrepreneurs. What kinds of new knowledge, skills, and attitudes need to be developed? What kind of areas should management education concentrate on?

The most important area is to develop the leadership style of managers. They have to be experts:

(1) in co-ordination;
(2) in adapting to change (sometimes to drastic change): not to cope with or avoid change nor to plan for future stability, but to accept change as a key element in shaping the future of the company;
(3) in deciding on radical actions when it is necessary;
(4) in living together with uncertainty, to take risk;
(5) in developing their capabilities to solve new types of problems, plan under pressure and in an uncertain environment;
(6) in building new corporate cultures, flexible organizational structures, future orientation, in using the collective

intelligence of the organization to mobilize for developing novel responses;

(7) in building new international relations, starting joint ventures; and still,

(8) think in terms of long-range strategic goals: to be strategists.

To explore these ideas I undertook some research three years ago which covered approximately fifty industrial public enterprises. The research tried to find out the correlation between performance and the strategy-making practice of the companies.

Having analyzed the situation in these companies I found that:

(1) the performance of companies with a healthy strategy-making system is better and more steady than that of companies not having built up a strategic-planning system;

(2) those companies having a strategic view are more innovative, risk-taking, more adaptive and faster to change.

In these companies the managers are more entrepreneurial. The companies, almost without exception have obtained new management in the last four to six years. Besides strong strategic thinking these managers have something more in common: they have put a great emphasis on human factors. They have tried to overcome the natural resistance to change of the people with challenging motivation systems, innovative organizational structures, and adequate continuous training. In these companies strategy-making is more than rational planning: it is a 'cultural phenomenon' as well, which shapes the firm's strategic direction, shapes the organizational culture, and builds up norms of behaviour and value systems. Unfortunately we do not have enough companies like these, and we have far too few managers who possess the desired features. This means that management education is a task which has to be in focus. Before summarizing the situation of management education let me turn briefly to another interesting research study dealing with the characteristics of private entrepreneurs and their education needs.

CHARACTERISTICS OF PRIVATE FIRMS, ENTREPRENEURS, AND EDUCATIONAL NEEDS IN THE PRIVATE SECTOR

To understand the situation concerning the same questions in the private sector I started a research study based on questionnaires. I sent 600 questionnaires to private entrepreneurs and got back 200 answers. So far I have evaluated 61 of them.[1] From the 61 I got only 5 answers without names which indicates that the entrepreneurs who filled in the questionnaire did not want to hide their opinion, in spite of the fact that they were given the option to answer anonymously.

The people in that segment of the sample I have already evaluated by age, family background, and educational background, are categorized in Tables 11.1–11.3. It is striking how young on average these private entrepreneurs are, how well trained they are, and the high percentage of them which come from intellectual backgrounds.

In order to gain some insight into their motivation when starting their own businesses, I asked two questions about the factors which influenced them. The results are shown in Tables 11.4. and 11.5.

The conclusion I come to is that these people are real entrepreneurs because basically they wanted to challenge themselves when they started their own businesses. But why did they want to do that? I got the feeling that the answers of the private entrepreneurs highlight a weakness in the public sector, i.e. the lack of entrepreneurship and the difficulties in being innovative within bigger companies.

These results support my previous findings concerning the basic issues to focus on in public companies:

(1) strategic thinking;
(2) innovativeness;
(3) entrepreneurship;
(4) building organizational and management cultures; and
(5) more human orientation.

It was interesting to see the answers concerning education needs – bearing in mind how highly educated they are – and the forms of education they would prefer (Tables 11.6 and 11.7). We have to take note of the answers. They want to learn, but do not prefer to do that in the established business schools.

Table 11.1 Age structure of subsample evaluated so far

	Number of people
18–24	—
25–34	16
35–44	25
45–54	12
55–64	8
65–	—
Total	61

Table 11.2 Family background of subsample evaluated so far

	Number of people	Percentage
Worker	16	26.3
Peasant	6	9.8
Intellectuals	31	50.8
Private	8	13.1
Total	61	100.0

Table 11.3 Educational background of subsample evaluated so far

	Number of people	Percentage
Elementary education	—	—
Secondary education	9	14.8
High school	10	16.4
University	42	68.8
Total	61	100.0

Table 11.4 Which factors motivated the private entrepreneurs most to start their own business?

The factors	The number of those who chose this factor
1. Desire to use my training and skills better	37
2. Be challenged by problems of starting a new business	30
3. Sense of adventure	26
4. Want to develop an idea for product	24
5. Be able to work with people I choose	23
6. Control my own time	23
7. Achieve personal sense of accomplishment	23
8. Work in an unstructured position	23
9. Be my own boss	20
10. Work with people who co-operate well	20
11. Take advantage of an opportunity I created	20
12. Not to work for an unreasonable boss	19
13. Desire for financial independence	17
14. Needed more money	17
15. Take advantage of an opportunity	16

Table 11.5 Which factors motivated the private entrepreneurs the least when starting their own business?

The factors	The numbers of those who chose this factor
1. Continue family traditions	—
2. Expected to continue the family traditions	—
3. Have sufficient time for family life	—
4. Escape unsafe working conditions	—
5. Step to achieve political ambition	1
6. Have more influence in the community	1
7. Be respected by friends	1
8. Desire to be wealthy	1
9. Follow the example of a person I admire	1
10. Contribute to the welfare of my ethnic group	1
11. Achieve a higher position in society	1
12. Apply lessons learnt from a previous business	3

Table 11.6 How many people in the sample felt a need for further education?

	Number of people	Percentage
Feel need for further education	51	83.6
Feel no need for further education	8	13.1
No answer	2	3.3
Total	61	100.0

Table 11.7 What kind of education did they feel useful?

Type of education	Number of people	Percentage
University	15	24.5
Business school (ie the type we have)	6	10.0
Chamber of Commerce	14	23.0
Special forms including private consulting firms	26	42.5
Total	61	100.0

THE STRUCTURE OF MANAGEMENT EDUCATION

The first business schools were founded in Hungary together with the economic reforms in 1968. We still have the same institutional system, basically with a central business school reporting to the Ministry of Education and Culture and with business schools reporting to the different branch ministries.

The system of management education is as shown in Fig. 11.1. The system is basically as it was built twenty years ago, although some new elements have emerged, like in-house company training centres (not very many), and private consultancies providing management education.

It is not surprising, therefore, that the system of education is in crisis. Previously, managers were sent to the different business schools regularly, at least in every fifth year, according to the five-year personnel plans of the supervising ministries. They were sent to different courses of the different business schools on the basis of their managerial task, duty, and assignment. The reason

147

Figure 11.1 The system of management education in Hungary

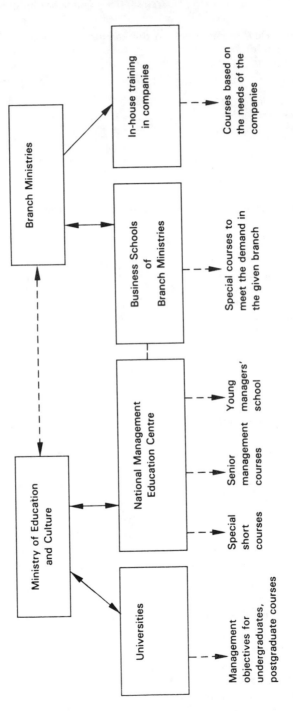

for this system was that those responsible for the appointment of managers had to be responsible for their further education, as well. As the top executives and their deputies were appointed and promoted by the branch ministries, it was evident that their training was scheduled by the same organizations. This system, too, has been modified by the recent economic reforms introduced in 1982. Now only in public-service enterprises does a clear responsibility remain with the branch ministries for taking care of the management development needs of top executives.

In the second and third group of enterprises it is not entirely clear who is responsible for the further education of management. It would be rational to say that the managers themselves have to feel the necessity for training, otherwise they would not be able to operate successfully as managers. However, this is again a rather long process. There are some encouraging signals: they try to find the appropriate kind of courses and if they do not find them in the traditional business school system, then they try to find other possibilities. And there are more and more possibilities in the form of private consulting firms offering consultancy combined with training. The other approach is to establish an in-house, in-company training centre. This is an increasingly popular solution, especially in the big companies, as it can build up a human resource strategy in harmony with the overall corporate strategy. This approach can be more creative and innovative, and can take into account the future needs of the companies far better than the business schools operating still mainly in the traditional educational system.

Finally there is the problem of business education in the universities, because, as far as the universities are concerned, we do not have business schools in the universities. I would like to mention, too, that although managerial subjects have been included in university education for several years both at undergraduate and graduate levels, there are still no departments of management in Hungarian universities.

It is an even bigger problem for the technical universities which have very limited curricula covering management subjects, like strategic management, marketing, organization design, etc. This is a very special and strategic problem: sooner or later the majority of the engineers will be promoted to be managers, and what is more, as you remember from the professional background of the practising managers, the majority are engineers at present, too.

149

CONCLUSIONS

To sum up the problems mentioned in this chapter, we have to emphasize that although there have been tremendous changes in the economic and institutional systems in Hungary, they have not been followed by similar changes in management education so far. Unfortunately, this problem has started to be a major obstacle to the ongoing economic reform process. The problem is complex: all levels of management hierarchy, including government institutions, badly need managers with sophisticated managerial knowledge, more creativeness, innovativeness, and risk-taking attitudes. To move ahead from a situation where the overall economic growth has been stagnant for some years already, and up to 30% of industry is estimated to be unprofitable, definitely makes it more important than ever that more attention than just lip service be paid to management education and entrepreneurship. It is especially the case now when more and more companies are becoming decentralized, new public companies and private enterprises are going to be established and within organizations also there is a decentralization process which demands more well-prepared managers. Right now good managers are still in short supply. It certainly takes a long time to solve this problem as we have started to think about it too late. Therefore, the only thing to do is to combine short-term and longer-term solutions to the problem at the same time. Short-term solutions refer to using different types of management education including on-the-spot training. However, in the long run there is only one way which strategically would lead to a solution: to introduce more management education in all universities. It is also advisable to loosen up the hierarchical system of present management education by allowing institutions to compete on the basis of better service. Private entrepreneurs have to be enabled to enter the education business much more easily than can be done at present. And at the least, management education needs an injection from abroad in the form of joint business schools established in Hungary. But to do all these things there is a very important myth to clear up: management selection and education, if it wants to bring grist to the mill of the economic reform process, has to become an economic and not a political concern.

NOTE

1. Having now reviewed all the returned questionnaires, the overall picture as described in this chapter is unchanged and the basic motivational factors are as set out.

REFERENCES AND BIBLIOGRAPHY

Csath, M. (1983) 'Strategic planning – A new arrival in Hungarian industry', *Long Range Planning* **16**(2).
Csath, M. (1986) 'Developing skills for successful joint ventures: New tasks of management development in Hungary', paper presented at the Management Development and New Economic International Environment Workshop, IIASA.
Csath, M. and Naylor, T.H. (1986) 'The Hungarian experience with deregulation', in Richard M. Burton and Borge Obel (eds) *Innovation and Entrepreneurship in Organizations: Strategies for Competitiveness, Deregulation and Privatization*, Amsterdam: Elsevier.
'Proposal for the establishment of a joint venture international business school in Hungary', a proposal in Hungarian which was given to several responsible people to make them interested in the ideas and get support from them, 1985.

12

Corporate social awareness and responsibility: implications for management education in Hong Kong

Joseph N.K. Tam

(Lingnan College, Hong Kong)

The current situation in Hong Kong suggests that there is a need for management education to tackle issues of corporate social awareness and responsibility.

In a free market-economy such as ours in Hong Kong, the traditional business function is economic and not societal in nature. Competing enterprises must be able to excel in product quality, innovation, market leadership, and overall productivity. They will otherwise be penalized by the market mechanism. Gaining enough profit for survival and growth naturally and logically becomes the dominant value and purpose of all business.

The self-serving, profit-maximizing behaviour of local entrepreneurs has long been justified on the grounds of the economic benefits they bring to our society. The enterprising spirit and style of management of these owner-managers have been highly spoken of as the capitalization of intuition in making prompt business decisions and the willingness to take risks for new opportunities with high monetary returns. Their behaviour resembles, in many aspects, the older generations of entrepreneurs in the United States or Europe, when the theory of the jungle still prevailed and 'the survival of the fittest' was the norm.

Public corporations in Hong Kong have long been regarded as extensions of the influence of the family businesses and as the means to make profitable use of other people's money. Family members are nominated as directors on the board and as top managers of these public corporations – after going public – whether they are professionally qualified or not. As Redding (1984) points out, the business ethics of these family-based businesses are limited to the organization's internal workings and to the staff on whom its survival depends. There are many cases where a company's name and goodwill have been abused by directors when they borrow money for personal speculation in the name of the corporation.

On top of this, our professional managerial system is not developing fast and effectively enough to cope with the rapid economic growth and ever-increasing international business and financial activities centred around Hong Kong. Many managers tend to remain loyal to the bosses of the family-based corporations, the so-called 'rice-bowl masters'. Also, recent cases of unethical business practices, which ended up in bankruptcies or government takeovers, reveal the lack of ethics in many business sectors and the urgent need to re-orient our existing managers and would-be managers to the broader concept of corporate social responsibility.

The concept of corporate social responsibility originated in the United States in the 1950s and spread to major Western industrial nations in the following decades. It should not be regarded as an isolated concept, but as a significant movement that has revolutionized managerial philosophies, theories, and practices. It has thrown light on social and ethical dimensions of the business environment which have been neglected by many established enterprises. What made an enterprise successful in the past does not guarantee its survival and growth in the future if the enterprise ignores social expectations and contravenes its social mandate.

In the early 1950s Howard Bowen suggested conducting social audits to evaluate the social performance of corporations. According to Bowen, businessmen 'are servants of society and that management merely in the interests of stockholders is not the sole end of their duties' (Bowen, 1978: 19–25).

In a free-enterprise economy, enterprises are established to provide goods and services to society under the profit motive. It is believed that such an economy functions well, usually with minimal government intervention. The traditional justification for such an economy rests on the basic assumption that perfect or vigorous competition will prevail. A main thrust of the competitive theory, as developed by Adam Smith and the classical economists, is that business enterprises will seek to maximize profit. By doing so, business helps to allocate society's scarce resources most efficiently under the market mechanism as if led by 'the invisible hand', and thereby serves the best interests of both capital owners and the general public. A competitive market system, therefore, reconciles private interests with public good. In this regard, the only responsibility of corporations is profit-maximization and nothing more. Milton Friedman is one of the most adamant defenders and spokesmen for this 'classical' or 'narrow' view of corporate social responsibility, which limits the corporate social responsibility of business to making profits for its shareholders. In the words of Friedman:

> In such an economy, there is one and only one social responsibility of business – to use its resources and engage in the rules of the game, which is to say, engage in open and free competition, without deception or fraud.

He concluded,

> Few trends could so thoroughly undermine the very foundations of our free society as the acceptance by corporate officials of a social responsibility other than to make as much money for their stockholders as possible. This is a fundamentally subversive doctrine.

> (Friedman, 1962: 133–6)

'The business of business is business.' Defenders of this narrow view like to cite this saying. In a pluralistic society, business, government, and other social organizations co-exist but each of them performs a different function in making profits and creating wealth. The chief danger to democracy and to individual freedom is the centralization of power in a certain group, especially government. Many concerned business persons therefore fear that calls for increased social responsibility on the part of business will only increase government control. The function of government is to look after the public interest. If business expands its function from merely making profit to looking after the public interest, it would be exercising duties only appropriate for government, and hence would put itself under government control. Other people fear that calls for increased corporate social involvement will put too much power in the hands of corporate officials, who, unlike government officials, are not legitimate representatives charged with determining the public good. Theodore Levitt echoed all these concerns about the dangers of excessive centralized corporate power or government power in a democratic society. He insisted that:

In the end, business has only two responsibilities, to obey the elementary canons of everyday face to face civility (honest, good faith and so on) and to seek material gain.

(Levitt, 1958: 41–50)

However, the rules of the game nowadays should comprise not only specific positivist laws but, as Bowie (1983) puts it, the moral constraints included in an implied contract with society. The social contract is an old concept in Western civilization. In the past the social contract called for business to produce and distribute products and services for profit according to the market mechanism. Changing social needs and expectations have given rise to the impetus to update the social contract. It now demands that business carry out its economic mission within new rules of the game. These may include requirements to produce useful and safe products and reliable services, to observe moral rules pertinent to free competition, to observe regulatory measures and laws, and to impose self-restraint and self-regulation. These all measure up to a very high ethical standard, in various functional areas of business, such as fair advertising and marketing, maintaining a safe workplace, avoiding environmental pollution, and so on.

Some writers, such as Simon *et al.* (1983), have attempted to draw bottom-line moral objectives for corporations. They make a distinction between negative injunctions and affirmative duties. A 'moral minimum' responsibility is to avoid negative social consequences of corporate decisions and take up all appropriate degrees of responsibility to eliminate the social injury or social ills they may help to create.

Social responsibility arises from social power. It arises from concern about the consequences of business actions as they affect the interests of others. Many contemporary scholars, including Keith Davies and Robert L. Blomstrom (1975), stress the importance of the socio-economic model in which an enterprise is not only an economic institution but also a social institution, having intimate interactions with other social entities within the domains of the greater social system. If business wishes to retain its long-term viability and significance as a major institution in society, it must be responsive to social issues by taking responsible decisions and actions. If business fails to respond, its power is likely to diminish. Davies (1983) calls this the 'Iron Law of Responsibility'. Along this line of reasoning, an enterprise

155

plays the social role of trusteeship of vast resources and it must serve the interests of all claimants on the organization, rather than just those of owners or customers or labour.

To summarize this discussion, we can see that the view of corporate social responsibility has expanded to encompass not only economic and legal responsibilities but also moral and discretionary responsibilities (Carroll, 1980). Managers must prepare to work to the utmost to fulfil their economic, legal, and moral responsibilities and exercise discretion whether or not to contribute more in other social endeavours. Although these responsibilities are conceptually distinguished as separate for the purpose of definition, they are often interrelated and should not be regarded as mutually exclusive.

Perhaps in the past it was appropriate to say 'what is good for GM is good for society'; but now, society requires that 'what is good for society is good for GM'. However, as the traditional values of Western management philosophy tend to over-emphasize profit maximization and efficiency, the social awareness of top management or managers at lower levels may be obscured from time to time by the pressing needs to meet challenges due to rapidly changing market/economic or technological environments. Moreover, existing business practice is to evaluate and reward managers based on relatively short-term performance criteria. Elmer Johnson, who is currently Group Vice-President for Operating Staff and General Council at General Motors, reported that GM established a corporate issues programme for dealing with issues concerning the company's responsibility for the protection of a whole variety of important social interests. Despite this declared purpose, management philosophy as expressed by Johnson is very much haunted by the traditionally limited view. Even though GM has taken some positive actions, its stance towards social obligations is more reactive than proactive or interactive. In Johnson's opinion (Johnson, 1986) the widening notion of corporate social accountability has intensified the adverse confrontation between business and government, particularly in the United States. The pursuit of social responsibility by American multi-national companies has escalated costs which have been passed on to the consumer, thus damaging the companies' competitive power in wrestling with foreign enterprises over the last decade.

Even if top management is convinced by the concept and put it as a major corporate goal along with traditional profit/market goals, they may encounter problems when they attempt to operationalize the concept in their own institutions. In recent years, there has been a growing emphasis on business ethics. Responsible companies try to enact codes of ethics which serve as administrative and behavioural guidelines for their managers and employees in an attempt to enhance social responsibility. Further, an application of ethical theory to aid managerial decision-taking is gradually gaining acceptance in the management education field, although it is less popular in intra-company management development and training programmes.

Within the multi-national context, existing practices in the training and development of many international organizations place great emphasis on the acquisition of technical skills, on raising competency levels in various operational areas, and on improving the man-management skills of selected candidates who will be sent to fill key managerial posts in overseas subsidiaries or joint ventures. This is not adequate, however. There exists a definite training need to improve managers' awareness of the different sociocultural and ethical environments of the destination country. It is my contention that it is equally important for the executives in charge of international divisions at corporate headquarters to think carefully about the implications of corporate social responsibility as one aspect of business policy and strategy formulation. Assuming that other strategic factors are equal, consciousness and awareness of social responsibility may help management to formulate and implement viable business policy and strategy, giving rise to high economic benefits as well as social benefits in the long run. I would therefore argue that the management developer owes as much to society as to the firm and the individual.

A recent survey of 1,200 colleges and universities in the USA (including 700 who were members of the American Association of Collegiate Schools of Business, an accrediting institution) indicated that the majority of schools of business administration in the USA do not offer courses in business ethics and/or in the social responsibility of business firms, either optional or required. Hosmer (1985) concludes that this is due mostly to the fact that faculty in the major disciplines and techniques of management do not recognize the complexity of ethical problems or the importance of ethical decisions in the overall management of large business organizations.

The same phenomenon appears to exist in the business schools of major institutes of higher education in Hong Kong. The concepts of corporate social responsibility and/or business ethics are kept in very low profile. Only one or two institutes are known to offer required or optional courses on these topics for the education of our business students. Perhaps the time has come for management educators and developers in Hong Kong to do something about this in a more responsive and active manner.

Robert Fell, the then Commissioner for Securities and Commodities Trading in Hong Kong, expressed a similar view when addressing the issue of how Hong Kong's businesses can meet the problem of unethical practices. He said,

> This requires proper development and training of our future managers, particularly the managers of public companies listed on the stock exchanges and to lay down the appropriate standards within a business.
>
> (Fell, 1984: 16)

While we expect the multi-national corporations operating in Hong Kong to behave as socially responsible citizens, we have every right to demand that local corporations behave in an even more self-disciplined manner. This becomes a very serious proposition when we look at the future role to be played by our free-enterprise economic system. Its proper function depends on non-government intervention and self-regulation on the part of business enterprises.

In order to maintain the momentum of our economic growth, Hong Kong requires more and more intelligent young persons to join our enterprises. How we educate and train this new breed of young managers and entrepreneurs to become socially responsible and yet proactive enough to meet the challenges from both local and international fronts is itself a challenge to the management development professionals in Hong Kong. By virtue of the Sino-British Joint Declaration on 19 December 1984, the current social and economic system in Hong Kong will remain unchanged after 1997. Our managers of tomorrow have to justify the viability of our free-market concept in the creation of wealth and contribution to the common good from now on to 1997 and beyond. Unless social awareness and responsibility are taken into account, this may not be possible.

REFERENCES

Bowen, H.R. (1978) *Social Responsibilities of the Businessmen*, New York.

Bowie, N.E. (1983) 'Changing the rules', in T.L. Beauchamp and N. Bowie (eds) *Ethical Theory and Business* (2nd edn), Englewood Cliffs, NJ: Prentice-Hall.

Carroll, A.B. (1980) 'Social responsibility as an objective of business: evolving toward a model of corporate social performance', in W.F. Gleuck (ed.), *Business Policy and Strategy*, New York: McGraw-Hill.

Davies, K. (1983) 'An expanded view of the social responsibility of business', in T.L. Beauchamp and N. Bowie (eds) *Ethical Theory and Business* (2nd edn), Englewood Cliffs, NJ: Prentice-Hall.

Davies, K. and Blomstrom, R.L. (1975) *Business and Society: Environment Responsibility* (3rd edn), New York: McGraw-Hill.

Fell, R. (1984) 'Problems and implications of unethical business practices in Hong Kong', a paper presented at the Conference on Business Ethics held jointly by the Hong Kong Management Association and the Independent Commission against Corruption.

Friedman, M. (1962) *Capitalism and Freedom*, Chicago: University of Chicago Press.

Friedman, M. (1970) 'The social responsibility of business is to increase its profits', *New York Times Magazine*, 13 September, 32–3.

Hosmer, La Rue T. (1985) 'The other 338: Why a majority of our schools of business administration do not offer a course in business ethics', *Journal of Business Ethics* 4(1), February: 17–22.

Johnson, E.W. (1986) 'General Motors Corporation: its constituencies and the public interests', *Journal of Business Ethics* 5.

Levitt, T. (1958) 'The dangers of social responsibility', *Harvard Business Review* September–October: 41–50.

Redding, G. (1984) 'Varieties of iron ricebowl', *Hong Kong Manager* May: 15.

Simon, J.G., Powers, C.W., and Gunnemann, J.P. (1983) 'The responsibilities of corporations and their owners', in T.L. Beauchamp and N. Bowie (eds) *Ethical Theory and Business* (2nd edn), Englewood Cliffs, NJ: Prentice-Hall.

159

Part IV

The challenges generated by questioning current practice

The papers in Part IV all question current practice in management education and development. Once again the issue is relevance, except that in this section it is not focused on from the perspective of cross-cultural transfer or of rapid social and economic change. The perspective taken is that of a Western standpoint critiquing itself.

The main assumption of the chapter by John Wallace is that management development is important, but that it can only be taken seriously if it can show what managers can achieve through management development and what the value of these achievements is. The author suggests that for management development to be effective it needs to relate specifically to particular problems at work; evaluation needs to be integral to any management development undertaken and the short-term effectiveness of any such interventions needs to be shown through what managers can say about what they have accomplished. Management development needs to be action-oriented rather than course-oriented; its purpose should be to help managers solve their work-based problems and to support them in finding solutions to these. Wallace suggests that two things need to happen for this kind of management development to become the norm. Decision-makers and funding agencies need to be educated as to what 'good' management development is – thus increasing demand for it; and management development professionals need to be trained in appropriate skills – thus increasing supply. The way forward is for committed professionals to run pilot projects which carefully monitor themselves towards success and record managers' achievements. Such projects can then influence the decision-makers and the management development professionals.

Wallace not only challenges a course-orientation to management development, but he also challenges us to identify and evaluate the outcomes of management development.

Dag Bjorkegren presents an in-depth case study of an open executive programme run by an independent training institute in Sweden, where this particular course has a high reputation. The overall aim of the programme is to transform specialists into generalists. Other features of the programme (which was dominated by lectures as well as assignments and cases) indicate that it is heavily influenced by the US model.

The author concludes that the programme he has observed is the traditional 'academic' model of management education, (quantitative/technical). He sees this as a one-way process which

163

results in improved general orientation and in the reinforcement of basic competence, but which is of very limited professional relevance.

He proposes an alternative (clinical/qualitative) model. This model is based on the notion of two-way communication and focuses on participants' own experience rather than on the teacher's expertise. This model has high professional relevance.

David Ashton's basic philosophy is that top managers have more need for the 'how' of developing high performance than the 'what'. In other words, they need skills that can be applied in specific situations, rather than general knowledge of such situations.

The author is opposed to the traditional view of managers' learning needs as being fixed according to level. Thus junior management needs personal skills development; middle management needs knowledge; and top management needs environmental, strategic, and knowledge-based broadening. Instead the author proposes that personal skills and broadening should be given alternately at each level of management. This he calls the squeeze-box approach.

Rae Andre describes some of the unplanned consequences of a training programme designed to internationalize the staff from twelve 'foreign' divisions of a major US company. Although the programme objectives were to foster mutual understanding of the international character of the business and to combat parochialism and rivalry across divisions, the author suggests that the effect of the programme was instead to assimilate foreign nationals into the American culture.

The results of the study highlight a warning for companies 'going' international. The unplanned consequences of the general and all-encompassing goal of internationalization are likely to be not internationalization, but cultural hegemony. The challenge this raises is whether cultural hegemony was not the real objective after all.

Ron Clarke describes a holistic approach to management development for people who work in low-income contexts and who do not necessarily see themselves as managers. The context of this chapter is secondary school management in Sierra Leone. The approach described is based on the view that resources can be material, human, and intangible, and can be found in environments, organizations and people. Furthermore, constraints are not seen as different entities from resources, but rather something can be either a constraint or a resource, depending on how you look at it. Managers are therefore encouraged to take a holistic view of the potential resources in their own particular situation and to assess what actions they can take to optimize these and minimize any constraints.

The approach is optimistic and humanist. It assumes that we can all develop creative resourcefulness in order to make the most of any situation. By working on releasing the potential in people, enabling them to see constraints as positive resources rather than as negative limitations, Clarke offers us an optimistic view of management development. It offers the challenge that management development need not depend on heavy financial and technological investment, but can be most effective and appropriate where it is grounded in managers and their contexts.

In Chapter 18 the authors describe the Institute of Social Management's recent experiences with an International Labour Office-funded development project. They present a single institutional success story set in the context of Bulgaria. This context is one of rapid industrialization, which has posed the dilemma for academics between maintaining their academic respectability and demonstrating their practical value to the economy.

The chapter focuses on the problems faced by management developers when introducing technological change at the same time as moving from an education–teaching style to a training–consulting style. The project reported introduced action-learning to the Institute of Social Management in such a way that dialogue between different groups in the organization was engendered and that learning was directly related to work in practice.

Thus in this section we move from a general call to action, to a critical stance to current practice, to offers for moving forward. Wallace calls for a general move within management education and development towards effectiveness through relevant – evaluated – provision. Bjorkegren, Ashton, and Andre all offer examples of how different programmes can lead to unintended consequences and ineffective outcomes – particularly where relevance and ownership are not directly addressed in the approach taken.

Clarke and Wallace et al. offer two views of how to conduct management education and development in such a way that it can honour and build upon the particular local context and the wants and needs of the particular managers. They offer us an optimistic note on which to close.

13

The promotion of effective management development

John Wallace
(*ILO, Geneva*)

THE SETTING

Management trainers and consultants (let us call them MD professionals for short) usually market their services poorly. Even when
their programmes are effective and innovative, they rarely
evaluate and publicize the results. This can contribute to low pay
and poor credibility.

For years, senior managers have been advising MD professionals to market their services better. For example, Donald Frey,
the Chief Executive Officer of Bell & Howell Company, has often
challenged the profession:

> My corporation and many others have applied your services.
> They have helped us improve performance. They generate high
> returns. But you are behind the door when large amounts of
> resources are being allocated; this is largely because you do not
> analyse properly what you have helped managers accomplish.
>
> (Frey, 1984: 7)

A way to improve the pay, credibility, and status of the
management development profession is to carry out effective,
action-oriented programmes, and to publicize the results managers
achieve. However, this requires special skills. In this chapter we
discuss several tools to help MD professionals acquire new skills
and use them with their clients. One type of tool is for training
trainers; this would increase the supply of MD professionals able
to organize effective management development programmes.
Another type, for decision-makers on how to work in partnership
with MD professionals, would aim at increasing the demand for
effective programmes.

New tools are needed to help MD professionals and the institutions which employ them to change the way they produce, evaluate, and market their services. With these tools, MD professionals would evaluate their work in terms of what managers achieve and the value of those achievements. Management development programmes would be promoted more in terms of what managers achieve and less on the basis of how well they had liked a programme or on how much they had learned. Moreover, since these tools would emphasize the design of programmes where managers take action to apply what they have learned, learning is increased and retained longer, especially if we are to believe the research that indicates that, unless applied, most of what is learned is quickly forgotten.

THE PROBLEM: A VICIOUS CIRCLE

A study by Tanton and Easterby-Smith (1985) indicated that most management institutions (in Africa, at least) find it difficult to escape a vicious circle. They found that since few management institutions collaborated effectively with industry, managers did not recognize the contributions the institutions could make. This lack of recognition resulted in a shortage of funds, facilities, and relevant training materials which, in turn, made it difficult to attract and retain professionals with suitable qualifications.

Should MD professionals and management institutions – the business schools, productivity centres, and management centres in which many of us find employment – market services differently? Should the annual reports of institutions describe what managers have been able to accomplish as a result of management development programmes? Do we need more MD professionals whose CVs describe this type of achievement? Many people in our field find this proposition controversial. To them the effectiveness of management development is long term and not subject to measurement. The effects are unquantifiable, and even if they could be quantified they could not be ascribed to management development alone. This paper does not debate these issues, it simply describes a strategy for those people in the profession who are not satisfied with the present situation and are looking for better ways to perform their functions.

The tools we are discussing are not for everyone. For example, those business schools whose good reputations attract more highly-qualified faculty members and students than they can absorb, or those short-course institutes that are oversubscribed, probably do not need the tools we are developing. Our target audience is one that is dissatisfied with its situation.

Dissatisfaction is only the first step toward change. Unless people and their institutions are able to look around and see others who are doing better, they tend to rationalize. People tend to accept their lot and comfort each other by saying that there is nothing to be done. Fortunately for us there are examples in the management development field where dissatisfaction has led to significant improvements. Let us consider a few.

The African management institutions surveyed by Tanton are not the only dissatisfied ones. In 1985, both the Manpower Services Commission (MSC) and the British Institute of Management (BIM) published surveys showing that few British managers believed human resources development to be a good investment. A key finding was that 'Few employers think training sufficiently central to their business for it to be a major component in their corporate strategy; very few of them saw it as an issue of major importance' (Coopers and Lybrand, 1985: 5). Such beliefs, while perhaps well founded, are dangerous. Nations that invest too little in their human resources in this competitive age risk lowering their quality of life. The MSC saw the complacency of British managers as dangerous and resolved to do something about it.

The MSC did not find British managers' low regard for the value of such services to be irrational. Clients and customers find it difficult to place a value on the quality and cost of services. Zemke (1985) reports that in 1985, for example, the Conference Board, a New York-based business research group, surveyed American consumers and asked them to rate nineteen products and nineteen services. The respondents reported that they were largely satisfied with the value of the products that they buy and use. Only three types of products were far below consumers' expectations: used cars, pet food, and children's toys. On the other hand, only two out of nineteen services provided acceptable value for money: air travel and electricity. Every other service they rated, from health care and hotels to educational and legal services, they judged overpriced and under-delivered.

Similarly, the surveys of the MSC and BIM indicated that management training and development did not meet the expectations of managers. What could they do? Realizing that the scepticism of British managers was not ill-founded, the MSC put forward a set of proposals that included a 'Queen's Award' for innovative management development.

The MSC set up its own demonstration programme to encourage British industry to spend more on this service. The MSC funded part of about 100 projects. To ensure that each one was effective the MSC laid down four requirements. Each project had to have:

(1) an analysis of training needs;
(2) suitable training materials;
(3) planned arrangements to ensure that skills acquired and lessons learned by managers during training were carried into practice; and
(4) arrangements for evaluating the effects of the programme on the overall performance of the organization.

In addition, organizations applying for funds had to indicate clearly in their proposals how the last two conditions were to be met.[1]

While it is too early to say whether the MSC's 100 projects will change the expectations of British managers, several lessons were learned. Charles Russell of the MSC produced seventeen short case studies from the projects. He found that specific organizational problems or business opportunities provided good opportunities for management development. These situations not only justified the investment in people, but also helped to ensure that senior management saw the results to be relevant. To reduce the risk of project failure, the MD professionals had to work hard to maintain the full support of top management. But, however good the teaching, without a well-designed follow-up programme much of the effort would be wasted.

Russell also found that most programmes took longer than expected because the time needed to complete the follow-up was difficult to estimate. He also found that evaluation, both of changes in organizational performance and of individual managers, was essential. Evaluation plans, therefore, should be worked out beforehand, not tacked on at the end.

A MODEL FOR PROMOTING THE MD FUNCTION

The ILO Management Development Programme has carried out similar studies. Perhaps the most controversial difference between our findings and those of the MSC lies in the realm of benefit/cost analysis. Russell concluded that since the organizations did not keep accurate records of the total costs of the management development programmes, it was impossible to calculate accurate benefit/cost ratios. This is an important issue. Properly designed and managed programmes can generate much higher short-term benefit/cost ratios than comparable investments in physical capital. Greater attention to this would help us put investments in human resources on a footing similar to investment in physical and financial resources. To start with we need a model to help us to communicate a clearer idea of the value of management development services.

$$\text{Value} = \frac{\text{Short-term effectiveness} + \text{Long-term effectiveness}}{\text{Cost}}$$

We can visualize the value of a service, including management development, as the relationship between effectiveness and cost. The higher the effectiveness and the lower the cost, the higher the value. The effectiveness of a programme has short-term and long term components. Short-term effectiveness is often simply what managers are willing to give the programme credit for helping them to accomplish.

Quality means different things to different people. Any professional, be it in medicine or management, moves onto thin ice when he begins to define effectiveness of service without considering the client's expectations and pocket book. Many managers go to training expecting to be entertained; our profession accommodates that expectation by handing out evaluation forms asking participants more or less, how they liked the show.

For the manager who merely wants to be entertained, a measure of short-term effectiveness is reflected in these end-of-course evaluations. However, as we will see in the examples below, a more relevant measure of short-term effectiveness can be obtained if we ensure that participants are given the opportunity to describe what they have accomplished as a result of an MD programme. This type of short-term effectiveness is often so significant in a properly designed and managed programme that we may not need to pay much attention to the long-term effectiveness. Short-term effectiveness, when measured in terms of accomplishments, is vital; it attracts attention to a programme and helps build up enthusiasm and momentum. Long-term effectiveness is usually measured in the increased capacity of an organization to improve performance. This capacity is created when managers build up their own confidence by implementing improvements.

To illustrate this model let us consider three examples:

Ethiopia: industry

Donarski *et al.* (1983) reported, that starting in 1980, with the personal involvement of the Minister of Industry, the Ethiopian Management Institute (EMI) launched a programme to improve production and maintenance in twelve corporations that controlled 250 manufacturing companies in the public sector. This programme cost on average US$200,000 a year to run. In the first year, twenty-six company teams competed to see who could most improve their maintenance systems. EMI provided them with training and consulting services. To allow the Minister to give awards to the best company teams, EMI arranged for each team to give a presentation followed by a plant tour. EMI then audited the results to ensure that the teams' claims were not exaggerated. By 1985 this programme had grown. Over 150 public enterprises were participating, and they were claiming almost US$50 million worth of improvements.

While the short-term impacts of this programme are important, the long-term impacts are interesting as well. EMI is now using this type of management development system to increase the availability of tractors on State farms and to improve the exportation of finished leather goods.

Kenya: building construction

In 1984, the National Construction Corporation of Kenya organized a series of programmes to help eighteen building contractors improve their site productivity. Participants were selected based on their past interest in improving their performance and on their willingness to learn. In May 1984 they were given a series of forms to complete and briefings designed to make them more conscious of the level of productivity on their building sites. In September they attended a three-day programme

172

where they learned to use work-study techniques to solve the problems they faced on their building sites. And, in December, six contractors gave presentations on the types of improvement they had carried out.

They claimed that between May and December they had together saved over US$180,000. They did this by changing the way they paid masons, by re-organizing the storage of building materials, and by improving the layout of the sites. The programme cost less than US$10,000 to run. Its long-term impact was that training (on other topics as well) became more popular with contractors in Kenya and that a modified version of the programme was launched in Botswana in 1986.

Philippines: transport

Beginning in 1983, the Provincial Bus Operators Association with the help of a productivity centre in the Philippines began organizing a series of business clinics with the managers of fourteen provincial bus companies. In the first year the managers of these companies reduced costs and improved services that they claimed were worth over US$1 million. Typical improvements came from setting up joint driver training programmes to improve maintenance and reduce wastage. This programme cost less than US$200,000 to run. In the long term, this business clinic approach has been adapted to other sectors in the Philippines such as furniture manufacturing.[2]

The benefit/cost ratios of these programmes exceed 2 to 1. However, only in the Ethiopian programme was there sufficient auditing of the benefits claimed to give us the confidence to defend the benefit/cost calculation.

To dispute the accuracy of such calculations, however, misses the point. Our objective is to help managers justify decisions to invest in people. In a world where investments in physical capital are expected to return at least 20% per year and those in financial capital at least 10%, what return does one need to justify investing in people? The returns on the Ethiopian, Kenyan, and Philippine examples all easily exceed 100%. These returns were obtained only because managers who took action gave credit to the MD professionals who had helped them. In order for such action-oriented programmes to displace academic, examination-oriented ones, much remains to be done. However, before we can devise a strategy we must look at why such action-oriented programmes are so rare.

BARRIERS TO EFFECTIVE PROGRAMMES

Two major barriers to making effective programmes more common are the need for MD professionals with new skills and the confusion among MD professionals and clients alike about the function of management development. First, there are very few people skilled at designing and managing programmes where needs are properly identified, training is designed to lead to action and participants are assisted in applying what they have learned and sharing their accomplishments. Many so-called trainers are really educators. They are skilled at passing codified knowledge on to young people; they are often good at teaching, but less so at helping managers improve performance.

Second, many people who make decisions about the design and execution of management development programmes appear to prefer educators to trainers because of long familiarity with education systems. Moreover, many organizations do so little effective training that these decision-makers have difficulty in distinguishing between education and training.

Thus an important first step in overcoming this confusion is to make a clear distinction among the various functions of MD professionals. What is management education, management training, and management development? Management education provides the broad, basic knowledge, skills, and values needed by potential managers. It is not as threatening as training.

We know of no examples where management education alone has helped to solve the immediate problems of organizations in developing countries. In fact, the difficulties of many management institutions seem to stem largely from using educational approaches to try to solve problems education was not designed to solve. Too often we fall into the trap that befell a regional official when he asked a national management institute to 'train those public enterprise managers how to make a profit'. Such problems cannot be solved by training or education alone. They first of all call for an analysis of the environment (Are price controls set too low? Are enterprises forced to absorb too many unskilled workers?), which should be followed by a coherent process that may include training and consulting.

What, then, is training? Most managers get most of their training on the job. This is usually supplemented by short courses designed to up-grade the skills of practising managers on defined tasks (e.g. finance, marketing) and to introduce new management tools.

Management development, on the other hand, is a management function. It aims to improve practice and support continued learning. It often combines formal courses, consulting, and on-the-job training to achieve general aims such as the growth and survival of an enterprise and specific aims such as reduced costs and improved quality.

Confusion between these different functions is a significant barrier to the promotion of our profession. This confusion leads to faulty procedures for funding management development and for reporting on its execution. Decision-makers too rarely allocate funds in such a way that programmes actually help managers improve performance. Instead, money is usually spent only on the classroom portions of a programme. Here people talk about problems and exchange views, but are rarely in a position to take action. This in turn leads to the symptoms of 'coursitis', so common among management institutions around the world. That is, people who decide on training as a solution pay institutions to run courses, not to help managers solve problems or to assist them while they implement solutions.

This confusion accounts partly for the poor administration of many management development programmes, starting with participant selection. With poor needs analysis and poor follow-up it makes little difference who is selected for training. When, as so often happens, the wrong participants are sent, institutions pretend that effectiveness is largely outside their control and that the beneficiaries enjoy some sort of sovereignty. That this bogus sovereignty is just an excuse and not a reason is illustrated in the recent experience of the Institute for Social Management (ISM) in Sophia. When the MD professionals at ISM realized that, to improve effectiveness, they would have to select teams from companies rather than just accept individual applicants, the clients resisted at first. They were not used to releasing several managers at once. ISM staff had to visit the clients and explain personally that the new approach would be more effective in solving problems in the companies. Most clients quickly saw the logic of training managers in teams and some clients then volunteered several teams.[3]

It is not difficult to overcome the barriers to effective management development, but we need a strategy for doing so.

A STRATEGY FOR OVERCOMING THE BARRIERS

First, we need to bring together examples of effective management development as the MSC is doing. With these we can train decision-makers how to distinguish between effective and ineffective designs. This is essentially a marketing exercise. It should increase the demand for effective programmes while decreasing the demand for programmes where people only talk about problems. To increase the supply of effective programmes, we must train trainers in how to help managers take actions.

One step in implementing this strategy is to change the procedures and reporting systems used to design and execute training projects. These procedures largely ignore the methodology of evaluation necessary for effective management development. Since 1954, for over thirty years, there has existed a well-defined hierarchy of effectiveness for training (Kirkpatrick, 1967). We need to apply it. The hierarchy is:

Attendance: Did the right people attend? Not how many attended.

Reaction: How well did the participants like the programme?

Learning: What principles, facts, and techniques were learned?

Behaviour: What changes in job behaviour resulted from the programme?

Results: What were the tangible results of the programme in terms of reduced costs, improved quality, and so on?

Where this hierarchy is ignored, management development programmes cannot be evaluated properly. Instead we are usually asked about 'efficiency', such as the number of participants per dollar. It is an old saying that people pay attention to what the boss pays attention to. Managers of management development projects are bright people; if their reporting system focuses on attendance, why should they be concerned about results?

Reporting systems that ask 'how many people attended?', but not, 'what did they do?' encourage decision-makers to allocate too few resources to needs analysis and follow-up. Such systems also lead us to do too little to ensure that participants are properly selected. They encourage decision-makers to view effective management development as too burdensome administratively.

Armed with examples of effective MD programmes we will need to ask key decision-makers 'Why are such effective programmes so rare?'. The answer will usually be that resources are allocated primarily to put managers into classrooms (attendance). The next question to ask is 'What can we do to change this?'. The answer should be that those who fund management development projects should take the stance of saying to us, 'I don't care so much about how many people attended, I really want to know what they did back on the job.' When monitoring and evaluation systems focus on results, then we MD professionals will be better able to organize more programmes that help managers solve problems, rather than ones where they simply exchange views.

DEMAND AND SUPPLY OF EFFECTIVE MANAGEMENT DEVELOPMENT

What tools can help decision-makers focus on results, identify good designs, and allocate funds so that more programmes are effective? Such tools should help decision-makers behave more like Jack Zigon, the HRD manager at Yellow Freight Systems in the United States who said, 'I usually look for someone who has organised performance-improvement programmes that helped managers improve quality, saved the company X dollars, reduced overtime by X, etc. I want to know if he bothered to evaluate a training programme's effect on employee performance.'

We in the training business are uniquely placed to train decision-makers how to get more for their money. Tools to train decision-makers to behave like Mr Zigon would cover topics such as 'the management development cycle', 'levels of effectiveness', 'opportunities for investment', 'needs analysis', and 'evaluating effectiveness'. A major theme would be that 'effectiveness requires partnership'. That is, a decision-maker cannot just send some managers to courses and expect to get a quantifiable return on his investment. Investments in people, like investments in physical capital, must be managed. By 'managed' we mean that the decision-maker who invests in a factory also sets up systems

177

for scheduling, for inventory, for quality, and so forth. Likewise when investing in managers, the decision-maker needs to be involved in defining needs and supporting change back on the job. Training for such decision-makers will need more than case examples. To be authentic it must lead to changes in the decision-maker's work. Such a decision-maker, 'godfather', or promoter of effective management development needs direct personal experience of how such programmes have improved his own organization. Such experiences make him an authentic promoter. He lets his colleagues know that he believes in training and that he wants people to do better as a result of an investment in their performance. He wants to be seen as someone to be counted on to fight for resources for effective programmes. He is good at helping his subordinates identify training needs and he helps them apply new skills in his own unit.

Managers who can give authentic testimonials about effective management development programmes are our best salesmen. We need to find and nurture such champions; to provide them with opportunities to feed back to us what we are doing right and wrong. Brian Bishop, a division manager at Prudential Assurance in the United Kingdom, is such a person. He frequently gives presentations to other managers in Europe about the way his company used action learning and the benefits they have reaped (Bishop, 1986). Such testimonials help generate demand for effective services.

THE SUPPLY OF MD PROFESSIONALS

Demand without supply leads to frustration. It would be foolhardy for us to train managers to identify effective management development and play their role in its production unless there are MD professionals who can deliver the programmes. To increase the availability of such people, we need new types of train-the-trainers (TTT) programmes. Most TTT programmes still emphasize classroom skills and the use of active learning methods such as role plays, training cases, and business games to replace passive methods such as lectures. But classroom skills are only a small part of an effective programme.

New TTT packages should be based on research into all the competencies of MD professionals who organize 'winning' programmes such as those mentioned earlier from Ethiopia,

Kenya, and the Philippines. What skills did the MD professionals have and what roles did they play so that managers took actions to improve organizational performance?

Key competencies include the ability to negotiate programme aims, to analyse work environments, and to organize support for action. Since successful marketing of future programmes depends on careful documentation of the benefits of past programmes, MD professionals need to negotiate quantifiable aims at the beginning of a programme and to arrange for managers to present their achievements toward the end. Another critical competency is the ability to carry out a needs analysis to distinguish training from non-training needs and to analyse the work environment to ensure that skills acquired and lessons learned can be applied on the job. Third, the MD professional must be proficient in organizing the support needed by managers to get permission and implement solutions.

Successful MD professionals are usually good negotiators. They assume a results-oriented posture when first negotiating with a client. This is illustrated by a story often told by Dennis O'Donnovan, the head of a management college of British Telecom: 'When a manager approaches me for help I ask him about the problems he'd like to solve. "I'd like to improve the productivity of my installations teams", one manager said. "Fine", I said, "by how much?" "By 30 per cent", he said. "Fine", I said, "By when?" "By the end of the year." "Fine", I said, "It'll cost you $11,000, and if you don't save three times that much, you'll get your money back."'

Good negotiation must be backed by good delivery. Such negotiations also often imply new contractual arrangements for payments for services and for selecting clients. This cannot happen overnight. When a management institution begins the process of improving its performance and repositioning itself in its market it must carefully select the initial set of clients to work with, negotiate a new mandate, and successfully carry out that new mandate. Success with the first set of clients is critical – if the institution fails with this group it may take a long time to generate another mandate. The key the first time around is to make success unavoidable.

If it succeeds in helping the client improve performance, new demands for service can quickly outstrip its capability to serve new clients. This process is illustrated by the Institut de Productivité et Gestion Prévisionnelle (IPGP) in Mali – an institution assisted by the ILO and the World Bank. In 1983 IPGP studied its market and selected several important clients. It then helped them improve performance. It helped the national tobacco company, for example, improve quality and reduce wastage by one third.

Several such assignments generated word-of-mouth advertising; the demand for IPGP's services increased. However, as civil servants in a government department, IPGP's professional staff had too little incentive to carry a heavier workload. The Institute then asked permission to become a semi-autonomous enterprise to give it more control over staff selection and terms of service. In effect, improved institutional performance brought 'success-generated' problems to IPGP.

Such problems can usually be anticipated from the beginning. At British Telecom, for example, as soon as Dennis O'Donnovan's approach began to work, he began to lose his trainers and consultants to line management positions. This, however, he saw as an opportunity to bring onto his staff other bright managers, young and old, as sources of further organizational change. So such success-generated problems lead to new opportunities to take on new roles.

MD professionals and their clients will need help in trying out the roles that are played in effective partnerships. Such a partnership is an 'action-chain'. The MD professional can see himself as taking on a series of roles complementary to the roles that the client is willing to play in order to solve a problem. At the beginning the MD professional must usually play a kind of 'detective', but he can play this role only if the client is willing to be the subject or 'suspect'. If the client buys the MD professional's analysis, he may need to be willing to play the 'student' to the professional's 'teacher'. Throughout the programme, the MD professional prepares the client to play the 'performer' to the professional's 'monitor' or coach. It is vital that the successful completion of one set of roles triggers the taking on of the next set. Failure to generate the next role-set leaves the original problem unresolved. So, in a sense, the new tools we need must help managers see the value of working with MD professionals to complete an action-chain and to train more MD professionals in the knowledge, skills, and attitudes to do so.

PUTTING THE STRATEGY TO WORK

Will new tools alone – some to increase demand among decision-makers and others to increase the supply of fully competent MD professionals – promote effective management development? Not without difficulty. The forces surrounding the trainer and the client, the organizations which employ them and the relationships between them will only change slowly. First, we must attract their interest, help them experience new ways of working, and then make it difficult for them to slide back to their old, easier habits.

Decision-makers should be the easiest to attract. Even though effective management development usually costs more than the ineffective kind, managers can usually find money for things they believe to be worthwhile. To attract managers, we need marketing tools that compare the return on investments in physical or financial capital with returns on investments in human capital. Managers readily accept the idea that where a bond might return 10% per year with low risk, a factory might return 20% per year. They also accept the idea that investments in factories must be managed – people must be hired, customers found, supplies purchased, and so on.

As our examples from Ethiopia, Kenya, and the Philippines indicate, investments in people, where people take action, can generate higher returns than are typical with bonds and factories. The final sales point comes when a manager asks whether we can guarantee such returns. The answer is 'no'. Just as with investments in factories, there are risks. Moreover, the investments must be managed.

We must therefore stress that effective management development programmes can be as difficult to manage as other business investments and unless there is continual commitment by senior management from start to finish, even the best-designed programmes fade away: conditions change, managers change, and there will be failures.

The greater challenge probably lies with MD professionals and the institutions which employ them. The weight of academic traditions in many institutions trigger many 'philosophical' propositions about the dangers of sacrificing long-term development for quick, bottom-line results. Research may be needed on whether managers learn best from lectures and from preparing for written examinations or from applying what they have learned to the job. However, no matter how rigorous the design, research

181

results have rarely convinced the die-hard lecturer.

This difficulty is illustrated in an editorial note in *Training* (1986). The writer, an MD professional in private practice, pointed out that university programmes in human resources development violated most of the principles taught there. MD professionals in the business world have come a long way by applying new performance improvement methods, but the professors who teach these methods and help companies apply them, do not use them in their own classrooms. They teach that instructional materials should be clearly written, but their own textbooks are often turgid. They teach that participative learning methods work best, but they themselves usually lecture. Their research shows that people learn best when information is divided into small 'chunks' and when students are tested on a step-by-step basis, but in typical university courses, students are tested only occasionally and on huge amounts of information. Their research shows that effective programmes are based on an analysis of needs, but their own courses are designed around pre-selected texts, tradition, and their own personal interest and expertise.

A SPECIFIC PROPOSAL

The tools and strategies we have been discussing should be combined in a programme to promote effective management development. This programme would consist of pilot projects carried out by MD professionals who are dissatisfied with the current situation, working with clients in enterprises where there is a good chance that performance can be improved. In developing countries, this programme could be backed by international agencies.

To start with, those MD professionals who are the most dissatisfied will have to form coalitions within management institutions to get permission to start small experimental exercises to demonstrate that their institutions can help clients solve real problems. Eventually, if done correctly, such programmes should replace those that are less effective but easier to manage. The institutions, rather than simply advertising their course offerings, would ask satisfied clients for short testimonials on how the institution had helped them and how much it had been worth.

For management institutions in developing countries, a powerful force is likely to be the international agencies. Funding agencies which insist on proper needs analysis, follow-up, and evaluation, as the MSC did, can help change the situation. However, as we said earlier, such agencies are part of the problem, as well as a possible key to the solutions.

Each agency (donor, development bank, multilateral agency, etc.) that wants to be part of the solution should begin by selecting a problem area of major concern (such as community development, water supply, etc.) and seek to part-fund several pilot projects on conditions similar to those of the MSC: a proper needs analysis, identification of existing appropriate training materials, and proper arrangements made for transfer back to the job. Part-funding may be essential to ensure local commitment to actually solving the problems.

To prepare the ground for each pilot project, training would be needed to ensure that MD professionals and their clients both share the model of management development, such as the one described in this paper. Such training is now possible. The ILO Management Development Programme has so far produced a score of case studies of effective management development programmes. Lecturettes, readings, quizzes, and glossaries of terms are also available.[4] These can be assembled in several ways to produce a variety of different training workshops and seminars needed to launch the pilot projects we have in mind.

Each of these projects will need careful monitoring to make success unavoidable. Otherwise, many old bureaucratic habits and procedures will create unnecessary failures. For instance, in many agencies the terms of reference for most needs analyses specify the writing of a report, but omit any mention of the processes to be followed to ensure commitment to the next step. Consequently the action-chain often snaps at the start of the management development process. Careful monitoring against milestones can overcome this.

The final step in this programme to promote effective management development will involve managers talking about what they have accomplished, thanks to MD professionals. These professionals in turn should give testimonials about how, by following this new path and exercising new skills, they have achieved higher status, more pay, and a better quality of life for themselves and their families.

NOTES

1. See Burgess (1986) and *The Employment Gazette* (1986) for information on this.
2. This project is discussed in more detail in Wallace (1985).
3. This experience is discussed more fully in Chapter 18 in this volume.
4. See, for example, Interfirm Comparison for Improving Performance: How Employers' Associations Can Help the Business Community (ILO, Geneva, 1986); The Role of Employers' Organisations in Promoting Management Development (ILO, Geneva, 1986); How to Design Interventions for Improved Maintenance Management (ILO, Geneva, 1983).

REFERENCES

Bishop, B. (1986) 'Action learning in practice', presentation for the HRD managers of posts and telecoms organizations, Oslo, 17 June.

Brown, M. (1986) 'Seven deadly sins', *Training* August: 78.

Coopers and Lybrand (1985) *A Challenge to Complacency: Changing Attitudes Towards Training*, Sheffield, UK: Manpower Services Commission.

Donarski, J., Heath, R., and Wallace, J. (1983) 'Results-oriented maintenance management', *Journal of European Industrial Training* September.

Frey, D. (1984) 'Human resources: The asset that doesn't appear on the balance sheet', paper presented at the ASTD Conference, Dallas, 22 May.

Kirkpatrick, D. (1967) 'Evaluation of training', in R.K. Craig and L.R. Bittel (eds) *Training and Development Handbook*, ASTD, New York: McGraw-Hill.

Tanton, M. and Easterby-Smith, M. (1985) 'International issues in management education: A preliminary survey of management education specialists from 21 countries', INTERMAN Symposium, ILO, Geneva, May.

Wallace, J. (1985) 'Fostering management growth in developing countries', *Training and Development Journal* January.

Wallace, J., Razvigorova, E., Kalev, J., and Boulden, G. (1988) 'Management and organisational development in technological transition' in J. Davies, M. Easterby-Smith, S. Mann and M. Tanton (eds) *Challenges to Management Development: Alternatives from Around the World*, London: Croom Helm.

Zemke, R. (1985) 'Contact! Training employees to meet the public', *Training* August: 41–54.

14

Some limitations in the Western model of executive training: a case study

Dag Bjorkegren
(*The Stockholm School of Economics, Sweden*)

INTRODUCTION

The importance of industry for Sweden's economic welfare has been increasingly emphasized in public debate in the 1980s and thus the spotlight has been turned on some of industry's principal actors – managers and executives.

Various types of executive training have emerged since the 1940s, aimed at helping emergent or established managers to meet the demands placed on them. From the 1970s and onwards, these training programmes have been subjected to increasingly severe criticism in the US. Leavitt (1983), for example, maintains, in a comparison between Japanese and American management, that US schools of higher education are responsible for the alleged deterioration (according to Leavitt) in the quality of corporate leadership.

As a result of this discrepancy between increasing demands on executives and the increasingly sharp criticism of the training of MBAs and executives, I considered that it was interesting to attempt to study how management training works and the relevance of such training for job performance – and this was the purpose of the study reported in this chapter.

METHOD

I limited the population studied to external, open management training. External, in this context, means training provided by an arranger who is independent of the customer-company, while open management training involves training programmes which are open to participants from all industries and companies.

From this population, I selected an external, open management training programme in Scandinavia which matched the basic characteristics of such training. The study was executed in the form of a case study.

I collected data about the training programme from written documentation (training programme brochures and internal documentation of courses within the framework of training), and from interviews with participants who had completed courses, representatives of major customer-companies, and course administrators. I asked questions about their experience of the training and I observed one training process directly.

My selection of interviewees was based on theoretical sampling principles established by Glaser and Strauss (1967) and Glaser (1978). The interviews and the direct observation were based on the clinical interview and direct observation techniques described by Athos and Gabarro (1978) and Roethlisberger (1977).

GENERAL CHARACTERISTICS OF PROGRAMME STUDIED

The type of training which I studied had been offered on a continuous basis since the 1950s, and, in the form studied, since the early 1970s. It was considered to be one of the leading programmes offered in Scandinavia. The training consisted of a number of courses offered within the framework of the training programme on an annual basis. The course length was six weeks, subdivided into three periods and involving five scheduled days of training per week. The timetable on working days ran from 07.30 to 21.00 hours, apart from Mondays when sessions started at 10.00 hours and Fridays when they closed at 15.00 hours. A normal scheduled day involved 8.8 hours of teaching – the remaining scheduled time was allocated for meals, social activities, and relaxation. There were over forty participants per course, mostly male. They worked in various industries and companies and their average age was forty-one. Senior executives were the target group for the programme (i.e. function-managers in industry and public administration who had recently transferred, or who were about to be transferred, to 'generalist' posts with multi-functional responsibilities or with senior management status). These function-managers normally had a technical education background, but were now about to be promoted, or had already been promoted.

The overriding objective for the training programme was the transformation of specialists into generalists. The areas normally covered were:

(1) Business policy
(2) Marketing and marketing strategy
(3) International business
(4) Financial analysis and strategy
(5) Organization
(6) Budgetary analysis, planning and control
(7) The corporation and society
(8) Information systems and data processing
(9) Administration of capital funds and materials
(10) Labour market questions
(11) Information and the media
(12) The manager's roles and work and personnel development
(13) Applied management (field-work project)

The emphasis in the training programme was on strategic and applied management. The fundamental pedagogic approach stressed an exchange of experience between participants at an advanced level. The teaching methods employed were a mixture of lectures, group assignments in connection with lectures, computer simulations, a corporate game, case studies, and a project assignment. Lectures were the dominant teaching form and occupied 70% of the teaching schedule. The remaining 30% of the time was mainly devoted to project assignments.

Formally, there was no teaching faculty – a programme-director was responsible for the basic design for course contents, which covered all courses within the framework of the programme. The programme-director appointed a course-leader for each course who was operationally responsible for the execution of each course and for the selection of guest speakers and teachers. Normally, the course-leader did some teaching in his own specialist area, introduced and thanked guest speakers, and linked and summarized the ground covered as the course progressed.

The teachers employed comprised university academic staff and teachers/researchers/consultants in specialist areas. Broadly speaking, the teachers were the same for each course. Informally, a teaching faculty existed in the sense that the teachers who were employed were usually responsible for the design and contents of their own components in the course and also arranged for guest speakers and other teachers to assist them. These teachers, together with guest speakers from industry and the public sector, performed the actual teaching.

The explicit forms of evaluation utilized were a questionnaire which used a 1–5 scale to measure how the participants viewed the design and execution of the various course components and what they had learnt, the morning meetings in which the course-leader discussed with the participants what they had learnt the previous day and a concluding evaluation of the whole course on the morning of the final day of the course.

ANALYSIS MODEL

I analysed the data on the basis of a model for educational processes in management training which I extracted from existing theories in the area in an interaction with the collection of data. In designing the model, I based myself on the learning-process theory of Argyris and Schön (1974, 1978) and Bion's (1959) group theory which I progressively adapted to the data. The analysis model has the following configuration:

Governing →Acting →Learning →Learning →Professional
values   climate   relevance

The reality studied involves educational processes in management training and the factors studied are governing values, the behaviour of the actors, the learning climate which is created, the learning process itself, and the relevance of the learning for management job execution.

The correlations in the model indicate that, in a specific situation, in this case management training, the actors' behaviour is governed by their evaluation of the situation. This behaviour gives rise to a learning climate which influences the learning that occurs in the training period. This learning may be relevant for the manager's work, to a greater or lesser extent, depending on how important the information, skills, and techniques which have been transmitted are in the specific job situation.

Governing values mean fundamental assumptions shared by a majority of the participants in a specific situation as regards what reality looks like and how things function in the real world – this is the basis for the actors' behaviour.

I regard the actors' behaviour (actions) as dependent on the governing values. The actors' behaviour in the training situation creates a learning climate – a general situation or environment for learning. I then subdivide this learning climate into an emotional and a cognitive climate which influence each other and, combined, comprise the total learning climate. The emotional learning climate expresses the actors' emotions, while the cognitive climate describes the actors' thoughts.

The emotional learning climate theory is based on Bion's group theory which describes how groups fluctuate between what Bion calls 'basic assumption groups' and 'working groups'. The basic assumption group avoids the concrete assignment and contact with reality, feelings predominate, and mental activities are at a low level – which influences any possible learning process in a negative manner.

Bion distinguishes three basic assumption states in groups:

(1) Dependency: The group leaves its fate to the leader, abandoning its responsibility for the task in hand (abbreviated as BaD).
(2) Fight flight: The group unites against a common enemy or deserts the task (BaF).
(3) Pairing: The group expects that some of the group members, irrespective of sex, will join up to give birth to the Messiah who will save the group (BaP).

The group climate and the defence mechanisms in the group assumption state are (according to Kets de Vries and Miller, 1984):

(1) BaD: The climate is characterized by exhilaration and trust in the leader, combined with feelings of guilt about the group's own inactivity. The defence mechanisms are idealization and downgrading of the leader.
(2) BaF: The climate is characterized by a lack of critical self-reflection and a tendency to place all blame for the anger, hate, fear, and suspicion that the group feels on the environment. The defence mechanisms are 'splitting' (that the world can only be experienced as evil or good and not both) and projections (the projection of non-desirable characteristics onto the environment by the group).
(3) BaP: The climate is characterized by optimism and enthusiasm, with open discussions without any direct leader. The defence mechanisms are fantasies and day-dreaming.

189

Characteristically, a working group is interested in development, operates realistically, and employs scientific methods – all factors which may influence the learning process in a positive manner.

According to Bion, the working group wins out in the end – the fluctuations swing in favour of the working group and, thus, in favour of reality and development. In an educational context, the emotional processes may support (the emergence of the work group) or disturb (the emergence of the basic assumption group) the thought processes – that is to say an emotional learning climate is created by the actors in a training situation which either supports or interferes with the cognitive learning climate, thus influencing learning in a positive or in a negative direction.

The cognitive learning climate theory is based on the Argyris and Schön (1974, 1978) theory of learning. Argyris and Schön distinguish between two learning and action models in social interaction: Model I, which is the normal case, characterized by a one-sided questioning of a situation with one-way control and an attempt to 'win' the interaction; and Model II, characterized by joint investigation of a situation, with mutual control, and an attempt to obtain correct information.

On the basis of this theory, it is to be anticipated in an educational context that the actors create a Model I learning climate, characterized by investigation of the applicable situation (in this case management) which is one-sidedly controlled and in which changes in behaviour are possible. Model II constitutes an alternative, ideal learning climate, characterized by investigation of the applicable situation which is jointly controlled and which permits questioning and changes in the actors' governing values – not merely changes in behaviour.

The cognitive learning climate is also influenced by how much information is transmitted. Due to man's limited information-processing capacity, over stimulation (excessive volume of information) results in a very extensive, self-protective filtering of mental impressions by the brain – the information input is reduced until it reaches manageable proportions.

When I speak of learning I mean knowledge or skills acquired as a result of study or education/training. According to Argyris and Schön, there are two types of learning: 'single-loop' which involves behavioural changes and 'double-loop' which means changes in values. Model II skills involve increased learning ability since the action model makes it possible to question values (e.g. how the problem is defined), while Model I only permits the questioning and changing of behaviour (e.g. how a problem which is already given can be solved). Model I skills are sufficient for 'single-loop' problems where a change in behaviour is sufficient for problem-solving. In the case of 'double-loop' problems, where solutions require value changes, Model I skills prove inadequate. Model II facilitates the handling of such problems since it permits changes in values. A shift in values can also occur in acute crisis situations.

Relevance means important and significant for the matter in hand. In this case, when I speak of relevant learning, I mean important and significant knowledge and skills for management, acquired through study and training. I assess the relevance of learning on the basis of a description of the manager's work and the knowledge and skills used in such work. My description, which is mainly based on Kotter (1982), indicates that social and technical (business) competence are required of a manager and that social competence becomes progressively more important the higher the manager advances in the organization. In his job, the manager primarily employs knowledge with a high action value. Two important components in a manager's work are the drawing-up of a plan of action and the execution of the plan by establishing a network of contacts. In strategic terms, this means the drawing-up and the execution of a strategy.

Therefore, if learning through management training is to be relevant, it should provide the participants with knowledge and skills in the drawing-up and execution of strategic plans of action which are both technical and social in character and with a special emphasis on social knowledge and skills. As regards the type of knowledge involved, it should be action-oriented in the sense that theories should not contain more concepts than can be applied 'on-line' and that the theories permit development so that gaps in knowledge can be filled in later in interaction with concrete situations. Kotter's concept of agendas and networks are examples of this type of knowledge. In the manager's work it can be assumed that a plan of action is required for what is to be achieved and, similarly, a contact network is required for execution of the plan. The exact contents of the plan and the exact configuration of the network are determined in an interaction with the situation which the manager is faced with.

ANALYSIS

In accordance with the analysis, the values which governed the planning and execution of the training programme were analytical, quantitative approaches to knowledge, in which technical knowledge was given priority. An analytical view of knowledge means that management was regarded as instrumental in problem-solving and that scientific experts supply knowledge which practical managers (practitioners) apply. The quantitative view of knowledge involves a value such as 'the more the better' in the sense that the more concepts and subject areas treated the better.

If we turn to the origin of the governing values, most of the teachers involved in the training programme came from universities where they taught undergraduate academic courses in economics and business administration. In such undergraduate courses, the students normally have very little working experience and therefore the bulk of the time spent in such courses is devoted to providing the students with basic knowledge about economics and business administration. This usually means that the education/training given is based on an analytical approach to knowledge – teachers in their role as experts in the subject transmit knowledge in their disciplines to the students.

The quantitative view of knowledge also probably has its origins in the university world and academic lecturing, with a large volume of concepts transmitted over a limited period of time. In academic undergraduate education, which is often of a general character, the emphasis is on covering as many concepts and subject areas as possible, since it is not clear exactly what assignments will face the students in the future. It is therefore considered desirable to provide as broad a spread of information/knowledge as possible on which a future professional career can be based.

The technical view of knowledge also seems to originate in the university world. Technical knowledge is the primary input in undergraduate education in economics and business administration, since the students are likely to have little job experience and they need, primarily, a fundamental economics/business apparatus of concepts to cope with their future professional occupations. The application of these concepts – the psychological and social aspects of economic/business activities – start to become relevant when the students start to translate their knowledge into practice.

As regards the management training which I have studied,

those responsible for directing the programme and the teachers who participated operated in the same manner as they did for academic undergraduate courses in economics and business administration. Thus the point of departure was academic approaches to management, transmitted by experts in the subject. The training programme attempted to cover as many subjects and concepts as possible with an overriding emphasis on technical knowledge about the business aspects of management.

Since academic undergraduate education is normally conducted in accordance with the above principles, it seems likely, in terms of the participants' reactions, that this approach to knowledge was reactivated for the participants when they found themselves in the training situation – in other words they expected analytical, quantitative, and primarily technical knowledge inputs.

The most obvious expressions of the influence of the analytical approach to knowledge was that forty guest lecturers participated in the course that was directly observed, lectures occupied 70% of the scheduled teaching time, and the teachers talked for 70% of the time in the lecture-sessions. This means that the teachers were responsible for the bulk of activities and that the participants were passive in the training situation. The quantitative approach to knowledge led to very intense scheduling with many informational components, expressed in the course which was directly observed by 8.8 hours of educational activities in a normal scheduled day's training which started at 07.30 hours and continued until 21.00 hours. A primarily technical transfer of knowledge led to a clear emphasis on technical knowledge components in the contents of the course, which was expressed in direct observations of the course by the fact that 5% of the scheduled time was allotted to the social and psychological aspects of management while the remaining 95% was devoted to business aspects.

If we now turn to the learning climate, the emotional learning climate was characterized by more or less strong tendencies towards basic assumption group formations (primarily BaD), expressed in excessive demands made by the participants on the teachers. The cognitive learning climate was characterized by cognitive tiring and exhaustion on the part of the participants due to the considerable flow of information and a one-sided control of the teaching situation on the part of the teachers, such control being encouraged by the participants.

The learning that the training course gave the participants was primarily increased general orientation, the learning of specific new

193

concepts, the reinforcement of fundamental competences, and a certain amount of training in coping with relationships with equals. Many of the participants considered that this learning increased their self-confidence.

The knowledge transferred was primarily of an academic nature, with low action values and an emphasis on technical knowledge – theories which consisted of many, often precise concepts which presumed control over the situation rather than interaction with it, and which therefore made on-line application difficult. Emphasis was on the business aspects of management. Since the participants primarily needed social knowledge with high action value in their jobs, but received technical knowledge with low action value, I assessed the relevance of learning for professional job performance as limited.

The learning in the training programme, viewed as a learning system, was of a 'single-loop' type. The training can be characterized as a 'single-loop' learning system which attempted to solve 'double-loop' problems with 'single-loop' measures – changes in behaviour rather than changes in values. As a result of the selective perception the governing values of the training programme created, the only possible changes were the replacement of individual lecturers and knowledge-elements, which hardly solved problems of excessive demands on teachers, the participants' cognitive exhaustion, or the low relevance of learning. The analysis is summarized in Table 14.1.

Table 14.1 Analysis of the training programme

Governing values	Acting	Learning climate	Learning	Professional relevance
An analytical quantitative view of knowledge in which primarily technical knowledge is transmitted	One-sided transfer of knowledge from teachers Participants passive Intensive schedule Emphasis on technical knowledge	Dysfunctional group-processes Excessive demands on teachers Cognitive exhaustion of participants	Improved general orientation Isolated relevant concepts Reinforcement of basic competencies Some training in handling relations with equals	Limited

AN IMPROVEMENT SUGGESTION

I now present an improvement suggestion for management training, based on the analysis model and the analysis of training
above.

What managers require in the training context is technical and
social knowledge: opportunities for training technical and social
skills and the articulation and consciousness of their professional
competence to enable them to improve and develop this
competence at a conscious level. To achieve these goals, management training might take the participant's job situation as its starting point, thus achieving the transmission of relevant knowledge,
the creation of exchanges of experience, and hence the refinement
of professional skills. In broad terms, this might involve the
transmission of social and technical knowledge and the training of
skills. Management training should probably emphasize social
knowledge. In connection with the training in technical and social
skills, the participants should be encouraged to articulate what
they do in order to improve and develop their professional
competence at a conscious level. As regards pedagogic methods,
Bakke (1958) indicates that case studies and fieldwork projects are
two methods which can realize the improvement suggestion which
has been outlined above in practice. In the terms of the analysis
model, the improvement suggestion can be presented in the
following manner:

Governing values

A clinical, qualitative view of knowledge is applied, in which
both social and technical knowledge is transmitted. I define a
clinical view of knowledge as starting out from the practitioners'
professional skills – the teacher's role is then to help the
practitioners to articulate and develop these skills further. When
I speak of a qualitative view of knowledge, I mean that a
reasonable number of areas and concepts is covered– which does
not exceed the participants' information-processing capability –
with the result that the participants remember the informational
components which have been dealt with after completing the training programme. A clinical view of knowledge is to be
recommended, since it is based on the professional skills of the
participants and develops them further, while emphasizing the

action value of the knowledge acquired. A qualitative view of knowledge is essential in avoiding cognitive and psychodynamic interference and in raising the quality of the knowledge. Social knowledge should also be included, since managers need to be able to implement knowledge – not merely to solve technical problems.

What I wish to do here, in relation to the training programme studied, is to suggest alternative governing values for the design of similar types of courses. This is a 'double-loop'(change of values). The programme which I studied attempted to increase its effectiveness, in the sense of increasing the relevance of teaching, by replacing teachers (i.e. 'single-loop' changes). However, the analysis indicates that the value changes are required to improve the relevance of learning (i.e. 'double-loop' changes). The fundamental problem in the training programme was that management training was placed on a par with academic undergraduate education in economics and business administration – none of the actors saw that two different educational/training situations were involved. Since the training situation is different, the analysis would indicate that it is necessary to change the governing values in order to achieve relevant learning.

Acting

The teacher acts as a discussion leader and summarizer, using such techniques as case studies and project assignments. The participants are responsible for the bulk of the activities. The teacher emphasizes the process rather than the final results and reduces any uncertainty he may have in the teaching situation by activating the participants and learning from their activity what is relevant knowledge for them, rather than reducing his uncertainty by one-sidedly controlling the training situation and being exposed to excessive demands from the participants.

Learning climate

The emotional learning climate can be improved if the participants become more active and are thus forced to deal directly with reality, reducing possible projections and excessive demands on the teacher. The cognitive learning climate is improved by

196

reducing the number of concepts and the participants' activity is increased, thus avoiding cognitive exhaustion.

Learning

The knowledge transmitted will be of higher quality and will also be more relevant since it will be based on the practitioners' professional skills and will emphasize action value.

Professional relevance

The relevance of learning in job situations will probably be high since the participants will receive considerable assistance in developing desirable technical and social competence – in the form of strategic planning and implementation capability. Such competence will, however, be of a 'single-loop' and Model I character if the training programme is not revised in a 'double-loop' direction by means of training in Model II behaviour. If this is the case, then the technical and social competence acquired will be of Model II type, with capacity for 'double-loop' learning. This line of argument is summarized in Table 14.2.

Table 14.2 Analysis of the improvement suggestion

Governing values	Acting	Learning climate	Learning	Professional relevance
A clinical qualitative view of knowledge in which both technical and and social knowledge are transmitted	Two-way communication Both teachers and participants more active Schedule with time for training of applications and reflection Both technical and social components treated	Functional group-processes Reasonable demands on teachers No cognitive exhaustion of participants	Improved general orientation Volume of concepts and their relevance increase Broadening of basic competence Training in handling human relationships and new implementation skills	High

CONTRIBUTION TO RESEARCH AND PRACTICE

The contribution made by this study primarily consists of a more cohesive theoretical approach in the area of management training in the form of an analysis model which can be used in the evaluation of similar training programmes and can provide a basis for suggestions for improvements, such as measures designed to lead to learning which is more relevant from the job point of view.

REFERENCES

Argyris, C. and Schön, D. (1974) *Theory in Practice*, San Francisco: Jossey-Bass.

Argyris, C. and Schön, D. (1978) *Organizational Learning*, San Francisco: Addison-Wesley.

Athos, A. and Gabarro, J. (1978) *Interpersonal Behaviour*, Englewood Cliffs, NJ: Prentice-Hall.

Bakke, E. (1958) *A Norwegian Contribution to Executive Development*, Bergen.

Bion, W. (1959) *Experience in Groups*, London: Tavistock.

Glaser, B. (1978) *Theoretical Sensitivity*, Mill Valley, California: Sociology Press.

Glaser, B. and Strauss, A. (1967) *The Discovery of Grounded Theory: Strategies for Qualitative Research*, London: Aldine.

Kets de Vries, M. and Miller, D. (1984) 'Group fantasies and organizational functioning', *Human Relations* 37(2/8): 111–34.

Kotter, J. (1982) *The General Managers*, New York, Free Press.

Leavitt, H. (1983) 'Management and management education in the West: What's right and what's wrong', The Stockton Lecture, London Business School, 16 March.

Roethlisberger, F. (1977) *The Elusive Phenomena*, Boston: Harvard University Press.

15

Management development in a British multi-national company

David Ashton
(*University of Lancaster*)

BACKGROUND

During the period 1978–86, I was involved in management development activities for a major multi-national company, with responsibility for the development and running of ten general management programmes each year. All were residential, with a typical national mix of twenty different countries out of thirty managers on any programme. The managers came from four very different industries (tobacco, paper, retail, and financial services), each with its own industrial traditions.

Although the Group employs around 350,000 people, it has both a small headquarters staff of 100 and an expatriate cadre of similarly small size. Because of the differences between the businesses, each is run on the basis of 'relative autonomy' in relation to the ultimate centre of the Group – although intervening levels in the organization, either geographic or industrial, may influence international or regional product or service policies.

However, in the area of management development, a central policy was developed by the Group's International Management Centre which identified criteria for all operating groups and businesses to consider and relate to their necessarily different systems and activities. The general management programmes I was involved in were designed to meet the demands of this central policy.

The national and business mix of participant managers made it necessary in the design and running of these programmes to understand and take account of two forms of cultural difference – national and organizational culture, respectively. Both forms have received increased attention in management and management-education circles in recent years. At the academic level, Hofstede's (1980) massive study of national differences among employees in a multi-national firm started several practical debates. These centred on the relevance of theory developed in one country's culture to the education of management in others. At a more popular level, the best-selling book *In Search of Excellence* by Peters and Waterman (1982) renewed interest in organizational culture – particularly since it linked overall business performance with strong and differentiated cultural features in an organization.

This chapter is written out of my experience of running the programmes described above. I first offer a view of international managers' learning needs which is specifically related to organizational culture. I then show how the traditional 'career' model of executive development fails to cater for these actual learning needs, and propose an alternative model which may be of greater relevance. Finally, I describe a specific experimental programme for chief executives which was designed to meet directly actual needs discovered within the business.

TAKING ACCOUNT OF ORGANIZATIONAL CULTURE IN MANAGEMENT DEVELOPMENT

The impact of organizational culture is both more difficult to control and more important to get right than any other single aspect in the design and running of management development activities.

I have come to believe that managers need less of the 'what' which they are offered in management education and development activities, i.e. the knowledge associated with the formal disciplines, functions, and systems of management, and more of the 'how' of management performance. A key feature of the 'how' is to develop an effective understanding of, and an ability to operate within, an organizational culture.

In the case of BAT Industries, it is particularly difficult to pin down and to make explicit statements about the organization's culture. The group is geographically very widespread; devolved in its style of management; it works in four industries with very little in common; and many of its individual businesses are relatively new to the Group. Yet the Group, as a whole, has a 'super culture'. By this I mean there are common ways in which top management tend to think, judge, and act in all aspects of business life, which affect their determination of organizational goals. These common ways implicitly reflect common organizational values. Many of the senior managers with whom I worked reflected continuing – and quite correct – concern about their personal effectiveness. They believe that their effectiveness will be improved both through a better understanding of this 'super culture' and through their individual ability to translate that understanding into appropriate behaviour in terms of their own 'local' business culture.

These organizational cultural issues of particular concern focus on the 'how' of management – that is, on understanding the informal rules of:

(1) how to get things done;
(2) how to be effective;
(3) how to get the resources you want; and
(4) how to deliver the results that are required, within the particular standards and values to the organization, at both local and overall levels.

Either from a content or a process viewpoint, trying to help managers become more effective in understanding and acting within an organizational culture may not necessarily be a straightforward task. It is not a simple matter of giving them knowledge, but rather of giving them exposure to a series of real situations, with opportunities to interact with senior management and to undertake real work – through projects and action learning – in different parts of the organization.

There are several kinds of teaching method which can enhance managerial effectiveness – including formal inputs, role plays, and structured exercises. However, one conclusion is that learning-by-doing is an even more powerful process than may have originally been suspected, because it will increase managers' sensitivity to organizational culture and consequently their effectiveness in getting things done. In project-based learning, groups and individuals work on real strategic problems. It is not enough for them to make theoretically attractive proposals, they must also carry back their proposals to real-life clients, who 'represent' the culture of their organization. These senior general managers, in their response to both the form and the content of ideas for the development and improvement of businesses, will demonstrate their perceptions about the organization's values. Thus management effectiveness in the specific organizational context – in the 'how' of management – is likely to be improved through this form of learning.

TRADITIONAL MODEL OF EXECUTIVE DEVELOPMENT

To what extent are current educational offerings likely to meet the specific demands of 'how to do things' rather than 'what to know'? Clearly the 'how' approach emphasizes the importance of effectiveness in a particular organizational culture; it also emphasizes the requirement for specific skilled behaviours by managers. Neither emphasis looks to be strongly represented in most current offerings. Business schools, management centres, and in-company institutions have, for many years, offered executive programmes designed to broaden managers. Although there have been a more limited number of programmes specifically designed for very senior managers, nevertheless these have been used by a wide range of organizations in both the private and public sectors. The focus of the programmes has tended to be upon providing these experienced managers with additional knowledge and understanding. Such knowledge may have possible general relevance to their industry – but on the whole the programmes have been geared to the notion of broadening or 'refreshing' the senior manager. There has been particular emphasis upon dealing with environmental changes, together with some attempts to teach more formal concepts of strategic planning and decision-taking. Organizations and their top managers may, by now, have come to expect that general management programmes are synonymous with broad environmental issues and increasing knowledge of several major management disciplines.

Because of this almost exclusive emphasis upon adding to knowledge, the senior manager's actual performance, in terms of the application of personal skills appropriate to their level of job responsibility in their organization, has been largely ignored. Yet appropriate personal skills may make a key difference to effectiveness in senior manager and chief executive roles. Further, it appears possible for these skills to be both identified and developed – although this may mean a significant challenge to traditional approaches to the design of general management programmes. In particular this skills approach may pose a threat to the 'heavy majorities' of subject/knowledge-based teaching

Figure 15.1 The career model for the executive

Management Level	Programme Focus
Senior	Knowledge-based 'broadening' – environment and strategy
Middle	Knowledge-based 'broadening'
Junior	Personal skills development

resources which are currently the core faculty in traditional business schools.

The design of programmes for chief executives seems most often to be based upon subjective judgement on the part of the designers – rather than upon real data about specific needs of chief executives. It may well also be true that both organizations and business schools are inclined to take less risk and to be less prepared to innovate in designing programmes for very senior managers. But the development of chief executives clearly is an important issue, and if it can be improved and other areas of their performance developed through new forms of programme, then the returns, in terms of improved organizational performance, are likely to be large.

I want now to review the traditional approach to chief executive development, and to offer a new model or framework with which to look at the development of chief executives.

We can describe the 'traditional' approach – which holds true for a wide range of institutions – as being based on an overall view of the career model for the executive, as in Fig. 15.1. This model reflects a simplistic belief that personal skills are best acquired at the junior entry levels of management; other development experiences thereafter are only concerned to broaden managers as they progress through their careers. At no point – except perhaps on a special, remedial basis – is there a requirement for the successful manager to undertake further skill training. Only in exceptional circumstances – for example, in the introduction of entirely new information technology, with organization-wide impact – may skills at any senior levels be contemplated within this model or approach.

This model also reflects a view of management skills which determines these to be limited to routine skills associated with junior manager performance – for example, interviewing, selection, appraisal, or presentation. These skills are required in the first managerial job, because they form a necessary part of the common role of the manager. They particularly focus on various forms of communication with individuals or small numbers of subordinates.

Management development programmes offered both within organizations and by outside institutions, such as business schools, are likely to reflect this kind of career general model of development.

In practice, however, it has often been found that experienced and very senior managers, find themselves in difficulty, particularly as they move into new roles, because they lack certain practical and specific skills essential to the successful performance of those roles. They are therefore forced to cope as best they can, picking up, in less organized or supported ways, key 'how to do it' skills in order to meet the demands of their job. While such casual and informal arrangements are usually perceived as inefficient and inappropriate, they are often not discussed with training and development staff. Thus the traditional executive development model of skills first, and only broadening thereafter, is perpetuated.

I would like to suggest an alternative model for manager education and development which, as shown in Fig 15.2, appears

Figure 15.2 The 'squeeze-box' model for manager education and development

Management Level	Programme Focus

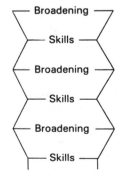

Senior — Broadening — Skills

Middle — Broadening — Skills

Junior — Broadening — Skills

more like a 'squeeze box'. What is key about this model is that the 'squeezed' points provided an opportunity for developing specific skills. In each case, skills are immediately pertinent to the performance of the job into which the manager is moving. We may therefore argue that, rather than skills training being a once and for all junior management experience, it is a regular require- ment for managers as they move through their careers. This will include the most senior management in an organization.

EXPERIMENTAL PROGRAMME IN CHIEF EXECUTIVE SKILLS DEVELOPMENT

In 1985 I had the opportunity to visit more than a dozen chief executives to discuss their own direct observations and conclusions about the skill-needs of top management. Each chief executive was leading a business in different parts of BAT Industries.

My approach to these discussions, armed only with two or three prompting questions, was to encourage these managers to talk as they wished into a tape reorder, about whatever dimen- sions of chief executive performance they believed to be important. Conversations would normally last for at least a couple of hours, and the transcripts were typed up in full for analysis.

Content analysis – which was developed and cross-checked with an academic colleague – revealed a surprising degree of similarity in terms of the identified key skill performance characteristics for a chief executive.

Very briefly, five key sets of skills emerged:

(1) the capacity for strategic thinking and decision-making;
(2) cross-functional empathy and understanding;
(3) effective team leadership and membership;
(4) effective appraisal and motivation of senior staff; and
(5) coaching and counselling skills for senior staff.

None of these areas of performance are surprising in themselves. What was more surprising was the relative uniformity with which a picture of needs in these areas emerged across three very different businesses at the general management level.

Managerial activity theory

Heartened by the positive skills identification which this survey of chief executives had thrown up, I followed this up with a survey of the key contributions in the research literature on chief executive performance. A summary of these findings has been published in Ashton (1986).

Mintzberg (1972), Argyris (1982), Kotter (1982), and Stewart (1982) have all addressed themselves, in part or whole, to the role and skill requirements of the chief executive. From their studies eight key areas of concern emerge for the effective performance of chief executives. All of these would appear to be amenable to skill development, rather than to broadening knowledge.

The key skills for the chief executive were seen by these leading contributors as:

(1) strategy change skills;
(2) on-line reasoning skills;
(3) interpersonal skills;
(4) unprogrammed decision skills;
(5) resource allocation skills;
(6) self-development skills;
(7) skills in determining the reality of managerial work; and
(8) skills in determining the effectiveness of individual manager performance.

The contributions of Stewart, Mintzberg, Kotter, and Argyris were based on extensive, practical research with chief executives and senior managers and, in broad terms, coincide with the findings of my own small study. Together, this would seem a fairly positive base on which to design a skills-development programme for chief executives.

Learning design for chief executive skills

The process of programme design was fairly lengthy and involved extensive collaboration and discussion with both chief executives and top personnel staff in the company as well as a network of possible programme faculty members.

An immediate concern was to identify the subsection of the management population for whom this particular programme would have a direct relevance. These were eventually defined as follows:

Within the BAT Industries Group, there is a relatively small number of "fast moving" General Managers, whose development to their best potential, is of particular concern to their Operating Groups as well as to the Group as a whole. For these managers, the development of their personal skills is likely to yield a significant return – and specifically those skills which are directly relevant both to their successful transition into larger general management roles and as preparation for future appointments.

In the development of the initial design of this programme, it was also felt important to agree a brief statement on the skills training approach, which was put over in the following way:

It is in the nature of skills development that any educational programme should restrict itself to certain key skills and, in a single-minded way, vigorously develop these. It is also important that such skill development is immediately relevant to the business and organisational context in which the delegates are currently operating.

Personal feedback will necessarily be a key feature of such a programme. This will both restrict the numbers of delegates on the programme, and underline the need for privacy during almost all working sessions.

Feedback is clearly a key feature of skills training, since practice and feedback represent the dominant, interrelated components of any skills-training activity.

Over time, the programme aims were also developed and were eventually spelt out as follows:

(1) To develop and test key skills in business strategy formulation, including environmental and competitor analysis and strategic decision making.
(2) To develop and test key skills in strategy implementation, including organizational communications and key staff appraisal and motivation.
(3) To provide opportunities for delegates to compare themselves with their peers within the BAT Industries Group and to learn and share experience with their peers.
(4) To provide opportunity for all individual delegates to undertake self-review and assessment of their potential for key senior, general management posts.

One key consideration in the design of the programme was the material on which these general managers would practice and develop their skills. Because the skills being developed were particularly pertinent to the chief executive level, delegates were asked to bring their own material on which they could practise. In each case, this meant identifying a major strategic problem on which the participant was currently working. This real problem was the main vehicle for their individual skill development throughout the programme. Additionally, there were introductory back-up exercises available, where necessary, though the main thrust of practice was reinforcement through work on managers' own existing strategic problems.

Programme structure

The structure of the programme was designed on a modular basis (Fig. 15.3). The first module primarily covers skills of strategic analysis, formulation, and reasoning. However, it was not intended that the first module should concentrate exclusively on

Figure 15.3 Modular structure of the experimental programme

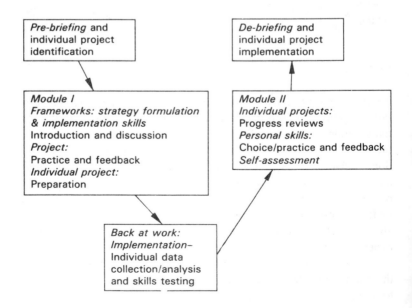

strategy-formulation skills, leaving strategy-implementation skills until the second module. The reality of the chief executive's world seems to be that strategy formulation and strategy implementation are very much entwined – it is therefore not intended that this programme would artificially break up this relationship into two separate parts. There is an intended time gap between the two modules, however, which gives opportunity for individual participants to return for a period of two or three months to their own businesses – committing themselves to practise and implement skills which have been the focus of the first module.

The second module provides opportunity for acquiring additional personal skills – in the areas of senior staff appraisal, coaching, counselling, and team membership – as well as reviewing progress on the application of strategic skills during the two modules.

The key role of feedback and review in skills improvement has already been highlighted. At the end of the programme, which is necessarily a relatively private workshop experience, a more appropriate way of giving feedback to their organizations is for the general managers themselves to return with their own self-assessment. They therefore prepare and undertake a detailed debriefing with their respective divisional boards – identifying the specific progress that they have made, as well as weaknesses which may need to be worked on.

CONCLUSION

Three groups of conclusions emerge from this chapter, all pointing up issues of concern for management development in the multi-national company. First, there is a need to understand better the learning needs of managers at different levels in the organization, bearing in mind the relevance of new skills to job performance at all levels of management. Associated with this recognition of differentiated learning needs is the insight that a further understanding of appropriate teaching and learning processes is also required – particularly further assessment of action- or experience-based learning.

Second, in a multi-national company, better understanding of the nature and effects of national cultural differences should help to improve communication and relationships among staff. That understanding should clarify what concepts about national differences are relevant, and how they should be learnt and applied by managers.

Finally, there is a strong case for arguing the importance of organization culture in managerial life – and this is made more complex in a multi-national company, where there may be a plurality of cultures within the whole. Not only should consideration be given as to how relevant concepts of organizations be put across to managers, but their motivation to become more effective in the 'how' of management should also be built on more directly as a central feature of management-development activities. This last conclusion presents a particularly strong challenge to most current learning-design assumptions in management education.

REFERENCES

Argyris, C. (1982) *Reasoning, Learning and Action*, New York: Jossey Bass.
Ashton, D. (1986) 'Managerial activity theory and the education of general managers', *Journal of General Management* 11(3): 27–36.
Hofstede, G. (1980) *Culture's Consequences*, New York: Sage.
Kotter, J. (1982) *The General Managers*, London: MacMillan.
Mintzberg, H. (1972) *The Nature of Managerial Work*, New York: Harper & Row.
Peters, T.J. and Waterman, R.H. (1982) *In Search of Excellence*, New York: Harper & Row.
Stewart, R. and Marshall, J. (1982) 'Managerial beliefs about managing: Implications for management training', *Personnel Review* 11(2).

16

Mixed-national training programmes: some unintended consequences

Rae Andre
(College of Business Administration, Northeastern University)

A Fortune 100 firm with over a dozen international divisions decides that it must begin to think like an international company. It believes it must integrate its managers on an international basis in order to foster mutual understanding of the international character of the business and in order to combat parochialism and rivalry among different divisions. As part of this effort to 'internationalize', the company decides to bring 50–100 high-potential young managers together in a one-year programme of study and travel in its home base, the United States. The programme is designed to continue indefinitely.

Over a three-year period, I had the opportunity to observe the mixed-national training programme just described, and I was able to do several different research projects in association with it. The research focused on the work and personal life adjustment problems of these middle management men and women and on the mixed-national character of their experience. Its purpose is two-fold. First, it is to give corporate and academic researchers interested in the relatively new and expanding phenomenon of mixed-national training programmes a preliminary insight into some of the methodological issues involved in understanding programme effectiveness. Second, its purpose is to provide some notes on practical issues in programme design. These studies directly address the issue of how the particular context of management influences the process of development for regular employees thrust into a mixed-national setting.

The approximately 55 high-potential managers who were studied[1] worked in a variety of fields – engineering, accounting, finance, personnel administration, and production management. Engineers predominated. Most were in their late twenties or early

Table 16.1 Countries of origin of the employees interviewed

Australia	6
Belgium	2
Brazil	4
France	4
FRG	9
Great Britain	11
Italy	1
Japan	2
Mexico	2
New Zealand	1
Portugal	1
South Africa	1
South Korea	4
Venezuela	2

thirties. All of the managers were in the United States primarily to familiarize themselves with the parent company, rather than to perform a particular job. Fourteen different nationalities were represented (see Table 16.1).

The managers were interviewed between five and six months after their arrival, or, in the case of the questionnaire study reported below, as late as possible in their tenure in the United States. Where the interviewing methodology was used, a structured set of open-ended questions was used in interview sessions that ranged from one to three hours.

ADJUSTMENT ISSUES

I was first interested in discovering how well the managers had adjusted on the job, both in the short term (the first day and first week) and over the longer term. It should be noted here that each of the managers had a specially-designed programme for his or her tour of the United States. In general, in addition to spending several months together at one site, each manager spent three months or more at other selected sites around the United States. Thus, the data we have here are a combination of many highly individualized experiences. The problems presented may in some ways be thought of as representing what a typical manager would be likely to experience in this company, or in other large multi-national manufacturing companies, in operations dispersed across the United States. Individual experiences, of course, may

Table 16.2 Problems in adjustment on the job

Total number of citations	Problem	Problem rated somewhat significant	Problem rated highly significant
30	Speaking basic English*	60%	40%
18	Lack of familiarity with work customs	72%	28%
15	Difficulty obtaining planning information	73%	27%
12	Lack of meaningful work	33%	66%
9	Lack of plant overview	44%	56%
8	Not being taken seriously	63%	38%
8	Adapting to different time perspectives	75%	25%
7	Driving long distances to work	71%	29%
7	Lack of manager and co-worker co-operation	43%	57%
5	Learning the technical language	100%	0%
4	Orientation to a type of department with which one is unfamiliar	75%	25%
4	Dealing with issues of intra-company competition and secrecy	25%	75%

* Of 42 non-English speakers.

differ. Not all visitors will encounter all the problems we note.

Our methodology was simple. The managers were asked to talk about their problems in adjustment on the job. Standardized questions and question probes were used. When a manager cited a problem, he or she was asked to make a judgement as to whether that problem was minor, somewhat significant, or highly significant. The results of the work-related segment of these open-ended interviews are presented in Table 16.2.

Several things are notable in these responses. To begin with, language is the overriding issue, cited by nearly twice as many managers as the second most-cited problem. Almost 75% of the non-English speakers cite difficulties with speaking basic English as a somewhat or a highly significant problem. In addition, even native English speakers cited learning the technical language as posing something of an issue for them. Clearly, more language training would have been useful for most non-English-speaking programme participants. One issue here is lead time in selection

213

for the assignment. Lead times were as short as three days, but generally were about six months. Unless an employee is relieved of other work responsibilities during this time (and even then six months is usually not adequate for learning a language), this is clearly not enough time to become fluent in another language.

A second important problem cited is the lack of familiarity with work customs. By this the respondents meant such things as how the power structure of the department works, what the 'real' working hours are as opposed to the posted working hours, and such other differences as one may expect to find in a new work culture. This suggests that some earlier training on cross-cultural work-related differences might have been of some use.

A third category of problems relates to the managers' direct on-the-job treatment. Such problems as obtaining enough planning information to do their job, finding meaningful work to do, and many of the other items listed in Table 16.2 refer to how well their new job experience had been designed for them. This job design issue was described by the managers as a problem for them on both psychological and practical grounds.

In general, the managers list three areas of concern: (1) language, (2) cross-cultural work-related differences, and (3) the design of their in-plant experience both in terms of the job that they are to do and their socialization to the plant. Whereas the first two areas are commonly discussed in the design of international training programmes, the third is seldom, if ever, considered. The experiences of these managers suggest that a variety of in-plant issues should be addressed.

Problems in personal life transitions were also explored, albeit somewhat differently. Although open-ended questions were used here as well, it was considered to be too obtrusive to ask the managers the extent to which personal problems were significant. In looking over the managers' response to this issue (see Table 16.3), it seems apparent that even given this cautious approach, the managers found that relatively trivial problems were easiest to talk about. Common sense would tell us that change of diet and eating customs, though a real problem for a few managers from Eastern cultures, was probably not a major issue for others even though it was the most mentioned. Furthermore, anecdotal data collected through my own experience with these managers suggests that at least a few serious problems did exist. For example, although the spouses of the managers formed a club that met frequently, some of the managers' wives did not join this club.[2]

Table 16.3 Problems in personal life transitions

	Number of citations
Change of diet and eating customs	18
Child-related: emotional adjustment, finding schools and medical care	16
Speaking and understanding English	12
Getting accustomed to banks and stores	11
Driving and arranging transportation	10
Wife has problems adjusting	8
Loneliness/lack of friends	8
High costs	7
Missing family	6
Poor housing	6
Difficulty in meeting Americans	4
Missing activities of homeland (culture, sports)	4
Speeding tickets	4
Wife and/or children not accompanying worker	3
Understanding and meeting women	3
Weather differences	3
Racism	2
Tendency (of the visiting manager) to overindulge	2
No problems	5

The generally accepted explanation for this was that these wives were at home involved with their young children and that they did not speak English, the predominant language of the club. It was also reported that wives not members of the club were often severely depressed, but because these women did not speak English, it was difficult for the other wives to help them to any significant extent. Some did assist them in their attempts to learn English. However, these women were not particularly motivated to learn. Actual crises did develop. On one occasion a wife who did not speak English contacted her husband at work to tell him their young child had fallen a storey and a half onto a concrete terrace. The husband, who had come from a culture in which the husband never leaves his job but in which, too, the wife is expected to and is fully able to handle problems at home, refused to come to help her. It was a couple of hours before the wife could communicate with her neighbours and get the child to the hospital. These problems did not show up strongly in our data. Overall, crises and other issues such as missing one's family and loneliness were probably more prevalent than the data would indicate.

We did not probe the managers to suggest ways in which these personal problems could be solved. Most appreciated any company efforts to assist them, however, and many would have preferred even more help for their spouses. It was our experience that often family problems were not mentioned by the manager until they became quite serious.

PROGRAMME RE-DESIGN ISSUES

In searching for ways to improve the programme, we focused on the workplace alone. We asked the managers how the problems they cited could be most effectively dealt with. Following are the ideas that they suggested.

Before the visit, goals and personal contacts for the job situation should be established. Goals of the employee's home management and of the local management should be discussed and co-ordinated before the visit begins. Often the managers would have brought relevant materials or knowledge with them, had they known what their job would be. A common complaint was that the managers did not realize the extent to which Americans would be curious about the visitor's own home work situation. The managers wished they had more time to learn more about the company's operations in their own country, and to prepare information and materials for dissemination in the States. One group of managers had been extensively trained in their own country about their own division, including plant tours at widely scattered locations, and their experience was the envy of many of the other participants from other countries.

Also, the managers wanted a personal contact within the sponsoring unit. They themselves, not merely their manager, wanted to be involved in planning their visit. They wanted someone that they could talk to informally, off the record, about what the work situation would be like.

During the first week on-site, several issues were seen to be important. First was introductions. It was suggested that these should be formal, and that they should include immediate co-workers, top management, and any other people that the manager would be likely to meet in the work environment. These introductions would serve several purposes. Even though the manager will not have remembered all the names of the people that he or she met, having been introduced, the manager will generally feel

216

more comfortable simply greeting people in the halls or around the plant. Likewise, other people will be comfortable greeting them and making them feel welcome. This is especially important because the manager may not make the same assumptions that Americans would make about who it is acceptable to approach and talk with. In some cultures, for example, managers seldom approach their bosses. The managers also noted that they felt excluded if they did not meet top management. However brief these meetings may be, they are important to the recognition and morale of these high-potential people. Finally, it should be pointed out that American employees will naturally be curious about the foreign visitor and will usually welcome the opportunity to meet him or her if the opportunity is provided.

Details of work programmes should be planned during the first week, and tailored to individual styles. Some managers preferred simply to observe at first, while others wanted to plunge right into some job. Many cited the need for some sense of direction. Yet, at the same time, inflexible hours and assignments could be a problem during the first week, when the managers often had many crucial personal arrangements to make outside of work, such as housing and transportation.

Managers wanted a plethora of specific information about their new corporate position. They often did not receive organization charts, or adequate product information. Sometimes they did not receive a tour of the facilities. In addition, a written guide to acronyms and technical terms was one set of information that was cited as potentially useful if tailored to the particular job and site. Also, the managers wanted more information on basic work customs, both formal and informal: When is lunch? Who goes to lunch with whom? Who pays? It was suggested that each manager be assigned a 'technical consultant' in his department. Busy bosses often became preoccupied with other matters soon after the managers' arrival. A peer who could be an on-going consultant (and, probably a friendly counsellor) was seen as highly useful.

Managers also wanted a physical space to call their own. Often they were allowed to float from office to office. But after having been physically uprooted from all familiar surroundings both at home and at work, having a physical niche to call one's own can be psychologically beneficial.

On-going language training was considered to be essential, as may be guessed from the ranking of problems suggested by the managers. Too often time was not allowed for this training once

Table 16.4 A general checklist for international exchange programme management

Before arrival
Have the managers from both countries established mutually acceptable goals for the visit?

Has the employee had intensive personal contact with at least one individual in the first department she or he will visit?

For the first week on site
Have formal introductions been planned?

Are work plans flexible enough to allow for the employee's input upon arrival – yet organized enough to give him structure if he needs it?

Have the employee's information needs been considered?

Does the employee have a place to call his own?

During the programme
What plans have been made to help the employee and his co-workers to cope with language difficulties?

How will the employee learn about work customs in the United States?

How will the employee's experience of challenge on the job be measured? How will his job challenge be maintained?

What plans have been made to help the employee with transitions in his or her personal life?

the manager was on-site. In addition, it was suggested that those with whom the visitor comes in contact be reminded themselves to adjust to the language problem and to slow down their own speech.

Description of American work customs, and of company-specific practices, was urged. The managers felt that often they appeared to be unassertive, when in reality they were only confused or cautious about what to do next. Work pace, union issues, working hours, and any other relevant customs needed to be explained. The extent to which such discussions are detailed, of course, depends on the manager's country of origin and the extent to which that culture differs from the American culture. For native English-speakers such descriptions may be reduced, though not eliminated. Often host country nationals assumed that work customs in Australia, for example, were identical to those in the United States, whereas in fact the work culture, even within the same company, differed significantly.

Finally, maintaining job challenge was seen as important. Positions requiring observation were only satisfactory for a short time. The managers sought the same, or even a greater, level of challenge in their job than they had in their home countries. Given their relatively short tenure on the job in the United States, providing this challenge is a challenge in itself. But many managers were bored and felt that their time was being wasted.

This research suggests that the context into which the managers enter, not merely the individual managers themselves, must be managed if the training experience is to be successful. A checklist summarizing the managers' suggestions as to how to improve the home country context is provided here for the practitioner charged with managing an international exchange programme (see Table 16.4).

THE LEARNING EXPERIENCE

In working with these managers it was also of interest to explore what indeed the managers learned from their experience. Of course, English-language skills were significantly improved. Also, an international contact network was developed. Further questions one might ask about the experience include: Did the fact that the managers often met in multi-national cohorts improve cross-cultural relations? Did it change their attitudes in any way? A questionnaire study focusing on the managers' attitudes toward each other and towards top management was conducted to explore these issues (Rae, 1985).

Did the experience encourage the managers to mix with other nationalities? The results indicated that the British were best able to integrate themselves with the other nationalities. This fact may be related to the close ties of the American and British cultures, but is just as likely an effect of speaking a quite similar language. Critical mass also seemed to be an important issue in whether a national group mixed well with other national groups. Often Germans were well-represented in a given year, and they were reported as mixing well with the other nationalities, in spite of (in this group) modest skill in speaking English. The nationality that was cited as mixing the least was the Koreans, who also had the most trouble with English.

When asked to rank in order reasons why certain groups mixed well with the other multi-national managers, the participants

219

listed the following: (1) mastering English (46% placed it first); (2) nationality (20% placed it first); (3) personality (18% placed it first); (4) economic class (10% placed it first); and (5) all other alternatives, including profession, being married to another nationality, or having parents of another nationality. Importantly, in this ranking procedure personality was volunteered in the 'other' category. This, along with a high non-response rate to questions asking the managers to rate each other using nationality as an identifying variable, indicate the managers' desire to be seen as individuals, rather than as representatives of their respective cultures. Marginal comments on the survey suggest that they wished to see other managers as individuals, rather than to stereotype them based on the culture from which they came. It is likely that individuals in the midst of experiencing the multinational setting are particularly sensitive to the detrimental aspects of national stereotypes. Despite the fact that national profiles may be predictive (Ferrari, 1972), many of them may have actively attempted to override the use of such stereotypes in an effort to be 'open minded'.

It was not clear from this study whether exposing managers to other nationalities made them in some way multi-cultural or cosmopolitan. Our research only addressed this issue in part, by comparing the managers' attitudes to the same case study both at the beginning and at the end of their stay. The case study reflected their approach to a top management problem involving what to do with a top manager who has been financially successful, but who in doing so has alienated his organization. It had been predicted in earlier research that being in the multi-cultural setting would make the managers less sympathetic to this top manager (Weinshall, 1977). However, in our research, the managers' attitudes did not change after their multi-cultural exposure. It remains unclear whether the multi-cultural experience changed the participants' attitudes.

CONCLUSIONS AND RECOMMENDATIONS

With a few exceptions, the problems that the managers in this company faced could not be characterized as severe, but neither were they insignificant. As we have noted, if anything our respondents under-reported their severity. At the same time, the learning the managers acquired was significant. They learned a new language, made corporate contacts, obtained a new overall view of the company, and were exposed to the American culture. However, we may question whether all of these add up to the company's stated goal of internationalization. This is both a theoretical and a practical problem. Clear theoretical models of internationalization – of individual cosmopolitans and of distinct corporate cultures integrating many nationalities – have been elusive. The company could not be expected to solve this problem in the design of a single programme. Nevertheless, the implications of these questions have importance to them.

Most importantly, perhaps, is the issue of whether the company was attempting to create an international corporate culture or whether it was trying to assimilate foreign nationals into its own American culture. The effect of the programme was primarily the latter. Evidence for this is, especially, the lack of attention to alerting American managers to the issues around hosting their foreign visitors. Basically, the visitors were expected to adjust to the system, not *vice versa*.

In my opinion, based on this study, management-development professionals and other practitioners interested in the multi-national, multi-cultural training setting should consider desired outcomes carefully and specifically when designing their programmes. Otherwise, unintended consequences that are counterproductive to the company effort may result. A programme such as this one may be casually designed on the simple assumption that 'mixing is better': throw people together and they will learn and grow and we'll all be the better for it. Although this is in some ways an attractive sentiment, in terms of actual learning that occurs and the utility that is gained by the sponsoring organization, hard questions have to be raised. In this instance, for example, important group effects were evident throughout the programme. Some nationalities banded together. The spouses' group had important influences. Most importantly, the fact that the visiting managers themselves formed a subgroup of the company had its repercussions. To what extent did the managers see themselves as an outgroup relative to the Americans they visited? To what extent did creating this international subgroup actually run counter to the goal of creating company cohesion? Although I collected no specific data on this issue, I believe, again from anecdotal evidence including many conversations outside of the studies reported here, that this was an issue of potentially high importance, and some threat, to the company.

221

On the practical side, the company must ask itself which of the aspects of internationalizing the company are most important to it. If these goals are identifiable and concrete, such as promoting better English and more contacts among young managers worldwide, could not these goals be met perhaps more inexpensively? Is a one-year programme in the United States, involving disruptions for entire families, as useful as shorter programmes in this regard? Is the cost justified? Most of the trainees would say that the programme was worthwhile for them personally. Whether it is also worthwhile from the company perspective is an issue that can only be addressed by thinking quite carefully about what internationalization really means . . . and about what it costs.

This chapter has provided some practical guidelines for use by management development professionals in designing an international managerial training programme. These guidelines have been suggested by an international set of managers involved in a training setting in the United States, and must be carefully re-examined if the training setting is elsewhere. Such training situations are complex, and further study of them needs to be done. Such research must consider the methodological issues of quantitative versus qualitative research if it is to be effective. In my opinion, researchers in this area have not yet done enough qualitative work to determine the pertinent variables for further, quantified, study. We do not yet know, for example, which attitudes are likely to change because of a mixed-national training programme.

Opportunities to study such programmes are rare. I wish to thank the anonymous company involved here for its openness and support in this project. I also wish to point out that although this chapter is in some respects critical of this particular programme, the programme represents an important beginning. At this point all efforts at managing multi-cultural management environments are experimental.

NOTES

1. The N-size for any individual study was either 50 or 58.
2. In all of the managerial groups studied, all spouses were female.

REFERENCES

Andre, R. (1985) 'The effects of multinational cohort training on attitudes toward other nationalities and toward management', *Management International Review* **25**(3): 4–15.

Ferrari, S. (1972) 'Human behaviour in international groups', *Management International Review* **12**: 31–5.

Weinshall, T.D. (1977) 'Communication, culture, and the education of the multinational managers', in T.D. Weinshall (ed.) *Culture and Management*, New York: Penguin Books.

17

Re-defining resources:
turning the minimum into the optimum

Ronald F. Clarke

(*University of Manchester*)

The approach described in this chapter has been developed over the past few years, particularly in public-service organizations in low-income countries, although the principles behind the approach should have wider applications. Much of the content of this chapter derives from experience of a workshop programme in management for principals of secondary high schools in Sierra Leone, which I helped to conduct with Professor Kwame Adjei and colleagues at the Institute of Public Administration and Management of the University of Sierra Leone over the past three years. As the approach has been applied in other circumstances it may be useful to provide some background before focusing on the particular features of the Sierra Leone situation.

BACKGROUND

In 1979 I ran a twelve-week study programme in Manchester for directors and heads of adult education and extension institutes and other non-formal education centres and programmes, as part of a regular programme of similar courses and workshops for administrators involved in various aspects of higher education.

They formed a varied group, mostly from low-income countries, representing a wide variety of work, but with a common core of interest and concern with adult and continuing education programmes and the need to manage them.

In common with a great many people all over the world, particularly in the public services, they had organizations and operations to manage, but would not normally regard themselves as managers. They had had no previous training in management, although some had attended short courses in aspects of administration. Also they had not previously thought of themselves as managers and indeed some were opposed to the whole idea of 'management' because of its associations with business and capitalist society, even if in some cases they were also personally attracted by the prestige attached to the term 'manager'.

We were concerned, therefore, to devise an approach to management which would suit the perceptions and needs of people in this kind of situation. In beginning to do this I thought back to my own earlier experience in similar situations in Africa, where I had been required to manage operations and departments and other functional units without any formal training or preparation in management or administration, and had to rely on a mixture of previous operational experience, observation, advice, and various kinds of experiential learning on the job. All of this was certainly useful but in retrospect I feel that I and my colleagues could have achieved more if we had been helped, at some stage, through a rather more structured experience, to view our roles in managerial terms. As it was, I never thought of myself as a manager in those days, and I doubt whether any of my colleagues did either.

If a managerial approach was needed on this study programme, it should not be managerialist. It should concentrate on the essentials of management, and not get bogged down in management jargon, excessive theorizing or over-emphasis on techniques. One of the basic problems in any management-education programme, especially for people who are new to the study, is where to begin. Another is how to give a conceptual sequence and unity to the programme of study that will not leave the participants more confused than when they began, from having experienced a mixture of theories and techniques that do not fit any recognizable whole, and seem to bear little relation to the problems they actually face in getting a job done.

It seemed clear, therefore, that we needed to concentrate at least initially on the basics of management in the broadest sense of the word, without the technicalities which might apply to people in large business organizations who were actually called managers and saw themselves as such. This would mean focusing on ends and means; on answering the basic questions: What is to be done? How? By whom? With what and in what circumstances? And supplementary questions such as when, where, and also why?

Shortly before this study programme began I undertook an assignment in Nepal, where I was asked to advise on the setting up of educational resource centres as part of an integrated rural development programme in four hill districts in the east of the country. This was a situation in which all kinds of tangible resources were extremely scarce, and in many cases what resources were needed would have to be created before they could be made available for use or distribution from the resource centre, which itself needed to be 'resourced' at least at a basic level in order to provide the required services to the community. This experience also helped to signal a way forward in our preparations for the study programme.

The need to focus on the significance of the concept of 'resource' in the Nepal assignment soon revealed the looseness with which the word is used. The 'resources' which the centres were expected to provide for education and extension work in the districts they served were obviously different from the 'resources' needed to set them up and run them. In the former usage, resources would be largely in the form of books and teaching/learning aids, and people to provide technical advice; in the latter usage resources would largely be money to run the centres, to furnish and equip them, and to pay the people in charge.

As we explored the significance of 'resource' further it seemed that while the concept was crucial to management in public-service units of the kind we were concerned with, the word was used loosely and variously, broadly or narrowly, almost always without definition, and according to the particular interests and vantage point of the user. We therefore moved towards a use of the term which would be comprehensive and would cover the means by which organizations and their managers seek to achieve ends: the 'how' and 'with what' aspects. This produced as a rough definition: 'anything which is able to *help* organizations and managers to achieve purposes'.

From these starting points and from our sharing of experiences with participants on the course, we began to develop what, for convenience, we have called a 'total resource' approach, and this has been further explored on subsequent programmes including the Sierra Leone workshops described below.

TOTAL RESOURCE APPROACH

Resources – as defined above – need to be balanced with constraints. Constraints (again broadly) are 'things' that can prevent or hinder what the organization and its members and managers are trying to achieve. But constraints should not be seen as necessarily opposites of resources, or as 'bad' while resources are 'good'. Nor should 'things' generally be considered as having in themselves some entity or qualities which categorize them as being resources or constraints; anything can be a resource or a constraint according to use and circumstances.

Resources and constraints

A resource is a potential; it is something that can help, or is available to help. What we conventionally think of as resources may be potential but are often hindering rather than helping our work, and thus act as constraints. A disaffected or untrained employee may be a constraint, as may a corrupt or inefficient manager, because they are hindering rather than helping the work of the organization. So may a defective piece of machinery, or an out-dated procedure.

At the same time what we conventionally regard as constraints within or surrounding the organization may be beneficial; thus certain legal or ethical restrictions which hinder some courses of action may, in fact, be to the benefit of the overall purposes of the organization; or some forms of conflict within the organization may be used beneficially to stimulate creative energy and dynamism. Where constraints are detrimental to the purposes of the organization they may, depending on circumstances, be minimized, by-passed, or converted into resources.

Categories of resource

Resources can be divided roughly into human, material, and intangible. There is not always a clear boundary between these categories; space, for instance, is literally intangible but has closest affinity to the physical objects that fill it; in some respects the line between humans and certain machines, such as computers and robots, is becoming increasingly blurred. Rather as organizational subsystems of various kinds are seen as dynamically linked and interdependent in systems theory, so the various kinds of resource are mutually influential. These linkages vary in effect and intensity according to circumstances and it is part of the manager's decision-making responsibility to assess various resource influences in relation to purposes when considering what to do in a particular situation. Is the time, money, and personal effort required to repair a machine or re-train an incompetent employee or introduce a new regulatory system justified? By taking a holistic, comprehensive view in assessing the total resource implications of a situation the decision-makers may be able to arrive at a more balanced judgement of likely effects and outcomes.

The primacy of people

People are inevitably at the centre of any resource network. In our approach people must be the primary resource. At its most elemental level an organization can exist without money but not without people, unless we are referring to non-human organizations. All kinds of resource have specific qualities, but people are unique in a number of ways. Above all they have, as individuals or groups, sets of intangible resources within themselves in addition to the physical or technical resources which they possess. They are individualized to a far greater extent than any other tangible resource. In effect, each individual person is a micro-organization. This uniqueness of people as persons can never be ignored by those who have responsibility to manage, even if it is sometimes forgotten by manpower planners and statisticians who do not have to manage the idiosyncrasies of individuals in the organizations they are planning for.

Balance

One of the main features of this total resource approach is a concern for balance. Even if people are the primary resource, they are not the only one; they are still a part of the total resource field of the organization, in relation to their tangible and intangible environment. Managing organizational resources is more than managing human resources. It is also more than managing money and materials. It involves managing time and information, and other intangibles such as systems and procedures, methods and techniques. Again, this implies other balances. For example, methods and techniques from this viewpoint are seen to be among the resources available to the organization. They are seen as the essence of management, which is a common managerialist position. Similarly, regulations and procedures take their place within the complex of resources without being elevated to the kind of predominance which they enjoy in most bureaucratic organizations.

Another form of balance is between the resources that are within the organization and those that are outside. This also applies to constraints. Perhaps, most obviously, people outside the organization can also be resources (e.g. the sympathetic adviser, the satisfied customer) as well as constraints, just as the people within it can fall in either category, or in between. Then there is balance at the micro level between the individuals, each with his or her set of resources (some of which are unique to the person and not to the organization as a whole) and the organization with its total body of resources. This in turn implies a balance between uniformity and variety, between commonality and uniformity, or between what people have in common and the respects in which they differ. People can in part be categorized and used, according to their capabilities, like working animals or machines. For the rest they act as individual persons or groups, often unpredictable, with unique sets of resources in themselves. This particular area of balance will become increasingly important as machines come to replace aspects of human work.

Encouragement of this sense of balance between and within the various resources of the organization, and between the organization and its environment, is an essential part of the total resource approach. Managers need a holistic appreciation of their organization, or at least of those areas for which they have overall responsibility.

MINIMAL RESOURCE SITUATIONS

To economists it is virtually axiomatic that resources are scarce. 'Resource allocation' implies an equitable distribution of what money (and perhaps also people and materials) is available to those who always need or demand more than they can be given.

229

This is particularly evident in times of financial cutbacks, such as the present, when in virtually every organization which is largely dependent on public funding there is continued complaint about inadequate resourcing.

The assumption that the demand for resources always exceeds supply is false and can be dangerous. This is an important aspect of our approach. It is possible to have too much money, too much equipment, too much space, too many people, or too much information; certainly too many regulations and procedures, and even too much time if we consider the total range of resources. Nations, like individuals, have squandered and misused sudden wealth; organizations in some countries are forced to take on extra labour they do not need and cannot afford in order to reduce the numbers of unemployed. Excess of resources can be as much of a constraint as scarcity.

However, lack of adequate financial, material, and human resources is a crippling constraint on many organizations and many countries. In the world's poorest countries the lacks in all of these areas are generally so great as to shame those in richer countries who constantly complain about the erosion of their own resources. The head of an average secondary school in Africa would marvel at the apparent richness of endowment enjoyed by his/her counterpart in Britain, and this would apply to most other organizations.

Sierra Leone was, and could be, a relatively wealthy country by African standards, largely because of its diamonds and other minerals. Why its people are in fact among the poorest is not a matter for consideration in this chapter.[1] Our immediate concern is with the managing and resourcing of secondary schools.

There are probably more secondary schools in Sierra Leone than is warranted by the size of the population or the economy. This means that tangible resources are spread even more thinly, and the jobs of the principals, teachers, and governors made more difficult.

Secondary schools in Sierra Leone vary from a few in the capital, Freetown, steeped in tradition and tracing their foundation back into the last century, to others, far inland, which spring up almost overnight under the sponsorship of a local proprietor. The average school may have little more than half the required number of staff, and possibly half of those are under-qualified for the level at which they are required to teach. They are poorly paid and there is widespread dissatisfaction, especially when salaries arrive late. Support staff are likely to consist of a clerk and a bursar, and a few labourers. Funding is mainly from the Ministry of Education, supplemented by school fees and anything extra that can be generated locally. Space is seldom a problem (except in the capital, Freetown) but buildings and equipment are generally inadequate and in a poor state of repair. Books and laboratory equipment are particularly sparse and ill-conditioned. Imported goods can cost many times the price of a local equivalent (if it exists) or the price in the country or origin; a single textbook can cost an average month's income.

This is the kind of situation that the principals who attend our workshops have to live with and try to manage. The material resources are minimal, and the constraints enormous. Several principals we have known are obliged to spend up to 40% of their time travelling, trying to get salaries for their teachers, food for their pupils, or petrol for their van, as well as driving to the capital or regional headquarters to attend meetings. Indeed, the chief resource in many of these schools is the combination of experience, wisdom, stamina, and dedication of the principals and some of their supporting staff.

This is one of our starting points. After virtually apologising for our own resource-rich backgrounds – the institute where the workshops take place is comparatively well endowed, even in relation to the rest of the university – we lead the participants towards a holistic view by asking them to reflect on all aspects of their school environment. They are asked to identify and describe all the resources available to them, in the broadest sense of the term, first to bring out their understanding of resource concepts, and then to explore their understanding and appreciation of the full range of resources available to them. This total resource analysis exercise can last up to two days in all, but is spread out after the initial description to precede study and discussion of means of managing the various categories of resource in relation to identified constraints.

There is a balance, in the workshop methodology, between technical and semi-technical inputs, individual analysis of back-home situations, and sharing of experience within the group. Thus individual analysis of school funding and expenditure at the beginning of sessions on financial management is followed by two days of instruction on basic budgeting and accounting procedures (always very popular, as principals often suspect that they are being cheated by their bursars), and this is followed by exchanges of experience, often anecdotal, but valuable not only for practical hints but also for confidence-boosting as individuals realize they are not alone in their troubles.

Gradually the focus of the workshop moves away from analysis towards synthesis, emphasizing the totality of the resource environment, within individuals, within the organization, and within the wider environment, and considers the resource and constraint linkages involved in a range of problem situations, most of which are presented by the participants from their own recent and often dramatic experience.

The focus now is on the optimum use (rather than maximum) of all available resources; on conversion, wherever possible, of constraints into resources (or otherwise finding ways of minimizing or by-passing constraints); and on stimulating creative resourcefulness in the principal and his colleagues. The term 'resourceful manager' can mean various things,[2] but in our sense 'resourcefulness' includes all of the above (best use, conversion, etc.) and in particular it involves actively seeking new resources or new ways of using or enhancing existing resources. It means the managers must develop themselves as creative, and imaginative thinkers.

Many and varied examples of creativity have been revealed and shared in the workshops, often showing remarkable ingenuity and persistence, and providing inspiration for others.[3] Extra funds have been generated in a variety of ways, most of them legitimate, especially through selling school produce. Various measuring instruments and other items of equipment have been made from old container boxes available at the harbour, at one tenth the cost of imports. Local community expertise has been discovered and used in the school. Unhelpful chairmen and members of governing bodies have been 'converted' into enthusiastic supporters. 'Difficult' staff members and pupils have become keen teachers and learners. Time has been saved by tactfully reducing casual visits without offending against social norms. Within the overall constraints of Government regulations, local procedures have been simplified to save time, energy, and paper. In some cases almost Machiavellian devices have been used: in one instance well-known deficiencies in the postal system helped to cover the intentional non-delivery of notices of meetings to a particularly obstructive member of a governing body.

These, of course, were the success stories: examples of resourcefulness already demonstrated or stimulated by the workshops. In a material sense they may make only a small dent in the general pattern of resource deprivation in which the schools fight a constant battle even to survive, and to fulfil their primary tasks of educating young people. Yet the overall message of this approach is optimistic, and strengthens the remarkable resilience and determination of the majority of the principals while encouraging those others who may have been in danger of sinking under the weight of constraints or allowing their schools to slide further towards chaos.

The workshops conclude with an action planning exercise where the principals are asked, within each resource category, to set out what action they plan to take or attempt over the coming year or other appropriate period, with the warning that they may be asked at the end of the period to compare actual achievement with intentions. Most of these action plans are both imaginative and realistic, and demonstrate the inspiration and new breadth of vision which the principals have acquired during the workshop.

This sense of new vision, of seeing the totality of their work as managers from a new perspective, and of realizing that they had more resource potential than they had ever imagined, is what comes through most strongly in the evaluation reports that have been presented at the end of each workshop.

RELATION TO OTHER APPROACHES

We are sometimes asked – though rarely by participants in the workshops – how this approach relates to the conventional and established approaches to management and management development.

It is important to stress that we do not suggest that this approach, by itself, is sufficient as a guide to the business of management, even for 'amateur' managers such as heads of educational and professional institutions. It is a way of beginning, a slip road from which one can lead into some of the more traditional highways of managerial analysis, viewing managers in their roles as, for instance, leaders or decision-makers, or delegates, or co-ordinators. These emerge naturally as we return to focus on the manager and his personal resources of knowledge and capabilities, after we have considered the various aspects of his resource environment and how they affect his work.

As the analyses of resources and constraints proceed, especially through examination of the managers' use of time, a picture of managerial work emerges which demonstrates a similar kaleidoscope of activity to that found by major researchers such as Stewart (1967) and Mintzberg (1973), and in subsequent studies such as that reported by Webb and Lyons (1982) on heads and senior teachers in a number of large secondary schools in the UK. These and similar studies of the actual behaviour of managers at work, mostly based on detailed diary accounts, have all shown that managers do not actually plan, organize, direct, and control in a systematic, sequential, and orderly fashion as Fayol and other early management theorists would have us believe. In fact their work is highly varied and fragmented, largely responding to immediate demands and pressures on their time.

Some institutional managers in developing countries, following a more autocratic and less participative manner of management than is common in most comparable Western organizations, seem able to insulate themselves from much of the hurly-burly of daily activity and work more steadily on strategic issues from behind large desks. Yet even here they are likely to be coping with a host of political and social pressures unknown to their Western counterparts and largely unconnected with the overt business of the college or other organization.

Within the established areas of approach to the interpretation of organization we clearly have a good deal in common with the open systems and contingency approaches, with their concepts of various aspects linked and mutually interdependent and interacting with the environment, and (in the case of contingency theory) much influenced by situational conditions.

One major concern in our approach, as already noted, is with balance, avoiding undue emphasis on any particular resource area. From this viewpoint, earlier approaches of the classical and 'scientific' schools – and their more modern successors – would seem to place too much emphasis on structures and on techniques, while the human relations school would tend to over-emphasize the human resource in relation to the rest of the resource environment. Within the range of metaphorical perceptions elaborated by Morgan (1986) we would see organizations primarily as living organisms, also in some ways as cultures, and as in flux and transformation. However, in our resource-centred approach we view the organization itself as a resource (or constraint), just as the individual person is 'a resource' and, at the same time, a micro-organization, a network of varied, interacting resources. From this angle there is no necessary conflict in our approach between open systems thinking and a phenomenological or existentialist approach which emphasizes the uniqueness of personal interpretations of reality (see, for instance, Gray, 1982). This is not intended to suggest that our approach offers 'all things to all persons', but that the holistic outlook and emphasis on balance between the various resource areas tends to convergence rather than divergence between different 'schools' of thought about the nature of management and organizations.

CONCLUSIONS

It is too early yet to assess the long-term impact of these workshops but, from what feedback has so far been received, it is clear that a good number of principals now approach their work from a different perspective, and have maintained at least some of the momentum they developed at the workshop.

I have also introduced and adapted this approach in other situations, including a UN workshop for scientific and technical officers in Pakistan, which will be used as the basis of new training material for people with this kind of background who become managers in scientific, technical, and other professional fields.

On present evidence the main advantages of this approach, in the circumstances in which it has been tried, seem to be as follows:

(1) It is relatively simple and jargon-free, and thus particularly suitable for those new to management, or those professionals and others who have to manage but do not necessarily see themselves as managers.
(2) It offers a broad holistic perspective of the manager's job, working from the definition of management as achieving purposes through the best use of available resources.
(3) It provides a conceptual framework on which individuals building their own understanding related to their own situation, the experience of their colleagues, and more universally applicable knowledge and skills, which can be adapted to a variety of organizational and cultural backgrounds.

(4) It moves from familiar to less familiar areas of resource management, from tangibles to intangibles, from basic concepts to more complex areas, and thus can provide a foundation for further study of the nature of managerial work and organizational structures and systems.

(5) It is a positive and optimistic approach which is particularly applicable in minimal resource situations, where those responsible for managing are struggling to make any progress or even to survive.

While the approach seems to be useful in the kind of situation described here we would make no further claims at this stage. Whether it has wider application, for instance in large government organizations or in private business, is a matter for speculation, and perhaps experiment. Other approaches may be more suitable in these circumstances. However, all organizations must be concerned with resources and constraints, and have at some time to answer the basic questions posed in our approach, however large and complex they may be, and these aspects at least should be more generally applicable.

NOTES

1. Some reasons are suggested in a report by the International Labour Organisation, 'Ensuring equitable growth: a strategy for increasing employment, equity and basic need satisfaction in Sierra Leone', Addis Ababa (1981).
2. See, for instance, Morris (1975) in which the author suggests that the three basic activities of management are (a) keeping things going, (b) doing new things, and (c) coping with failure. Each of these is highly relevant to the Sierra Leone situation, even if the emphasis and balance are rather different from those common in industrialized countries.
3. See Schumacher (1973) for an extended discussion of this kind of resourcefulness through applications of intermediate technology in developing countries.

REFERENCES

Gray, H.L. (ed.) (1982) *The Management of Educational Institutions*, Lewes, England: The Falmer Press.
Mintzberg, H. (1973) *The Nature of Managerial Work*, New York: Harper & Row.

Morgan, G. (1986) *Images of Organisation*, Beverly Hills, CA: Sage.
Morris, J (1975) 'Developing resourceful managers', in B. Taylor and
  G.L. Lippitt (eds) *Management Development and Training Handbook*,
  London: McGraw-Hill.
Schumacher, E.F. (1973) *Small is Beautiful*, London: Blond & Briggs.
Stewart, R. (1967) *Managers and their Jobs*, London: MacMillan.
Webb, P.H. and Lyons, G. (1982) 'The nature of managerial activities
  in education', in H.L. Gray (ed.) *The Management of Educational
  Institutions*, Lewes, England: The Falmer Press, 85–108.

18

Management and organizational development in Bulgaria

John Wallace (*ILO, Geneva*)
Evka Razvigorova (*IISA, Austria*)
Jack Kalev (*ISM, Bulgaria*)
George Boulden (*ALA International, UK*)

INTRODUCTION

This chapter describes the recent experiences of the Institute of Social Management (ISM) in Bulgaria; a project funded by the United Nations Development Programme (UNDP) and organized by the International Labour Organisation (ILO). It began in 1983 with a three-week seminar for the forty staff of ISM. Today new philosophies and mechanisms are an integral part of ISM's working practices and the model developed there has been used to train trainers in other institutes in Bulgaria, and in Cuba to train 400 management development staff.

The chapter is set against a background where rapid industrialization in a socialist society puts special demands on management development professionals. These professionals experience the pull of academic respectability while trying to find mechanisms for delivering value-for-money to practising managers. We try in this chapter to highlight the conflicts that arise when management development professionals, recognizing the need to be seen as up-to-date, attempt to introduce computers and closed-circuit television while moving from an educational–teaching style to a training–consulting style.

MANAGEMENT IN BULGARIA

Management and organizational development has a short history in Bulgaria. The People's Republic of Bulgaria began industrializing only after World War 2. Before then, Bulgaria was primarily agricultural; its industry was limited, mostly to textiles, forestry, woodworking, tobacco, and foodstuffs. Three-quarters of its people were peasants. Today, the situation is reversed: only one out of four Bulgarians work in agriculture while 75% live in urban areas.

Bulgaria industrialized rapidly: gross national product increased 22 times and national income 14 times between 1983 and 1984. New industries – heavy chemicals, metallurgy, electronics, and electro-technology – have been introduced. Traditional industries – textiles, machine building, tobacco, and foodstuffs – have been modernized. Since 1939 Bulgaria's industrial production has increased 89 times, while agricultural production has increased 319%.

Industrial development has helped government fulfil its social policy and solve some fundamental social issues, while continuously increasing the population's standard of living. According to the 12th Party Congress appraisal, Bulgaria has created a material and technical base for future development. The Party aims to increase the standard of living by increasing productivity and efficiency through technological innovations. Bulgaria's scientific and technical policy is now directed to satisfying society's needs, to increase international competitiveness, and to improve Bulgaria's position in the international division of labour.

A new system of management and organization was introduced. The July 1968 decision of the Central Committee of the Bulgarian Communist Party concerned improving management systems and creating a new system for management development. Different governmental bodies are radically revising management and organization in industry. The Ministerial Council created a special department in the early 1970s to improve continuously Bulgaria's management systems. In 1968, the Ministry of Labour's Management Training Centre was created, with a computer centre for training top-level managers. At the beginning of the 1970s, the Academy of Social Sciences and Management Development and its Institute for Social Management were established. Since then, the Institute for Social Management (ISM) has been the main co-ordinating body responsible for management development in Bulgaria, including that of top-level executives.

Management and organizational development in Bulgaria is dynamic. Since 1982, improvements in national management have aimed at increasing companies' business initiative. Earlier, companies mainly implemented and executed ministerial requests. Today managers must change from simply executing plans. They must become risk-takers and strategists. Bulgarian organizations are now introducing new methods for strategy development, for increasing flexibility, for rapid problem-solving in order to change direction when necessary.

MANAGEMENT DEVELOPMENT AND TECHNOLOGICAL CHANGE

Management development needs can be defined by two groups of factors: the stage of economic and social development and the internal organizational factors, such as the organization's development, history, and culture, top management's personality and style.

These needs often take a long time to formulate, but once formulated it takes even longer to develop the facilities to satisfy these needs. Should an institution such as ISM wait for managers to realize themselves what their needs are or should it help managers formulate their needs and understand them fully?

Bulgaria uses both approaches; its management development system offers training to different managerial levels. At the same time, Bulgaria proactively helps managers recognize their needs through TV, broadcasting, lectures, brochures, special information courses, even obligatory courses for some managers, literature, and consulting assignments. It is often a mistake to wait for individuals to realize their own training needs. Facilitators should help managers understand and accept the need for management and organization development. When technological change is rapid, managerial development needs to change rapidly as well. Training offerings rapidly become obsolete.

Bulgaria is experiencing rapid technological change which requires greater decentralization of decisions and greater use of sophisticated management methods, such as modelling, simulation, quality control systems, and methods to stimulate creativity. This decentralization has also created several new organizational problems. For example, the opportunity to develop their own strategies has created the need for new in-company departments to forecast and plan. Managers want to learn about systems and procedures for strategic management. An operational mentality must become a strategic one.

State decisions have opened up new opportunities for companies to increase profitability and to develop new activities.

Small and medium-scale enterprises are being set up to accelerate technological innovation.

Small-scale enterprises and joint ventures have created other organizational challenges. Bulgarian enterprises must overcome organizational boundaries and hierarchic barriers and create joint ventures to introduce new technologies. New co-operative forms require new management skills.

Between 1980 and 1984, more than 150 joint ventures were created successfully, but not without problems, for example, in the production of advanced welding techniques and bio-products. Research production units, institutes, universities, and the Academy of Sciences often enter into joint activities or agree to co-operate in commercializing technologies. A good example of this is a company called Research Technology Centre–Metals Technology created jointly by an institute of the Academy of Sciences and a production company to explore original Bulgarian technology for casting by contrapressure. Everywhere in Bulgaria small-scale enterprises are using new technologies to process raw materials and to reduce waste.

The ISM must satisfy new needs and help managers recognize and understand their needs themselves. Questionnaires have been distributed at regular courses asking about new training requirements, and the Institute's consulting department has studied new needs as well.

BACKGROUND OF THE ISM PROJECT

The need for change in management development was felt strongly at ISM. The first reaction in 1975–80 was typically academic: we emphasized the subject matter and spent much time developing new curricula. ISM also increased its offerings. But by September 1980 it had become obvious that we had to change not only what we were teaching but how we taught it.

So we looked not only for new subjects, but for new methods. The easiest way seemed to learn from the industrialized countries. Immediately, two questions arose:

(1) How relevant are these Western management development experiences?

(2) Since Europe and North America have attained their present standards over a long time and even today their

241

management is imperfect, is their model really appropriate for us? After all, management is a social mixture which always reflects material life.

We concluded that since we are at different stages of development, the Western model was applicable but we should adapt it. We should learn not the mistakes, but from them. By drawing from the wealth of expertise we would accumulate knowledge and skills which we could adapt.

The programme

In 1981 the ISM got an opportunity to update its teaching methods under a UNDP project. We decided to buy microcomputers, CCTV, and specialized training materials. Staff would learn modern management training methods through two major seminars. The first, Modern Management Training Methods (MMTM), would demonstrate participative styles of training in use in the West. We would also look at ready-made packages and how to adapt them to Bulgarian situations. The second, originally called Computer-Aided Instruction and later Computers in Management and Management Training in order to broaden its scope, was intended to help ISM staff to see how they could apply the recently acquired computer equipment in their work.

Two ILO-appointed external consultants and a senior member of the ISM staff managed the Bulgarian side. We adopted a management style of consensus where the consultants and the ISM staff worked together first to develop the project and then to run it.

In the spring of 1983 two important factors were identified which significantly influenced the way the programme developed and the results that were achieved. We realized that we needed ownership and commitment by the participants. Both consultants had considerable experience in similar programmes where technically good seminars had failed to meet participants' needs. We were determined to avoid that if possible. Second, since most of ISM's work was educational rather than training, some time was needed to develop basically different skills. Most of the staff were teachers, not trainers. To be successful we needed to change our way of doing things. We therefore needed to highlight the difference between teaching and training and the role of both, and provide opportunities for people to change.

242

We therefore adopted a broader approach than originally planned. To make the programme as relevant as possible, we analysed the training needs of ISM staff (consultants should practise what they preach: do needs analysis before designing the programme). To enhance ownership and commitment through involvement we set up preparation groups among the most experienced staff. They were sent on fellowships to various European countries to examine training methods, packages, and simulations, decide which approaches and packages were most relevant, and prepare materials to use on the MMTM course with the consultants.

While this approach would get commitment to the seminar, alone it would not enable the participants to develop skill in using MMTM. Thus, we decided to use the following model. The seminar would kick off the programme and produce a six-month Action Group Programme to help the delegates improve their MMTM skills.

By June 1983 we had a broad outline of the seminar which have five sections:

(1) the systematic design of training programmes;
(2) the use of 'aided instruction';
(3) computers in management and management training;
(4) real-time methods in organizational development; and
(5) the setting up of seven design groups involving all participants based on their 'institutional chairs' to enable them to develop new programmes based on the materials demonstrated in the seminar.

The consultants took responsibility for sections (1) and (5) jointly with ISM senior management. The other three were handled by preparation groups of ISM staff assisted by the consultants. Fellowships were organized during the second half of 1983 in Britain, France, and Italy. These allowed the groups to see a range of MMTM techniques relevant to their projects and to choose some to present to their colleagues in Sofia. This part of the project ran in three stages:

Stage 1: A three-week residential seminar. The first five days covered the theory of designing training programmes. The next nine days were run as three blocks focusing on the MMTM activities chosen by the preparation groups. The final four days

243

on evaluating the experience and organizing the design groups for Stage 2.

Stage 2: A six-month action group programme. Design groups were to be created based on the seven ISM chairs to apply something from the seminar to an existing programme, or to new programmes.

Stage 3: Evaluation. A one-week programme to assess the work of the design groups and to award certificates of competence in the use of MMTM. At this stage a special permanent group was to be set up with representatives from all the chairs to provide on-going feedback to ISM on developments in MMTM and to act as a focal point for ISM to sell its MMTM expertise in the market place.

Stage 1 started in December 1983. The consultants were responsible for the first five days and the last four. The three-day modules on MMTM techniques were run by the three preparation groups who had been on fellowships. The three groups were on audio-visual-aided, computer-aided, and real-time methods.

The seminar was attended by all ISM staff, some sixty-five people, including the preparation groups. The opening sessions highlighted the difference between traditional teaching and modern training methods and introduced a 'process' method for developing training programmes which served as the basic model for the rest of the seminar:

Needs ⟶ Training ⟶ Programme ⟶ Implementation ⟶ Feedback
analysis   aims   design

The audio-visual-aided group demonstrated an action maze, a presentation analysis exercise, behaviour analysis in training, interpersonal negotiation using simulations, and instructor-free training using video packages. The real-time problem-solving group demonstrated methods for group problem solving and an approach to management/organizational development using large-scale simulations of a total business. The computer-aided design group demonstrated the use of computers both to help managers manage and to train managers. The group used software such as VisiCalc and Wordstar, some simple decision-making exercises, and a business simulation from Sheffield Polytechnic. In the final days the design groups produced action plans for Stage 2. These were presented to the management team of the ISM.

Stage 2 began in December 1983 and, as far as the project was concerned, ended with the review in Sofia in March 1985. This was considerably longer than planned for several reasons, not the least of which was due to the consultants not taking into account the need for Academic Board approval for course changes. The consultants provided monitoring and on-going support throughout this period with a total of eight on-site visits including direct support to the personnel group to run the MMTM seminar, first in Varna in September, and in Cuba in February 1985. In addition, several specialist fellowships were arranged to satisfy particular needs.

Stage 3, the formal review of the project, was held in Sofia in March 1985. Seven design groups presented the results of their work over the fifteen months of the project. These included the running of in-plant action-learning programmes by two groups, the adaptation of many of the simulations and original designs of specific material by others, and ISM running its own MMTM seminar in Cuba in February 1985. Even though the project is officially finished, ISM intends to go on.

ACHIEVEMENTS

For the Institute and its personnel the programme has undoubtedly been successful. Six of the action groups have done major new work directly related to the project, and several individuals have achieved significant personal development.

(1) The economic mechanisms group developed and ran new programmes for exporters and adapted computer-based simulations for training Bulgarian managers in the use of economic mechanisms.

(2) The personnel group adapted and ran the MMTM seminar themselves, firstly inside Bulgaria, and then helped ISDE (Instituto Superior de Direccion de la Economia) in Cuba to train 400 management trainers nationwide.

(3) The strategic planning group developed a new type of action-learning programme to enhance their existing work.

(4) The theory of management group developed nine simulations covering all the basic aspects of management theory for use in first-level training.

(5) The quality group developed and ran a series of seminars for middle and senior managers to create in-plant action groups to solve quality problems.

For the consultant, some forty people have worked for fifteen months under the considerable pressure of their normal jobs and have coped with their own personal development and through that the development of ISM. They did not have to; no one would have been fired for not working on this project.

It worked because it had the ingredients for success: ISM's management saw the project as an opportunity to develop their people and their organization. ISM management helped the staff not only to learn but how to apply their learning. They were concerned that it should not just be a seminar where people turn up for three weeks and then forget about it. The preparation groups ran their own three-day programmes. The design groups developed new programmes based on their experience. The participants were motivated, most had realized that conventional teaching methods were ineffective with experienced managers, and saw how the project could help them solve some current problems.

The consultants' style enabled them to use the opportunity effectively. They engaged in frank and free discussion between all parties. All opinions were considered before decisions were made. These were always agreed at the highest level in the Institute before action was taken. This enabled us to harness the abilities of all parties and at the same time provide support for the courage to make things happen. This process was used to develop the programme, to run it, and to evaluate the results. This was an environment of mutual trust and openness; from this we got commitment and ownership which enabled the rest to happen.

Here we used existing positive conditions to create the right environment. We learn that it can be done, but like all good cakes it not only needs the right ingredients, it also needs the right cooks. The lesson for the ILO is that it is important to get the background conditions right before starting projects in order to get positive results. If these are right then both task and environment must be managed to ensure success.

246

Statistics from *Philip's Modern School Atlas* (1986), London: George Philip & Son Ltd.

Basic statistics

This table presents information about all countries referred to in this book, and also includes USSR, Australia and Canada.

Country	Population (000s)	Life expectancy (yrs)	Urbanization (%)	Land area (000 km²)	Food supply (calories per day)	Education % Total school-age group Primary 6-11 yrs	Secondary 12-17 yrs	Trade Import (US$)	Export (per cap)	GNP US$ per cap	Growth per cap	Loans and debts End '83 (US$M)	(% of GNP)
Algeria	21,272	57	46	2,382	2,586	93	36	484	602	2,400	2.4	12,942	28
Australia	15,544	76	86	7,618	3,055	100	90	1,507	1,529	10,780	0.9	773	0.5
Bahrain	400			0.6									
Bulgaria	8,961	70	67	111	3,622	100	82	1,414	1,432	3,800	1.1	1,535	0.5
Canada	25,150	76	75	9,221	3,346	100	95	2,942	3,455	12,000			
China	1,051,551	67	21	9,326	2,426	100	35	19	21	290	4.5	6,899	18
Colombia	28,217	64	66	1,039	2,494	125	46	181	112	1,470	2.7	1,223	26
Ethiopia	35,420	43	15	1,101	2,149	46	12	27	12	140	0.7		
Hong Kong	5,364	76	92	1	2,771	100	67	5,329	5,283	6,000	6.8	224	0.8
Hungary	10,665	70	55	92	3,484	100	73	760	803	2,150	5.6		
India	746,742	55	24	2,973	2,056	79	30	18	11	260	1.8	21,277	11
Japan	120,018	77	76	371	2,852	100	92	1,137	1,148	10,100	3.3	4,319	0.4
Kenya	19,536	57	17	569	2,011	100	20	73	52	340	1.0	2,384	43

Basic statistics contd.

Country	Population (000s)	Life expectancy (yrs)	Urbanization (%)	Land area (000 km²)	Food supply (calories per day)	Education % Total school-age group Primary 6-11 yrs	Secondary 12-17 yrs	Trade Import (US$)	Export (per cap)	GNP US$ per cap	Growth per cap	Loans and debts End '83 (US$M)	(% of GNP)
Malawi	6,839	44	11	94	2,208	62	4	47	33	210	1.1	719	55
Nigeria	92,037	49	22	911	2,378	98	16	151	127	760	0.7	11,757	18
Philippines	53,351	64	39	298	2,405	100	64	153	96	760	2.9	10,385	30
Sierra Leone	3,536	38	23	72	1,938	40	12	47	42	380	0.3	359	35
Swaziland	649	46	20	17	2,553					890	0		
Sweden	8,337	78	85	412	3,146	99	85	3,159	3,518	12,400	0.8	*737*	*0.8*
Tanzania	21,062	51	14	886	1,955	98	3	40	18	240	0.1	2,584	59
Turkey	48,265	63	45	771	3,002	100	39	224	147	1,230	1.4	15,396	30
United Kingdom	55,624	74	91	242	3,249	100	83	1,775	1,628	9,050	1.0	*1,432*	*0.3*
United States	236,681	75	74	9,127	3,641	100	97	1,376	921	14,090	1.5	*8,698*	*0.2*
USSR	275,000	69	65	22,272	3,360	100	97	293	333	5,300			
Zambia	6,445	51	47	741	2,146	96	16	88	100	580	2.5	2,638	84

Notes:

Population: UN estimate for mid-1984.

Life expectancy: Average for men and women – expectation for child born today if levels of death last throughout life.

Urbanization: % of total population in urban areas.

Land area: Total area minus lakes and rivers.

Food: Average daily intake per person 1979-81.

Education: % of school-age group.

Trade: 1983/84 figures: total figures divided by population.

GNP: Estimate of average production per person in US$ for 1983. It measures value of goods and services produced plus the balance, positive or negative, of income from abroad. The rate of change (growth) is the average annual percentage change during 1973-83 in the Gross Domestic Product (i.e. GNP minus foreign balances).

Loans and debts: External public debt at end of 1983 in US$ millions. Figures in italics show official development assistance made by developed countries and percentage of donor's GNP.

Index

absentee rates 73
academic education 192–3
academic standards 41, 43
action learning methods 140, 141, 173–4, 196, 201–2
Adjei, Professor Kwame 224
Africa 75–83; *see also under individual countries*
African Development Bank (AfDB) 79
agriculture 97, 239
aims of management education/training 130, 187, 205–6
Aldemir, C. 131, 136
Algeria 66–74
'alternative' management technologies 52–3
American Association of Collegiate Schools of Business 157
AMT (Angewandtes Management and Training) programme 132, 134, 135
analysis model 188–91
analytical view of knowledge 192, 193
Argyris, C. 188, 190–1, 206
Ascolfa (Colombian Association of Management Schools) 44
assertiveness training 79
assets 99
attitude change 140
authoritarian values/management style 69, 72, 73, 131, 133
authority 57; economic 99–100, 104–5

Bahrain 29–39
Bakke, E. 195
Barbato, R. 21
Barnard, Chester 109
barriers to effective programmes 174–6; strategy for overcoming 176–7

'basic assumption groups' 189, 193
BAT Industries Group 200, 207
behaviour 58, 63, 188, 189; changes in 190–1, 194
Beijing Optical Instrument Factory 106
Bell & Howell Co. 167
benefit/cost analysis 171, 173
Berry, J.W. 59
Bion, W. 188, 189, 190
Bishop, Brian 178
Blomstrom, Robert L. 155
Blunt, Peter 67
'bonus coefficient' 105
bonuses 105–6
Botswana 13, 173
Bowen, Howard 153
Bowie, E. 155
Brazil 1
British Institute of Management (BIM) 169
British Telecom 179, 180
'broadening' approach 202, 203, 204
building construction 172–3
Bulgaria 4–5, 238–46; management development in 240; management in 238–40; technological change in 240–1
Business Administration Program (Turkey) 130
business schools: and evaluation 15, 168, 171–2, 176–7, 192–4; beginnings of 13; growth of 14; in Bahrain 32–8; in Bulgaria 241–6; in Colombia 42–4; in Hong Kong 157–8; in Hungary 147, 149, 150; in Sweden 185–8, 192–4; in Turkey 130–2, 134; in USA 1–2, 157; quality of teaching in 128; weaknesses of 51–2; *see also* MD professionals

249

Capital Iron and Steel Co. 98, 103, 104, 105, 110
career model 203–4
case study of executive training: analysis model for 188–91; analysis of 192–4; characteristics of programme 186–8; improvement suggestion for 195–7
Central Bank of the West African States (BCEAO–COFEB) 80
centralization 108, 137, 138; of power 154
Centre for the Study of Management Learning (CSML) 2
challenge, need for 219
change, resistance to 140, 143
China 1, 112–24; development of management in 113–15; 'economic responsibility system' in 97–111; history of management in 113; management education in 19, 117, 118, 119–24; present situation in 115–16; problems of management in 117–18; 'scientific management' in 3, 109, 113, 114, 115–16, 117–18
Cladea (Latin American Council of Graduate Management Schools) 41, 44
class discussions 133
clinical/qualitative view of knowledge 195–6
coal miners 63
cognitive learning climate 190, 193, 196–7
Colombia; business schools in 42–4; research into management in 45–50
Commonwealth Development Corporation (CDC) 82
competitive environment 141
Conference Board 169
Conference on International Management Development 2

conformity, socialized 59, 60, 62, 69, 140
considerate leader style 88, 89–90
'consolidation' phase of management education 15, 17, 20
constraints 227, 230–1
consumer research 169
contact network 191
contingency approach 234
Continuing Management Education Programme (COMEP) 36–7
Coopers & Lybrand 169
'counter-industrial tradition' 67
'coursitis' 175
creativity in problem-solving 232
credibility/status of management training 167
cross-cultural milieu 125, 126–7, 133, 134, 135
Cuba 245
cultural factors 58–60; and clashes between cultures 132–5; and 'considerateness' 88, 89–90; and organizational effectiveness 67–8, 72–3; and teaching methods 4–5; in management development 61–4; in Moslem organizations 69–70
'Cultural Revolution' 114–15, 117, 120

Davies, Keith 155–6
decision-makers; attitude change among 140; attitudes to training 176–8, 181; skills required by 205, 206
defence mechanisms 189
democratic approach of MD professionals 246
dependency, in groups 189; see also conformity, socialized
design of programmes 186–8, 192–4, 195–7, 206–8
Deutsh, Karl 67
development, management see

management: development/
  education/training
development tasks of LDCs 51
developmental stages of
  management education 12–18
DIA programme (Germany) 132,
  134, 135
diploma v. degree courses 32–4,
  35–6
disciplinary sanctions 69

Easterby-Smith, M. 168
Eastern and Southern Africa
  Management Institution
  (ESAMI) 81
eating customs 214
economic analysis 80
Economic Development Institute
  (EDI) 79, 80, 81–2
economic differences between
  countries 5
'economic responsibility system':
  and state 99–103; assignment
  of responsibility in 103–4;
  economic authority in 104–5;
  effectiveness of 108–9; future
  development of 107–8;
  ideology in 109–10;
  performance evaluation in
  105; profit distribution in
  105–7
economics 120, 121, 122, 123,
  229
education, management see
  management: development/
  education/training
educational approach to
  management development 174
effectiveness, organizational
  60–1, 66; cultural factors in
  67–8, 72–3
effectiveness of managers 201
effectiveness of training
  programmes: barriers to
  174–6; long-term 172;
  overcoming barriers to
  176–7; short-term 171–2
'effects' method, French 80
egalitarianism 98, 109
elders, respect for 71

electronics firms 87–8, 90
emotional learning climate
  189–90, 193, 196
engineers as managers 141, 149
enterprises, socialist see socialist
  enterprises
entertainment value of courses
  171
entrepreneurs 144, 152;
  characteristics of 145–7
entrepreneurship 140, 142, 143,
  144, 150
environmental issues 202
'establishing' phase of
  management education 14,
  16, 19
ethics 58; corporate 153, 155–6,
  157, 158
Ethiopia 172
Ethiopian Management Institute
  (EMI) 172
European Economic Commission
  (EEC) 81, 125
evaluation of management
  development 76, 78–82, 168,
  170, 171–2, 176–7, 188,
  192–4, 244
expatriates 32
experiential learning 133, 134;
  see also action learning
  methods
experimental programme in skills
  development: aims of 205–6;
  design of 206–8; structure of
  208–9
exporters 245

faculty: recruiting of 54;
  shortage/inadequacy of 41,
  123
family businesses 12–13, 152–3
family problems 215, 216
Fayol, H. 109
feedback, personal 207, 209
Fell, Robert 158
female attitudes in Moslem
  cultures 71–2
fight/flight reactions 189
Fijardo, H.R. 73
'floating wage' 106, 107

foreign working environment: adjustment to 212–16; problems in 213
free-enterprise economy 152, 153–5, 158
Frey, Donald 167
Friedman, Milton 154
funding agancies 75–83, 182–3

General Motors (GM) 156
Germany, West 125, 128–9, 132, 134
goals of management 86–7, 88
governing bodies of schools 232
government 57–8; control of business 154, 156; support for business training 14
'great leap forward' 114
group effects 221
group theory 189
'growing' phase of management education 13–14, 16
guest-workers 125, 128–9, 132, 134
Gulf Polytechnic 31, 32–4

Handy, C.B. 15
Harvard Business School 127
Heyel, E. 60
hierarchical system/structure 69, 138, 139, 150
history of management: in Bulgaria 238–40; in China 113; in Hong Kong 152; in Hungary 137–40; studies of 49–50
Hofstede, G. 200
Hong Kong 89, 152–8; private-sector companies in 152–3, 158
Hosmer, La Rue T. 157
human factors in organizations 131, 143; see also cultural factors
Hungary 4, 137–50; characteristics of entrepreneurs in 145–7; history of management in 137–40; management

education in 147–9; private-sector companies in 144–7; public-sector companies in 140–3, 149; reforms in 138–40

ideology 109–10
income tax 102
independence, socialized 59, 60, 62, 140–1
India 63
industrialization 112, 239
initiative, lack of 98
innovation 143, 144, 150
Institut de Productivité et Gestion Prévisionnelle (IPGP) 179–80
Institute for Social Management (ISM) (Bulgaria) 175, 238, 239, 241–6
'integrating' phase of management education 15, 17, 18
integration with other nationalities 219–20
Intermediate Technology Group 53
international agencies 182–3
International Fund for Agricultural Development (IFAD) 79
International Labour Organisation (ILO) 180, 238, 242; Management Development Programme 170–1, 183
international networking 18
internationalization of companies 221, 222
introductions to new colleagues 216–17
investment in human capital 177–8, 181
'iron bowl' 106
'Iron Law of Responsibility' 155–6
isolation, sense of 62
Istanbul University 127, 129–30, 133
Italy 1, 60

Japan 1, 3, 87, 91; management
style in 87–8, 90–1
job-related training 80; see also
learning-by-doing approach
Johnson, Elmer 156
joint ventures 241

Kenya 82, 172–3
key competencies of MD
professionals 179
kinship 70–1
knowledge: approaches to
192–3, 195–6; levels of 52
Koç Holding 130, 131, 135
KOGEM programme (Turkey)
130–2, 134, 135
Kohn, M.L. 60
Kotter, J. 191, 206

labour relations studies 48–9
language problems 213–14,
217–18
Latin America 40–56
LDCs (less developed countries)
1; 'alternative' management
technologies in 52–3; and
funding agencies 182–3; and
technology transfer 50–3;
development tasks of 51;
minimal resource situations in
230–3; research into
management in 45–50, 52,
53–6; teaching methods in 5;
see also under individual
countries
leadership 85–91; considerate
88, 89–90; goals of 86–7,
88; skills needed for 142–3
learner-centred approach 83
learning climate 188, 189–90,
193, 196–7
learning on courses, types of
193–4, 197
learning theory 190–1
learning-by-doing approach 140,
141, 201–2; see also action
learning methods; job related
training
Leavitt, H. 185
lectures 182, 187, 193

Levine, Theodore 154–5
Lupton, Tom 67
Lyons, G. 234

McGuire, J.W. 29
Malawi 81
management development/
education/training: aims of
130, 187, 205–6; and
minimal resource situations
230–3; and organizational
effectiveness 60–1; and
technology transfer 50–3,
75–6; barriers to effectiveness
of 174–6; case study of
185–98; cultural model of 61-
-4; developmental stages of
12–18; effectiveness of
programmes 171–2;
evaluation of 76, 78–82, 168,
170, 171–2, 176–7, 188,
192–4, 244; in Africa 78–83;
in Bahrain 32–8; in Bulgaria
240–6; in China 117, 118,
119–24; in Hungary 140–3,
147–50; in Latin America 40-
-5; in Sweden 185–8, 192–4;
in Turkey 127–35; in UK
199–209; of conservative v.
progressive managers 140–1;
of teams of participants 175;
principles for 76–7;
promotion of 167–83;
strategic choices for 30–1;
surveys of 169–70; values in
44–5, 188–9, 192, 195–6;
see also under individual
headings, e.g. effectiveness
of training programmes;
relevance of training
managerial activity theory 206
Managerial Grid theory 85
'managerialism' 225
'Managing By Wandering
Around' (MBWA) 86
Mananga Agricultural
Management Center (MAMC)
82, 83
Manpower Services Commission
(MSC) 169–70, 171, 176, 183

marketing function 141
marketing of management
    training 167, 168
materialistic outlook 62
MBA programme (Turkey)
    129–30
MBO (Management By
    Objectives) 110–11
MD professionals: and
    achievements of management
    168; and function of
    management development
    174; credibility/status of 167;
    democratic approach of 246;
    in Swedish case study 187–8;
    key competencies of 179;
    marketing by 167, 168;
    negotiation skills of 179;
    roles of 180; supply of
    178–80
measuring instruments 115, 116
micro v. macro perspectives 61
Mintzberg, H. 206
Misumi, J. 87
mixed-national training
    programme 211–22;
    adjustment issues in 212–16;
    learning experience in
    219–20; programme re-design
    issues in 216–19;
    recommendations for 220–2
Modern Management Training
    Methods (MMTM) 242, 244
modular structure 208–9
'moral minimum' responsibility
    155
morality 70, 72; see also ethics
Morgan, G. 234
motivation of workers 108–9,
    110–11, 141
multi-national companies 21,
    128, 156, 157, 158, 199–210

National Association of Schools
    of Public Affairs and
    Administration (NASPAA) 78
National Construction
    Corporation of Kenya 172–3
national stereotypes 220
nationalization 63

negotiation skills 179
Nepal 226
networking, international 18
numbers of students 40–1, 42,
    119, 120–1, 122, 123, 128
Nystrom, P.C. 59

O'Donnovan, Dennis 179, 180
Ohio State leadership research
    programme 85
'One Best Way', notion of 85–6
open management style 69–70, 72
open systems approach 234, 235
organizational culture 200–2,
    210
Oriental culture 60, 62–3
ownership of companies in
    socialist countries 68, 138–9

'pairing' 189
Pakistan 13–14, 235
part-funding 183
'particularist' models 2
Paul, K. 21
performance evaluation 105
personal problems of employees
    89, 214–16
personality development 58–9
Peters, T.J. 86, 200
Philippines 173
philosophies of management
    education 15
physical space, personal 217
pilot projects 183
plan of action, manager's need
    for 191
pluralism 29
political system 66; see also
    socialist enterprises
postgraduate studies 122
poverty 45, 230–1, 233
private-sector companies 126,
    144–7, 152–3, 158
problem-solving, creativity in
    232
production, industrial 114, 115,
    141
'profit delivery quota' 100, 102
profits: distribution in socialist
    enterprises 105–7;

maximization motive for 152,
153–4, 155; sharing between
enterprises and state 100–3;
short-cuts to 109
profit-taxing system 102
project appraisal 80
project assignments, on courses
187
'projection' 189
'proto-industrial culture' 67
Prudential Assurance 178
public-sector companies 126,
140–3, 149

quality: concept of 171; of
teaching 128; problems with
245
quantitative view of knowledge
192, 193
questionnaires 131, 144, 188

records of production 115, 116
Redding, G. 152
reforms, economic 138–40
relevance of training 191, 194,
197
reporting systems 176–7
research into management
181–2; and teaching 55–6; in
Colombia 45–50; in LDCs
52, 53–6; priorities of 55
'resourcefulness' 232–3
resources 224–36; analysis of
231–2; and constraints 227;
balance between 228–9, 234–
5; categories of 227–8;
concept of 226; excess of
230; lack of 78, 230–1, 233;
minimal resource situations
229–33; primacy of people as
228; 'total resource approach'
227–9
responsibility see 'economic
responsibility system'; social
responsibility; corporate
results of management training,
unquantifiability of 168
'rice-bowl masters' 153
roles in training 180
Rostow, W.W. 11–12

rural communities 70, 72–3
Russell, Charles 170, 171

Sawyer, J. 59
Schipers, F. 73
Schlossman, S. 21
Schön, D. 188, 190–1
Schumacher, E.F. 53, 236
'scientific management' 3, 109,
113, 114, 115–16, 117–18
secondary schools 230–3
selection of participants for
training programmes 81, 175
selfishness of manager husbands
215
seminars 134, 243
Shanghai 116
short-term v. long-term
effectiveness 171–2
Sierra Leone 224, 230–3
Simon, H. 109
Simon, J.G. 155
Singapore 14
'single-loop' v. 'double-loop'
learning 190–1, 194, 196,
197
Sino-British Joint Declaration
(1984) 158
skills approach 202–3, 205–9
small-group work 82
Smith, Adam 153
social change 125, 126–7
'social contract' 155–6
social knowledge 191, 194, 195,
196
social responsibilities, corporate
153–8
socialist economies 4; see also
under individual countries
socialist enterprises 68–70,
72–3, 97–103; authority of
99–100, 104–5; distribution
of profits 105–7; inflexibility
of 137–8; principles of
108–10; profit-sharing with
state 100–3; relationship with
state 99, 137, 138;
responsibilities of 99, 103–4
socialization 59–60
Southern African Development

Co-ordination Conference (SADCC) 78
'splitting' 189
'squeeze-box' model 204–5
staff development 19–20
standard of living 97, 239
Starbuck, W.H. 59
'starting up' phase of management education 12–13, 16
steel plants 116
Stewart, R. 206
strategic choices for management education 30–1
strategy-making skills/systems 143, 191, 207, 234, 245
structure of programmes 208–9
Sun Wu 108
supervisors 81, 86, 88, 90
Swaziland 83
Sweden 3, 185–98

Tanton, M. 168, 184
taxation 102–3
taxi drivers 109
Taylor, B. 67
teaching, and research 55–6
teaching materials 81, 128, 133, 134, 182
teaching methods: and cultural factors 4–5; in Africa 78; in Sweden 186–8, 192–4; in universities 182, 192–3; in USA 4, 21; skills approach 203, 205–9; see also action learning methods
team approach to management training 175
technical view of knowledge 192, 193, 194
technological change 240–1
technology of management, transfer of 5–6, 50–3, 75
testimonials about programmes 178
time, use of 234
timekeeping, good 90
'total resource approach' 227–9
trades unions 48

trainers/consultants, management see MD professionals
Training 182
training, management see management development/education/training
train-the-trainers (TTT) programmes 178
transferability of management education 37, 79; see also relevance of training
transport 173
treatment of foreign managers, on-the-job 214
Turkey 125; management education in 127–9; role of management in 126–7

UK 1, 3, 4; management education in 18, 199–210; notions of 'considerateness' in 89; withdrawal of government funding in 15
undergraduate courses 192–3
unethical business practices 153
United Nations Development Programme (UNDP) 81–2, 238
United States Agency for International Development (USAID) 78, 79–80
Universidad de los Andes 46–7, 48
Universidad Javeriana 47, 48, 49, 50
universities: academic approach of 192; establishment of management education in 14; in Botswana 13; in China 119–24; in Hungary 149, 150; in Latin America 40, 46–7; in Turkey 128, 129, 135; non-adherence to principles taught in programmes 182
urbanization 62–3
USA 1, 3, 60; consumer research in 169; corporate social responsibility in 153, 156; mixed-national training

programme in 211–22;
notions of 'considerateness' in
89–90; present state of
management education in 18;
teaching methods in 4, 21

values: changes in 190–1, 194;
conformist/conservative 70,
72, 131–2, 133; cultural 58,
59, 62, 64; in management
education 44–5, 188–9, 192,
195–6; *see also* cultural
factors; ethics

Wales 88
Waterman, R.H. 200
Webb, P.H. 234

welfare of employees, concern
for 88
wives of managers 214–16
work customs: information about
217, 218; lack of familiarity
with 214
'working groups' 189, 190
work place: importance of 217,
218; unfamiliar 217, 218
World Bank 75–6, 82, 180

Yellow Freight Systems 177

Zambia 80
Zemke, R. 169
Zigon, Jack 177